ROADMAP

The GET-IT-TOGETHER GUIDE *for* FIGURING OUT WHAT TO DO *with* YOUR LIFE

by **ROADTRIP NATION**

Created by Nathan Gebhard, Brian McAllister,
and Mike Marriner
with
Jay Sacher, Alyssa Frank, Annie Mais, Jamie Zehler,
Willie Witte, *and* Mara Zehler

Second Edition

CHRONICLE BOOKS
SAN FRANCISCO

Library of Congress Cataloging-in-Publication Data:

Names: Marriner, Mike, author. | Gebhard, Nathan, author. | McAllister, Brian, 1975- author.
Title: Roadmap : the get-it-together guide for figuring out what to do with your life / created by Nathan Gebhard, Brian McAllister, and Mike Marriner.
Other titles: Road map
Description: Second edition. | San Francisco : Chronicle Books, [2020] | Includes index.
Identifiers: LCCN 2019010636 | ISBN 9781452173443 (pbk. : alk. paper)
Subjects: LCSH: Career development. | Vocational guidance.
Classification: LCC HF5381 .M39623 2020 | DDC 650.1—dc23 LC record available at https://lccn.loc.gov/2019010636

MIX
Paper from responsible sources
FSC™ C008047

Manufactured in China.

Design by Jennifer Tolo Pierce.
Illustrations by Matthew Allen.

Interviewees' quotes from the Roadtrip Nation Interview Archive appear throughout this book and have been edited for print purposes. Videos of interviews can be viewed at roadtripnation.com.

10 9 8 7 6 5 4 3

Chronicle books and gifts are available at special quantity discounts to corporations, professional associations, literacy programs, and other organizations. For details and discount information, please contact our premiums department at corporatesales@chroniclebooks.com or at 1-800-759-0190.

Chronicle Books LLC
680 Second Street
San Francisco, California 94107
www.chroniclebooks.com

WE WROTE THIS BOOK FOR YOU, SO MAKE IT YOURS.

Scrawl notes in the margins, dog-ear chapters, stain pages with coffee, throw it against the wall if you feel like it. You're steering the wheel, so take charge.

Above all, be honest. Everything you do in these pages will be about silencing the din you hear from others and turning what makes you unique—the interests, values, motivations, and peculiar quirks only you know and understand—into a life you want to live. It's an investigatory journey that'll lead you to a path that's most true to who you are, but it's bound to stir up some deep questions in the process. Don't ignore those questions. Examine them. Build on them. And let us know what you find.

See you on the open road.

—Roadtrip Nation

#RoadmapBook
@RoadtripNation
facebook.com/roadtripnation
instagram.com/roadtripnation

contents

About Roadtrip Nation 6

Roadmap Online 9

Introduction 11

PART ONE: LET GO

CHAPTER 1   THE INVISIBLE ASSEMBLY LINE 26

CHAPTER 2   SHED THE NOISE 41

CHAPTER 3   WHERE YOU COME FROM DOESN'T DETERMINE WHERE YOU GO 52

CHAPTER 4   BUILD A LIFE, NOT A RÉSUMÉ 69

From the Road | Right or Left? 82

CHAPTER 5   LIFE IS LINEAR ONLY IN THE REARVIEW MIRROR 88

CHAPTER 6   LIVING IN BETA 99

CHAPTER 7   WHAT IS SUCCESS? 108

CHAPTER 8   THE BLANK CANVAS 119

PART TWO: DEFINE

CHAPTER 9   PURSUE YOUR INTERESTS—NOT AN OCCUPATION 130

CHAPTER 10   DEFINING YOUR FOUNDATION 147

CHAPTER 11   ROADMAP 154

CHAPTER 12   YOU MIGHT NOT BE CRAZY, BUT MAYBE YOU SHOULD BE 165

From the Road | The Internal GPS 176

CHAPTER 13   WHAT ARE YOUR SUBJECTIVE TRUTHS? 182

CHAPTER 14   SKILLS PAY BILLS 195

PART THREE: BECOME

CHAPTER 15 DRIP. DRIP. SPLASH. *212*

CHAPTER 16 SHIFT YOUR SKILLS *223*

CHAPTER 17 HUSTLE *238*

CHAPTER 18 RISK OR REGRET? YOU CHOOSE. *255*

From the Road | You're the Center *264*

CHAPTER 19 GET TO FAILING *270*

CHAPTER 20 FIGHTING DOUBT *279*

CHAPTER 21 PRACTICE, SCHMACTICE. IT'S DOING THAT MATTERS. *288*

CHAPTER 22 WHEN TO VEER AND WHEN TO U-TURN *301*

CHAPTER 23 DISTINCTION IS EVERYTHING *310*

////////////// PROJECTS //////////////

Project #1 Talk with Someone Who's Living Your Roadmap *320*

Project #2 Sell Your Goods/Services Online *328*

Project #3 Travel to a New Place *334*

Project #4 Create Your Own Semester *339*

Project #5 Find Your Niche *346*

Project #6 Invent Your Own Project *350*

Acknowledgments *356*

Index *358*

ABOUT
ROADTRIP NATION

We're Roadtrip Nation, and we're here to provide anyone who's facing uncertainty about their path in life with the courage to be true to themselves.

We were born of that same uncertainty, and we're here to help. We started our journey in 2001, as a group of friends unsure of what to do with our lives—and most of all, worried that the path we were on was wrong. More than wrong. It felt as though following the path laid out ahead of us threatened to flatten who we were, bury it, and cover it over with something false.

We were looking for a better way. So we hit the road to find the people who had forged a path forward that was authentically their own. They'd pursued lives and careers based on what mattered to them, following their interests where they led, even through failure, criticism, struggle. We met them in high rises, at home, in wide-open pastures, and on boats at sea—and we asked them real questions about how to build a life on your own terms. And what we found in their stories was bigger than our journey alone.

Ever since, we've been building on this movement and this mission to empower people to define their own roads in life. We've handed the keys to our big green RV over to countless new teams of roadtrippers: real people, poised at a turning point, looking for guidance. In getting outside of what they know and listening to the life stories of the people they meet on the road, as we once did, the process of building a life guided by their interests unfolds.

These stories and advice from the road fuel our award-winning documentary series and films on public television, career exploration resources and tools, books (like the one you're reading now!), self-discovery programs for the classroom, and a vast video archive of two decades' worth of stories—all dedicated to helping people build lives around their interests.

We send these stories rippling out to show you what's possible when you listen to yourself and go relentlessly after what matters to you.

ROADMAP ONLINE
THIS BOOK IS JUST THE START

When it comes to defining your own road in life, this book is just the jumping-off point. Visit our website to use the companion Roadmap tool to discover thousands more Roadtrip Nation Leaders and careers that match your interests.

Then immerse yourself in stories from our two decades on the road. On our website, you can watch the interviews from this book (and explore thousands more!) and check out all of the episodes from our long-running documentary series on public television centered on uncovering how truly successful people have created authentic lives for themselves.

Follow along as you read this book by going to **roadtripnation.com**.

INTRODUCTION

This book is about answering an old question in a new way.

The question itself is unavoidable; no matter who you are or where you're from or what you've been through, you're going to reach a moment in life when you're anxious and confused, unsure about the path ahead. And you're going to hear that voice, from outside and within, asking you, "So, what are you going to do with your life?"

It's not easy to admit that often the only honest answer to that question is "I don't know." It's tough being lost. We speak from experience—and we're not just referring to heading down the wrong street or being in the wrong city or even state (although we've been there plenty of times, too). We're talking about that deeper meaning of lost, the one that prompts the scary questions about life and work and lasting satisfaction.

When you're facing the future, when those questions are barreling down on you and the knots in your stomach are tightening, you can feel incredibly isolated. We're here to remind you that you're not alone.

Back at the beginning of our journey (just as now) we craved the breathing room, the thinking space, and the fresh perspectives that the open road had to offer. We felt that there must be more options than what we'd been exposed to, more examples of people out there that we could learn from. Adrift, without a steady paycheck or a backup plan, we jumped into an RV with nothing but a nagging sense that how we'd been taught to think about our futures was in fact deeply wrong.

We wanted to talk to people who'd made it to the other side—the people who were actually living lives that were deeply satisfying. We painted a twenty-year-old RV an electric shade of green and scrawled on a name—Roadtrip Nation—then spent months crisscrossing the United States, talking to more than eighty people along the way. Some of them were the leaders of the biggest companies in the world; others were filmmakers, designers, a lobsterman in Maine, and even a U.S. Supreme Court justice.

We were in search of the answer to one big question—How do you build a career that's true to who you are?

But that first question led to lots more. Where were you at our age? How did you get to where you are today? Were you ever scared or unsure? Did you ever feel like you were pressured to conform? How do you deal with the uncertainty and ambiguity of life? What exactly is "success" to you? Are you happy? When have you failed? What do you wish you'd known when you were our age? How did you turn your beliefs into action?

Hearing their stories was astounding. There wasn't as much distance as we'd imagined between where they'd started and where we were now. We just hadn't heard these parts of the story before. We'd hit the road to get distance from the expectations all around us—to create space from what we knew—so that we could see ourselves more clearly. What we didn't expect was to find a whole new way of thinking, a whole new approach to how we could build a life guided by our interests—an approach that would kick-start our journey, but also steady us for every single step, bump, and turn in the road that came after.

The people we've met and continue to meet are living with intention—they're not just choosing one career and fitting themselves into it. They're actively pursuing their interests every day, not just when they're twenty-two and not just one time; they're growing and changing and expanding what they're capable of throughout their lives. These Leaders we've met on our travels all around the country provided us with new answers to old questions. And, frankly, those new answers arrived just in time.

The world has changed. What you do with your life is no longer something you figure out just once. And when you're bound to face change—chosen or not—shrinking away from it is not the answer. What we've learned from people who took great risks, made hard decisions, and faced uncertainty and failure is that change is never easy, but being open to where change leads is essential. Inevitably, you will face changes. How will you use that change as a power source and move yourself forward?

Every time you pick up this book, you may be facing a different kind of change. It might feel outside of your control—industry trends, where this career is up and that one is down. It might be the economy or even what "work" looks like. You might be the one who's changed. Maybe you've lost someone important to you. Maybe you have a new family to support. Or maybe your version of success or happiness just looks different than it used to.

When things are shifting around you, and you're not sure what the future will look like, all you can do is go back to who you are and what matters to you. It's exactly why we took the first road trip. And it's why we wrote this book.

That first road trip was a launchpad for the movement that Roadtrip Nation has become. We've learned that it's absolutely possible to live a rich and authentic life—one that will grow and thrive along with your interests, your values, and your vision. We know it because we've sat down face-to-face with people who

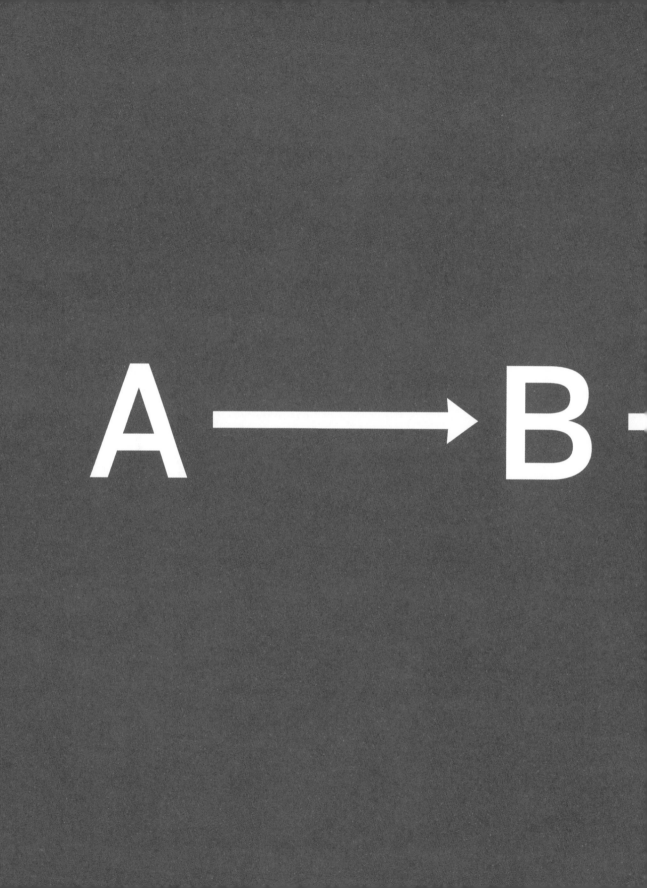

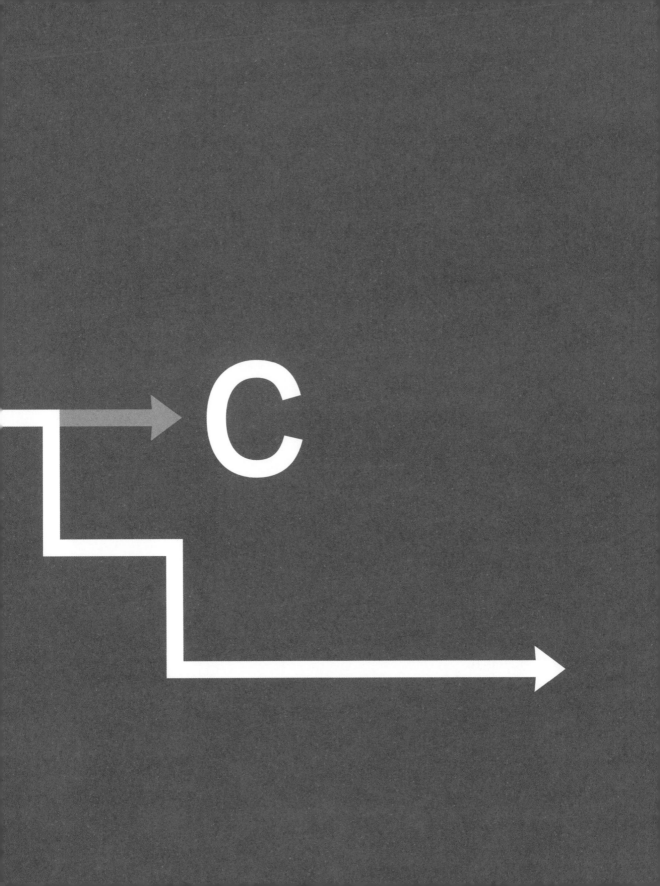

are doing just that, and we've straight-up asked them what it takes to live a life that's true to who you are. That was nearly twenty years ago, and since then, we've been sending new roadtrippers out on the road every year to take transformative journeys and ask these questions for themselves.

Those conversations are the foundation of Roadtrip Nation, and as you turn the pages of this book, you'll hear more and more of the insights and stories that have been shared with us on the road.

In this new edition, we have even more wisdom to share, and we're more energized than ever. In the five years since we first wrote this book, we've sent our green RV out around the country dozens more times. The roadtrippers who've helmed those trips aren't just lost twentysomethings—though some still fit into that category, too. They've come from all over the country, and their backgrounds represent all kinds of stories and struggles. A twenty-eight-year-old military veteran injured in the line of duty; a thirty-eight-year-old mother of three who's going back to school; a roadtripper team in their forties and fifties facing a changing workforce; eighteen-year-olds fresh out of high school and looking ahead to college, trade schools, and more.

We've filled this volume with as many ways of living and building a life as possible, to show that the challenges and triumphs from these stories hold lessons for anyone. Our roadtrippers have been educators, veterans, DREAMers, people living with learning and attention issues, students who beat incredible odds to make it to college, and more—and we've followed them all over the country, exploring industries as diverse as design, business, technology, auto trades, insurance, and cybersecurity.

We've mapped their pathways, from self-made successes to high-school drop-outs to trade schools and apprenticeships, community colleges, graduate schools, and doctoral degrees. And along the way, we've crossed paths with inspiring Leaders like bestselling author Chris Gardner, who wrote *The Pursuit of Happyness*; Paralympian Scout Bassett; *MythBusters* host Kari Byron; LA Sparks COO Christine Simmons; Grammy Award–winning singer-songwriter John Legend; and more. Their advice and lessons are infused throughout this new edition.

We're proud of how many more experiences we've captured, but even more than that, we feel more confident than ever in the process we've laid out in this book for how to build a life that's meaningful to you.

This approach isn't about choosing a career or distant future goal and reverse-engineering yourself into it; it's about following your interests and making choices every day that move you toward a wider and ever more flexible view of your future.

What we've learned about how to do that—what we are still learning—is at the heart of this book. It's all centered around something we've come to call self-construction, and it's all about giving you a framework and the tools to build a life that's true to who you are and what you care about. This isn't a recipe for success or a detailed checklist; this is a process of evolution that you'll find yourself revisiting anytime you need to remind yourself of who you are and what you care about. Self-construction is made up of three distinct phases, and we'll go into them in the three sections of this book.

Let Go is about releasing the expectations that have been put on you—who you should be or what you should do. It's about shedding the Noise you've heard for your whole life, clearing away what doesn't feel right, and beginning to understand what success truly means for you. Your life is yours to define. This is where the work starts.

Define starts with your interests and guides you in combining and exploring them to find ways of living and working that you never may have imagined for yourself. This isn't about finding one career, it's about starting from your Core Interests and giving you the freedom to grow in any direction you choose.

Finally, **Become** is all about what it takes to put your dream on the street. Facing fear, doubt, failure—it's all there. But no matter what setbacks or challenges you face, your actions and the work you do to get to your own version of success are what define you.

And that's the key: Self-construction starts with you. Let go of what's expected, define what matters to you, then become who you want to be. It's an interactive, ever-evolving process that only you can start and only you can finish. You'll have to ask yourself some difficult questions and confront the answers you get, no matter how challenging they may be. Because it's not your parents' life, not society's, not what anyone tries to tell you your life should be—not even what we say it should be. It's yours. Self-construction is about focusing on the core of who you are and what matters to you. With hard work, and plenty of course correction, revisiting this process will lead to the most meaningful experiences, the most enriching work, and the most fulfilling life.

LET GO
DEFINE
Become

But we also understand that no matter what your circumstances are, forging a life path that's right for you can sometimes seem impossible. Most people, ourselves included, find big, high roadblocks between where they are and where they want to be. Responsibilities, expectations, self-doubt, and the grind of everyday life can make us feel trapped and confused. We get worn down and worn out, and we feel tempted to give up. We start to believe that maybe there is no realistic way (beyond dumb luck) to live a life that's both fulfilling and financially sustainable.

One foggy morning, when road-tripping through the redwoods of Northern California, we expressed these exact feelings to a man named John Perry Barlow.* This free-thinking, philosophizing Renaissance man had traveled many different roads in life. From early beginnings as a cattle rancher and lyricist for the Grateful Dead to pioneering internet activism and cofounding the Electronic Frontier Foundation, John's rambling life story had our heads spinning. We came to him panicked and paralyzed by the confusion ahead of us, and like a modern-day mountaintop mystic, his thoughts gave us peace and clarity: "I think the most important thing is to recognize that everybody else is scared, too. It's not like you're the only ones who feel like they don't get it. Nobody really gets it. It's not gettable. **All you can really do is try to make a warm peace with all the rest of your confused and frightened peers, and take courage and comfort in that.**"

Much of this book is about courageously taking comfort in our collective confusion and finding refuge in the guidance and wisdom of those who have gone before us. John told us, "I think it's important to place a different value on what you connote when you say 'getting lost.' As long as we assume that that means we are helpless, and adrift, and abandoned, then very little good

 roadtripnation.com/leader/john-perry-barlow

can come of it. But start to think about being lost in a positive way—[it's about] exploring and opening yourself up to possibilities that you wouldn't have otherwise considered."

"If you're not lost," he told us, "you're not much of an explorer."

We value exploration, and thus we value getting lost. Since you're reading this, there's a good chance you do, too. Because the flip side of the landscape before us today is an immense space for creativity and flexibility, and endless possibility for experimentation and exploration. The world is changing rapidly, and it is ripe for us to shape to our liking. We can create livelihoods that have never been seen before. And that may be the most exciting thing of all.

Immersed in the stories we've heard, we feel compelled to share them, but we also feel a powerful sense of responsibility to find our own ways. It's impossible to listen to the people we've met and not be provoked to act, to move, to become something more than we were yesterday. That's the energy and enthusiasm we want to share with you.

Self-construction never stops. There is no finish line. Life is an open-ended pursuit that constantly leads us to new truths, and those truths can only come from within ourselves. We don't have the answers for you. This book is a guide to your own self-construction. Interact with it. Question it. Question us. Ask the questions you find here of the people in your own life. Use this book as you see fit. Use it, then step back and reevaluate your life. Then reuse it. Then step back and reevaluate your life. Then reuse it . . . you get the idea.

Repeatedly revisiting the ideas on these pages will challenge the way you see the world. Let these concepts help you continually build a life that is wholly yours.

Come get lost with us. You may be surprised where you find yourself.

PART ONE

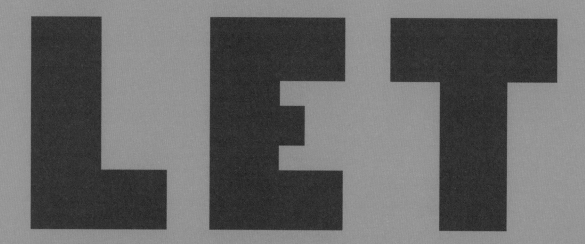

LET

CHAPTER 1

THE INVISIBLE ASSEMBLY LINE

Here's a big, goofy cliché: *You can be whatever you want to be.* We just cringed as we wrote that, but nevertheless it happens to be true.

So how did this corny afterschool-special cliché become a tired trope rather than an empowering truism? Maybe because the world we navigate forces us to ignore its underlying truth. In the name of security, we put aside what we might truly want. We pay our dues. We put our heads down and work hard, chugging along on a preplotted path that promises stability, security, and comfort. But in the quiet moments, we have a nagging feeling. Is this the path we're supposed to be on? Are we fulfilled? Satisfied? Are we living our lives or are our lives living us? Are there choices we could be making that better speak to who we are? Are we on the right road?

For some people, finding the "right" road is easy (or at least it seems like it to those of us standing off on the side). They seem to be living the life they want to live, they appear to be successful, thriving, and happy in the roles they've chosen. For most of us, however, finding that road feels like an exercise in impossibility. We get stuck. And lost. We feel afraid of the unknown or incapable of bold action. We become bogged down by the responsibilities we face and the choices in front of us.

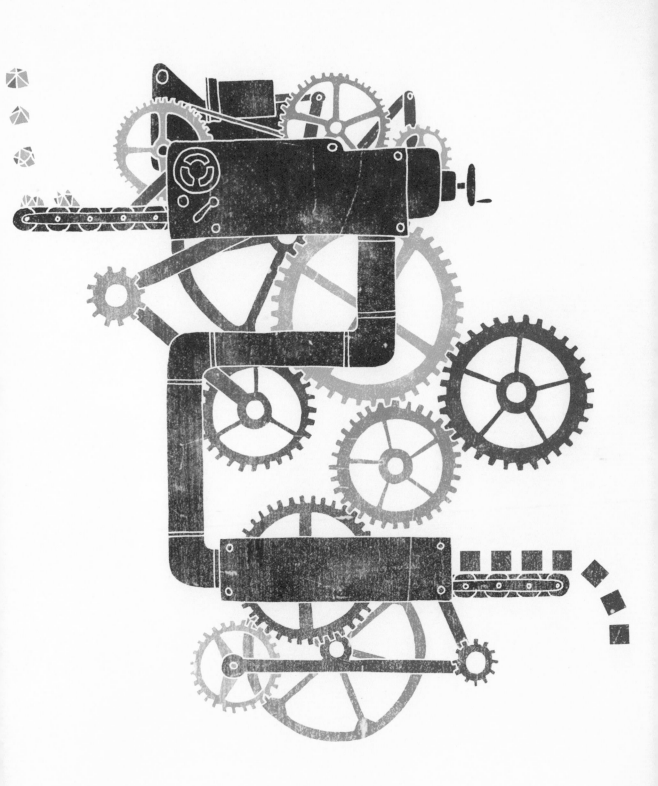

If the road belongs to us, why is it so difficult to get on it? Why can't we force that cliché back into truth? The answer lies in a particularly sneaky aspect of human nature. Just as a deluge of rain pounding a dry hillside will form rivulets that trickle downhill—beating tracks of least resistance into the earth—as individuals, we tend to fall into the paths that society has already created for us. This process starts early in our lives and is devilishly hard to shake. And while there can be value in the tried-and-true (there's nothing wrong with everybody wearing pants, for instance), following by rote restricts individual experience and inhibits potential.

Think about it this way: If you live on the North American continent, outside your door is a road that will get you to New York City. You can pull out a map and take any route you want, winding through purple mountain majesties and amber waves of whatnot and stopping at as many roadside tourist traps as you'd like. You can explore sleepy towns off the beaten path, you can stop off for a few cheesesteaks in Philly or roll up to the Grand Tetons, and no matter where you happen to be, you will still be on the road to New York City. But if you punch your destination into your phone, it will lead you directly to the closest highway. It will tell you exactly how far it is to New York and estimate exactly how long it will take you to get there. And it will be a nonstop march that's as straight as possible. You'll have certainty but no cheesesteaks, no time for

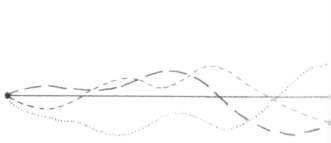

exploring, just you in your car on the very same highway that everybody else takes. This is exactly what society's formula for "success" is like: a one-size-fits-all, bumper-to-bumper haul that ignores the nuances of who you really are.

This is the Invisible Assembly Line, and chances are you're on it.

Our personal Assembly Lines are built cog by cog from all the expectations, education, social norms, well-meaning advice, and preprogrammed choices that we've absorbed from the day we crawled out of the sandbox and wondered what we would be when we grew up. Whether we're pushed to become doctors or lawyers or to work in the family business, or told that our aspirations are beyond us, all those fears and all that conditioning define our decisions and our expectations without our being aware that it's happening. But it *is* happening.

That's where we began—on the Assembly Line. Our first road trip was forged by a numbing fear that we were locked into preplotted career destinations: a doctor, a business consultant, or the next in line to run the family business. None of these options had anything to do with who we really were, but they had everything to do with the expectations we had absorbed. And it filled all of us with a jittery sense of panic. We were afraid we'd wake up one day with the devastating realization that we'd been living someone else's life.

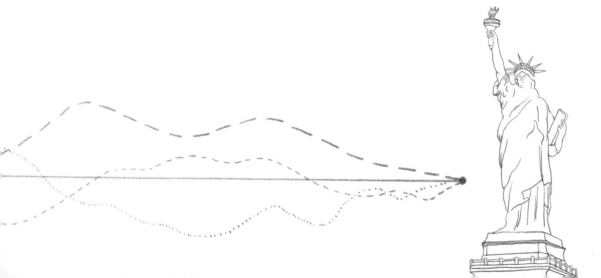

Of course, staying on the Assembly Line offers the seductive perceived comfort of safety in numbers. After all, if everyone is taking the same path, it must be the right one. That's the trickiest part: When you're on the Assembly Line, you often don't even know what your options are. The machinery of the Assembly Line does the work of defining happiness for you; it dictates every step along the way, and in what order, but it's not made for you as an individual. The folks we've met on the road, the Leaders—each with their own constellation of interests, experiences, talents, and ambitions—have all discovered ways to escape the Assembly Line and find their own way forward.

Rewriting the script you're handed can be one of the most difficult acts in your life. It might upset people close to you, it might shake the foundations of your worldview, and it might be scary. The political activist and BET host Jeff Johnson* remembers rejecting the Assembly Line while he was in college on a track scholarship.

As Jeff became more involved in student politics at his school's Black Student Union, his track coach confronted him: "I didn't bring you here for that. I brought you here to go to class and to run track." Jeff's Assembly Line was starkly clear: star athlete, not justice-minded activist.

Much to his coach's surprise (and his father's dismay), Jeff made the tough choice to reject the scholarship so that he could pursue his interests in school with a clear conscience. In rejecting the preprogrammed route, no matter how scary doing so was, Jeff found an important lesson that he continues to share with others.

* ▶ **roadtripnation.com/leader/jeff-johnson**

"Most people who are successful . . . didn't do what everybody else did. They didn't go the same routes everybody else went. It is the people who think outside the box in whatever discipline they are in who shake the world. No one's looking around at the people who followed a manual saying, 'My God, they followed that manual in a way that was just inspiring.' It is the people who throw the manual away and say there is something beyond this that I can share, or that I can give, or that I can invest, who become successful."

—JEFF JOHNSON, *BET host and political activist*

Being stuck on the Assembly Line often manifests itself as a nagging feeling in your gut that things should be better than they are. That gut feeling is what launches the first phase of your journey. It's time to get to the root of what's causing that anxiety.

Start by asking yourself questions—not just about the road you're already on, but deeply personal questions about who you are and what you want. In short, at this moment, it's time to be selfish. It's time to focus inward to uncover your individuality and to spend some time asking the questions that will reveal what is *authentically* you.

Are you heading toward a destination you really want to reach? Is whatever goal you're striving for worth the work you're putting in? Take some time to think honestly about yourself. Don't think about who you are "supposed" to be, or who your friends think you are, or the persona you've crafted. Who are you really, right now? Asking these questions of yourself can be a tool for change, both for you and the world at large. It leads to a more honest understanding of what makes you different from others and what unique contribution and perspective you can offer. Don't worry about the answers; think about what questions you *haven't* been asking yourself.

What truly excites me?

IF I hAd A hAll pASS on FAiluRE, FEAR, OR . . . whAt would I bE doing?

WHAT WOULD LIFE LOOK LIKE FOR ME TO GET TO THE END AND NOT REGRET DECISIONS I'VE MADE?

When you're on the Assembly Line, those questions can be really challenging. You might be afraid of the answers, or troubled by how far you are from where you thought you wanted to be. Or you may find that answering questions about yourself leads to those three frightening words: I don't know.

Don't worry. There's more power in saying "I don't know" than you might think.

WHAT IF AND WHERE TO?

Coasting along on the Assembly Line carries many dangers. One of the most serious is the curse of "What if?" that was hammered home to us by the spoken word poet Airea D. Matthews.* When we met her in a theater in Detroit, she had just finished her MFA in poetry. Before that, however, Airea was on the Assembly Line.

"I think I was born a poet and performer," Airea says. "But I was not doing what I knew I should be doing." Growing up, Airea's home life felt chaotic, with a father who was an alcoholic and addicted to heroin. Airea's mother pressed her to get a business degree and do something where she would make money and always have what she needed. So she went to college, studied economics, and got a master's in public administration before taking her place in a corporate account executive job. Security and certainty, right? But eight years went by, and the only thing that was certain was that she was miserable.

* ▶ **roadtripnation.com/leader/airea-dee-matthews**

"There's a great weight that's placed on your shoulders . . . when you are not actually doing what it is you should be doing," Airea says. In the end, security held only so much power. She was stuck doing something that didn't speak to who she really was or what she really wanted. "You come to a cliff and you jump off," Airea recalls. "For me, that cliff was the realization that I just hated my job. It wasn't fulfilling."

Once you know that what you're doing isn't lining up with your vision, it's time to act. Every day longer is a day wasted on a path that's not your own. She turned to poetry and writing, which had fascinated her since she was a child. When a friend invited her to an open mic night, Airea discovered that other people connected to her words.

Spoken word was a hobby, but Airea needed to commit. Instead of following the Assembly Line, Airea asked **"What if?"** and took a chance. Taking those two simple words seriously is what nudged her off the Assembly Line.

"I had to get to the point where I just had to make my own life. My decisions were independent of other people's decisions—I'm not your mirror. It doesn't matter what other people's expectations are. **Strive to be the version of you that you see in your head, that you know you can be."**

There can be any number of self-created reasons for staying on your own Assembly Line, and they don't have to be bad, by any definition. There's nothing wrong with wanting security and a steady paycheck. There's nothing wrong with wanting the house with a view or a healthy 401(k). The danger arises when you haven't asked questions about why you're doing what you're doing and striving for what you're striving for.

So let's ask some questions about why—starting with, where are you headed?

The Assembly Line of _____.

(your name)

The voices around me are saying

"I should be a _____"

"I have to_____."

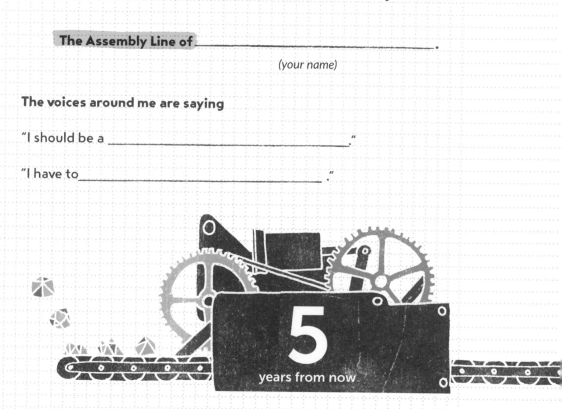

And if I stay on this Assembly Line . . .

Five years from now I will be _____.

(busy, lost, afraid, excited, curious, employed)

Is my job interesting?

Do I live for the weekends?

Am I having fun?

Who is with me along the way?

. . . and in ten years, I will be _____.

(struggling, having fun, afraid, working hard, building, off track, tired, excited)

Am I good at what I do?

Am I challenged?

Do I feel like I'm going somewhere?

Is there momentum in my life?

Do I have a wife/husband/partner? Kids?

Am I happy?

Am I where I thought I would be?

Am I playing as much as I hope to?

. . . and in fifteen years, I will be _____ .

(happy, confused, afraid, excited, stuck, accomplished, proud, regretful)

Where will I live?

What does my work look like?

Do I like the people I spend time with?

Does the work I do give me pleasure and meaning?

Am I a better person than I was fifteen years ago?

Am I proud of how I've lived life thus far?

Are the answers you've given to these questions freaking you out?

YES

NO

We felt the same way.
And just as it was for us, this
is a great place to start.
Keep reading.

The road ahead looks pretty good.
You're one of the fortunate ones.
Keep reading. This book should
confirm what you're thinking and
help you stay on your own road.

Taking risks in your life and stepping off the Assembly Line will not, as we've been told to believe, automatically lead to missed rent payments and subsequent financial ruin, but that doesn't mean it won't be a challenge.

So many of the people we've interviewed and been inspired by, the folks we refer to as Leaders, found true success, both financially and psychologically, after years of being stalled on the Assembly Line. They broke free from the Line by asking the big, embarrassing questions, the touchy-feely New Agey kind of questions that can seem like they have nothing to do with the predicament you hope to solve. But asking "Who am I?" will instantly slow down the wheels of the Assembly Line. The slower the Line, the easier it will be to jump off.

Judge Penny Brown Reynolds* puts it simply: "Tapping into your purpose takes a great deal of discipline, because you have to ask yourself the question every day when you open your eyes: 'Who am I?'" Penny grew up in poverty in Louisiana, overcoming homelessness and abuse before she got to law school. This step was enough to showcase Penny as someone who didn't take the path laid out for her, but what's amazing is that Penny has never stopped questioning her choices and path to make sure they still align with her interests. For Penny, her road was about helping people fight oppression and abuse. She became a judge, presided over a television show courtroom, and now is an ordained minister, all in the name of following her own road. She sums it up: "I know now in my heart my road is constantly evolving—that it's about keeping your heart open. Stop watching your life from the sidelines."

Learning what you don't know about yourself will reveal the ways in which the path you're on diverges from the path you will ultimately want to take. As you question the road ahead, the gears of your personal Assembly Line will start to rattle and slow. It's time to leap.

✱ ▶ **roadtripnation.com/leader/penny-brown-reynolds**

CHAPTER 2
SHED THE NOISE

- -

In order to leap from what's expected, you have to be able to hear yourself. That begins with dividing who you are from what other people want you to be. Self-doubt, external pressures, false ideas of what success is and isn't—we call all that the Noise. To become the version of yourself that you want to be, you have to block it and listen to yourself. The Noise may come from family and friends, teachers, coaches, counselors, and from society at large. It can come with equal force from friends or rivals, strangers or family. It's in the books we read, the social media we consume, the shows we watch, and most dangerously, it's within ourselves.

For some of us, the Noise might be a reminder to make money above all else, or to follow in the footsteps of a successful sibling. For others, the Noise is that we'll never be good enough to make it in a chosen pursuit, or that we'd be crazy to try something different. Whatever the case, the Noise is the furnace that powers your personal Assembly Line. These messages keep the Line moving, and keep us on it.

Different as it is for each of us, the Noise is also every person's individual starting point. Virtually every Leader we've spoken to on the road has described the Noise, in one form or another, factoring into their lives.

"When I was a senior in high school [at a Catholic boarding school], two days before my graduation I was told by this nun, 'Get a good job pumping gas in a gas station and stick with it. That's your life.'"

—*Gerard Baker, first Native American superintendent of Mount Rushmore National Memorial*

"Well, society told me go to school, white picket fence, get the house, get the girl, have kids, have a dog—so simple. It wasn't that simple for me; I wanted something different."

—*Dominick Cruz, professional MMA fighter*

"Because of where I grew up, the Jewish suburbs of Baltimore, you were expected to prepare yourself to go to medical school . . . what else would I do? That's what people did if they were smart: They became doctors!"

—*Ira Glass, host of* This American Life

"I was a girl in India in a small place. The entire community was up in arms. There were people—neighbors, relatives, you name it, people I hadn't even seen before—coming into the house and trying to talk my parents out of this crazy decision to send their daughter alone on this journey at the other end of the world to pursue something called astronomy."

— *Mansi Kasliwal, assistant professor of astronomy at Caltech*

"When I decided to take auto shop, my guidance counselor, friends, parents of friends, all of them gave me the same pushback. A) Why would you want to take auto shop 'cause [you're] a girl, and B) But you're smart, you're going to college, why do you need auto shop? Both of those things are horribly insulting, right? One said I can't be an auto mechanic 'cause I'm a girl, and the other one said being an auto mechanic is for stupid people."

—Bogi Lateiner, founder of 180 Degrees Automotive

"When I decided to leave the academic track and try being a cartoonist— [I had] that feeling: You told everyone you were getting a PhD and you wanted to be a professor, so what are they going to think of you if you don't do that?"

—Jorge Cham, roboticist turned cartoonist of PHD Comics

"My community is in poverty, mostly farm workers. My parents worked in the fields, and they don't have a high school education. . . . When I was in high school there were some folks who told me to pick up a trade, and not pursue my dream of furthering my education because I would fail."

—Raul Ruiz, physician, congressman, and first Latino to earn three graduate degrees from Harvard University

"When I called my family and said I'm going to apply to NASA, my dad said, 'No, you shouldn't, those people are really smart.' I think he was trying to tell me, they're going to break your heart—so don't apply. Sometimes parents are overprotective in a bad way. Be overprotective—don't let me fall—but let me jump."

—Diana Trujillo, aerospace engineer at NASA's Jet Propulsion Laboratory

What should strike you about the Noise in these examples is that it's not necessarily malicious. For the most part, it's just well-meaning advice, blanketed by good intentions and persuasive in its persistence. The trick becomes distinguishing the Noise from genuinely helpful guidance. We can all agree that advice from peers and elders is an essential way to fact-check yourself and gain insight about your road, but we've also all been subject to boilerplate wisdom that doesn't take into account who we are as individuals, and that advice isn't helpful—it's just the Noise.

Adding to the danger is that the Noise can also give us a way to avoid our fears and insecurities. Listening to what we "should do" can make us feel like we have our very own emergency parachute. The perceived security of groupthink keeps us insulated. If we're simply following a mapped-out path, we're not to blame when it runs off a cliff or doesn't take us where we were told it would go. The parachute of the Noise doesn't, of course, provide any real safety; it only keeps you from examining how your day-to-day decisions have brought you to this moment and this identity. It keeps you from facing your doubts. But examining the root of those doubts will open up new ways to discover who you really are.

The Oscar-nominated filmmaker Richard Linklater* describes overcoming the Noise as akin to ordering a meal that's not on the menu. Growing up in a small town in Texas, he remembers wanting to be a writer. But his desire to enter the arts was met with prickly disapproval. "It was, 'Well, yeah, you could study literature, but you'll never achieve anything. I mean, we don't do that.'"

The menu in front of Richard was pretty clear. Take a safe route, get a law degree, scrap the arts. "And that's just the practical advice that your loved ones, the people closest to you, will give you," Richard says. "Everyone around me was

* ▶ **roadtripnation.com/leader/richard-linklater**

44

saying, 'You should go to medical school, you should go to law school.' Do they really want you to be a lawyer? No. It just sounds good. I remember thinking, 'Anything everyone wants to do can't be right. I don't want to live like them. I don't want their life.'"

Richard chose to rebel against the path in front of him. He went to work on an oil rig, saving as much money as he could so that, after a couple of years, he was able to enter what he calls a "monkish, dropout, total-devotion phase." He ravenously ingested everything he could about filmmaking. He watched ungodly amounts of movies, read books, bought editing equipment (and taught himself how to use it), and cultivated his skills. Success for Richard was never a foregone conclusion, but with his inner voice guiding him through the many setbacks and challenges he faced, and no shortage of hard work, Richard has become one of the most critically acclaimed independent filmmakers in the business, making such lauded films as *Dazed and Confused* and *Boyhood*.

Bogi Lateiner* faced the Noise from family and friends when she decided to start fixing up cars after college. During that time, her greatest challenge was letting go of expectations and learning to be confident in who she is. "Listen to your inside voice," she says, "that gut voice that tells you what's going to make you happy." She ran her own automotive shop, 180 Degrees Automotive; hosts *All Girls Garage*; and is constantly dreaming up new projects to empower other women who wrench. "People told me I couldn't be a mechanic because I'm a girl," she says. "Don't let anyone tell you your dreams aren't good enough or that they're not the right dreams to have. Use people's naysaying as fuel for your fire. Dream wildly and then go do it."

As BET host Jeff Johnson reminded us, **"Whether people agree or disagree with you, so what? They don't have to live your life."**

* ▶ **roadtripnation.com/leader/bogi-lateiner**

When we first began speaking about the Noise at public events, we got a lot of flak. Teachers would quietly take us aside. Parents would stand up in the middle of our presentations feeling threatened, saying: "Let me see if I'm getting this straight. Are you telling our kids not to listen to their parents and teachers? Because I've got a problem with that." To them we'd say that rejecting the Noise isn't about shutting everyone out like a rebellious teen who's determined to get a face tattoo. Rather, it's about taking an honest look at the influences, expectations, and constructive criticism in your life and making informed decisions. Sure, in a perfect world, everything we do would warrant high fives and praise from our parents, bosses, and random people on the street, but we have to accept that our missteps will be numerous and hearing an outside perspective can help. Sometimes the critics might have a point.

And that's why it's important to truly think about what you're hearing. Is the message you're getting asking you to change who you are? Or is it something that can help you on your path? It can be hard to listen to the feedback, but it can also be a motivator. Entrepreneur Gary Vaynerchuk's* life looks like a picture of success now, but he went through years of rejection and criticism before he made it to this point.

"Go read all the reviews of my first book, the negative ones," he told us. "Being underestimated is such a gift. People spend so much time trying to talk themselves out of it. I would let it fester. Put all that pushback, all those nos, just put it in a little pocket. Let it grow."

"Self-awareness is the ultimate drug," Gary says. "You have to figure out who you are and you have to tune out all the other voices. All of them—especially the ones that are closest to you. You're better off to have issues with your parents now and love them forever than to appease them in the short term and then have resentment for the rest of your life."

* ▶ roadtripnation.com/leader/gary-vaynerchuk

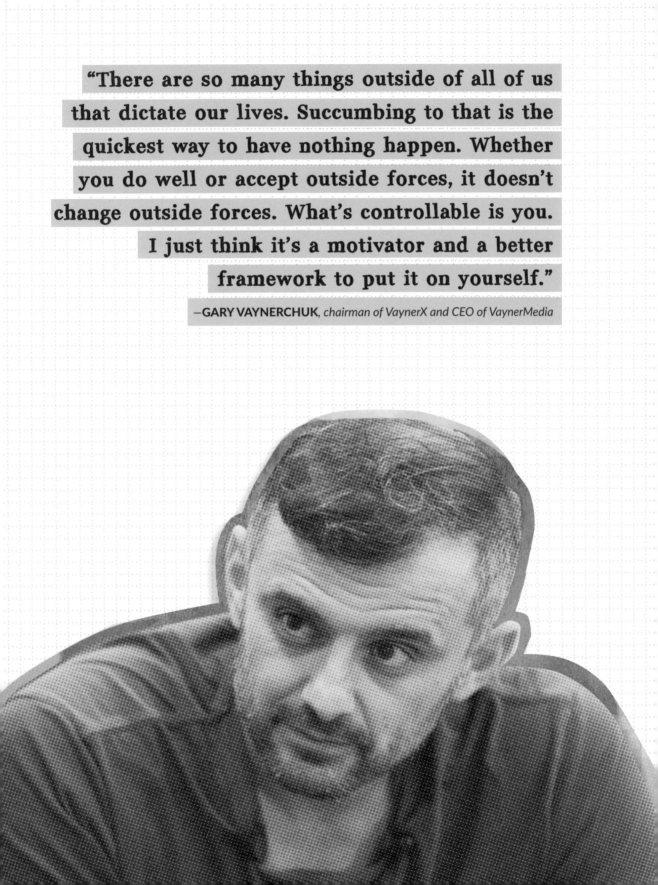

"There are so many things outside of all of us that dictate our lives. Succumbing to that is the quickest way to have nothing happen. Whether you do well or accept outside forces, it doesn't change outside forces. What's controllable is you. I just think it's a motivator and a better framework to put it on yourself."

—GARY VAYNERCHUK, *chairman of VaynerX and CEO of VaynerMedia*

STUDY YOURSELF

How can you distinguish between negative Noise and useful feedback? You filter it by being honest with yourself. When Richard Linklater decided to do his contrarian swing away from all the advice he was receiving about his life, it wasn't that he was able to immediately replace it with a clear vision of what he wanted. But he did know that the conventional spiel wasn't connecting with basic truths about himself. This awareness of the expectations Richard had for his life led him to take a self-reflective step away from the Noise. To get to that self-reflective step, you need to start studying yourself. Unearth your true interests, values, and aspirations in order to see how the Noise is inconsistent with who you are.

The basic rule is: If the message you're hearing takes into account who you are as an individual, and it rings true, chances are it isn't the Noise. If the message raises that gut-churning feeling of "This is not me," it's the Noise. The great thing about pinpointing the discrepancies between your authentic self and the clamor of the Noise is it will help solidify your value system, which in turn helps you more clearly identify new Noise when it comes down the pike.

Want to try this out? Play with the flowchart. Reflect on your day, your week, or even the past year. What comments, advice, and feedback did you receive from others? Was it Noise? Punch your findings through the flowchart. As the data drops through, you should, like a sort of psychological coin sorter, end up with a big, heaping pile of Noise in the Noise column.

Write down all that Noise somewhere—on the next page, in a journal or a notebook, or on a mirror. Take a "before" photo of your Noise so you have a reference to look back on. It's time to destroy it.

IS IT NOISE?

"_____"

Write an example of your Noise here.

Does this comment take your own individuality into account?

YES

NO

Is it valid?

Do you trust this person's opinion?

YES NO NO YES

This is constructive criticism. What should you be taking into account?

_____

_____

_____

Is there some truth to this comment?

NO YES

This is Noise but there might be something to learn from it. Can you think of anything?

_____

_____

_____

THIS IS NOISE. SHED IT.

Erase it! Burn it! Smash it to bits! Attach it to a brick and drop it into the sea, send it into orbit—whatever method of destruction feels best to you. Take an "after" photo, or record a video of the whole experience. (And use **#RoadmapBook** so we can see, if you do!)

What you've just done is create distance between yourself and the Noise. This is crucial, because if you don't flush it out, the Noise will infiltrate your psyche. Your uncle's gentle chiding that "you're just not cut out for that" will slowly morph into "I'm just not cut out for that." **Internalized Noise affects our belief systems and erodes our sense of self, killing our confidence and dreams. Then we pass that corrupt view of the world on to others like a bad cold.**

Elaine Kwon,* a celebrated concert pianist, five-time U.S. Tae Kwon Do champion, and music-theory lecturer at MIT, is not—by outward appearances—someone whose life has been dominated by the Noise. But the fight against self-doubt is something she has dealt with her entire adult life.

"My father just wanted us to succeed," says Elaine. "He said, 'Not only are you Asian and a minority, but you're also female, so you have to work doubly hard and be doubly better.' It was really tough when it came time to make a decision about college, and what I was supposed to do. I was supposed to become a medical doctor. My parents had a vision of me being stable and secure and having a nice profession."

Elaine had to choose between fulfilling her parents' expectations and chasing her own dream of becoming a pianist. She faced a crucial challenge. "I was already set up to go to University of Washington and enroll in pre-med. But I just didn't want to go into medicine," she recalls. "So I had a very tough conversation with my father. And I just decided, I'm going to follow my heart. Because otherwise I'm gonna feel sick inside. So I didn't listen. I went into music."

✳ ▶ **roadtripnation.com/leader/elaine-kwon**

The massiveness of this choice is powerful, and it's something Elaine probably understands only in hindsight. "If I had just followed the regular path, I probably wouldn't be playing at Carnegie Hall right now," she told us.

But Elaine's story holds another, perhaps more important lesson. Elaine's struggle against internal Noise is not a long-resolved struggle from her college years. "I felt so much pressure," Elaine says, "and I still feel that pressure. But it's mostly, myself . . . It's mostly—" here Elaine pauses, as if realizing something for the first time—"Maybe, maybe it's a habit from when I was a kid. . . . The pressure comes externally and then, I internalize it, and now I still put pressure on myself."

There it is. There is no lifelong vaccination against the Noise. It's rough for us, but, like distressed denim or tax day, it is never wholly banished. That might sound like a grim pronouncement to end this chapter on, but it's actually comforting.

Consider the Noise an equalizer. Every successful person, from rulers of nations to innovative engineers to mustachioed cocktail mixologists, has to overcome the Noise. Every day. Before our road trips, we didn't imagine that successful people from all walks of life struggled with the same doubts that afflicted us, but hearing the stories of others helped normalize our own struggles. We— and you—are not alone, even if the struggle never ends. Want proof? Here's a glimpse at our internal monologue when we were first writing this:

Is this chapter working? Does it make sense? Are we smart enough to be writing this book?

CHAPTER 3

WHERE YOU COME FROM DOESN'T DETERMINE WHERE YOU GO

What are you supposed to do when you're battling something greater than Noise? Not just self-doubt or misplaced advice, but hurdles that feel insurmountable? How can you "let go" of institutional blocks like racism, classism, or discrimination; or personal circumstances like financial insecurity, loss, or addiction? Things that will stay with you your whole life, and fundamentally shape how you see the world? Things that just don't seem to be . . . "let go"-able?

A few years ago, when we sent a group of young adults (who were out of school and struggling to find meaningful work) on the road, these were the questions they needed answered. The *Ready to Rise** road trip yielded some of the most powerful conversations in Roadtrip Nation history, but for roadtripper Ryan, there was one standout interview: Chris Gardner, the entrepreneur and author whose story inspired the film *The Pursuit of Happyness*.

* ▶ **Watch the documentary *Ready to Rise*: rtn.is/ready-to-rise**

All roadtrippers are typically at turning points, looking for guidance. (And if you're holding this book, we're guessing you're in a similar spot!) But Ryan was facing something more daunting than not knowing what to do with his life: He had grown up in a violent household, watched loved ones struggle with addiction, and was now fighting just to find steady housing—he needed a spark.

Chris Gardner's* story is familiar to anyone who's seen the Will Smith movie: He grew up in an unstable home with an abusive stepfather and joined the military as a way out of his environment. After finishing his service, he was working a dead-end job when he decided to pursue his dream of becoming a stockbroker— sacrificing his financial security and ultimately his home along the way. But he broke through, winning a position at one of the largest stock brokerages in the world and eventually starting his own wildly successful firm.

The roadtrippers met Chris at his luxurious office in Chicago, but the conversation revolved around his and Ryan's shared experiences spending homeless nights sleeping in the same Oakland, California, train stations. Chris proudly told Ryan that he secured his first big contract with Bay Area Rapid Transit (BART) by impressing them with his knowledge of their public transit system. "I used to live on [their] trains, and because of that, I got the business. They aren't gonna teach you that at Harvard; you have to learn that in Oakland!"

* ▶ **roadtripnation.com/leader/chris-gardner**

"You're gonna get your mother's eyes, your father's nose, and there's nothing you can do about it. But the spirit of who you're going to become as a man or a woman, I believe you can choose. I <u>did</u> have a choice. We all come from some place we didn't necessarily choose, but we can choose where we're going."

—CHRIS GARDNER, *entrepreneur and author*

It was a point Chris reiterated over and over: He'd found success because he'd decided he wouldn't let his circumstances define him. Instead, he'd used the hard-learned lessons from his past to push him in a positive direction.

That doesn't mean he didn't face setbacks; he made mistakes and missteps that easily could've landed him right back in the cycles of abuse and poverty. But he'd made it through, and now he was able to inspire Ryan to break out of those same cycles.

If you're thinking there's no way you'll ever get past the hurdle you're facing, or no way to get out of the hole you're in, we're here to tell you: That's. Not. True! This stuff doesn't just go away—but it definitely doesn't have to stop you. Like Chris, you might find that the lessons learned in the toughest times are actually the ones that will carry you forward.

Reflecting on Chris's story, we saw a new flame alight in Ryan. He'd seen some-one in his exact situation who hadn't just made it through, but had gone above and beyond to create a life that was extraordinary by any standard. "It gives me the perspective just to try harder and just keep going on," Ryan told us. "I'm gonna follow my heart and dream big."

YOUR STORY HAS POWER

When you're going through something impossibly hard, it often feels like you're the first person ever to encounter a roadblock. But even if you feel alone in your struggles, there's probably someone out there with a similar story who can give you the encouragement you need to keep going.

It's a huge part of why we send people out on the road—sometimes it just takes seeing someone climbing the mountain ahead of you to realize that even when it does get hard, it's possible to press on. Often, the second you hear the story of someone like you who's made it, you finally give yourself permission to dream and let yourself envision the life you've always deserved.

When *Beating the Odds** roadtripper Estephanie hit the road, she needed that encouragement. A second-generation American and first-generation college student from the Bronx, she had big dreams of pursuing the performing arts professionally. But she didn't see many people like her on Broadway or the big screen—and she was starting to question if her dream was worth the financial burden of college. Most of all, she didn't want to let anyone down.

The first leader she met was Elaine Del Valle,** whose impressive credits as a producer, actress, casting director, writer, and director wouldn't hint at the fact that she'd fought tooth and nail to make it out of her environment and into show business—even though that's exactly what she did.

Elaine grew up not far from where Estephanie did, in Brownsville, Brooklyn, a notoriously violent and impoverished neighborhood in New York. There wasn't much arts-focused education available, but when the gym teacher cast her as Sandy in a makeshift production of *Grease*, Elaine immediately caught the theater bug.

* ▶ **Watch the documentary *Beating the Odds*: rtn.is/beating-the-odds**

** ▶ **roadtripnation.com/leader/elaine-del-valle**

Pursuing theater in community college, she learned that a fundamental part of acting and writing was the concept of "speaking your truth." So she did: Elaine wrote the first act of an autobiographical play so powerful it prompted a teacher to pull her aside and tell her, "You **must** keep writing this."

That play bloomed into *Brownsville Bred*, an intimate one-woman show about growing up in the projects and watching her father struggle with heroin addiction. It was so personal that Elaine initially resisted performing it, but when she finally did, she was floored by the reaction. Telling her story wasn't just facilitating her own healing process; it was helping others process their upbringings in ways she'd never thought possible. "People were really relating to me. Writing that play empowered me beyond words."

Estephanie was equally amazed by Elaine's story: She'd thought no one could relate to her seemingly unique struggles, yet all her life, a role model had been just a short train ride away. "[Elaine] had to embrace her truth to not be a victim of it," Estephanie recounted, echoing her own struggle. "And sharing it helped her accept herself."

I DIDN'T SEE IT, SO I HAD TO BECOME IT

Can you only succeed if someone's set a precedent for your success? Or is it possible to define your own road through obstacles you've never seen anyone overcome, as difficult as it may seem?

We wanted to write this book in the hopes that the stories we've collected would connect with you and help guide you over your specific hurdles. But . . . we also acknowledge that sometimes you have to be the first to make the leap.

"I had a lot of insecurities about what I'd be able to achieve because I've never seen anyone else achieve it that looked like me. But I came to a point where I was like, I need to be that person that I'm looking for. I'm going to be the face for other young Puerto Rican women who are first-generation college students, who need to see that there's a place for them in business and there's a place for them in tech. Even though I didn't have that person to look up to, I became that person for someone else."

—**JESSICA SANTANA**, *cofounder, New York On Tech*

Code Trip* roadtripper Robin hit the road with a mission that should've been simple: She wanted to conduct an interview with a fellow Native American working in tech. But after 3,600 miles, 26 days, and who knows how many cold calls, she still hadn't found anyone who shared her background. Nevertheless, there was someone who made a huge impact: New York On Tech cofounder Jessica Santana.**

Growing up in New York City, Jessica watched classmate after classmate drop out of school, let down by the lack of local resources. Something within Jessica kept driving her to "make it out," but she knows this made her one of the lucky ones—some of her friends didn't even realize that was an option.

Years later, when she jumped into the corporate world of finance, she became increasingly uncomfortable with the fact that most of her peers were wealthy white males. While looking for a mentor at her company, she realized none of her superiors were from low-income backgrounds—how could any of them possibly understand her perspective or give her the advice she needed?

It led to an epiphany—she'd accrued enough of her own experiences to be a mentor to the people who really needed it: the kids back home! So she quit her job and, along with her college classmate Evin Robinson, founded New York On Tech, a nonprofit that connects New York City students with mentorship opportunities and access to tech education.

* ▶ **Watch the documentary *Code Trip*: rtn.is/code-trip**

** ▶ **roadtripnation.com/leader/jessica-santana**

After hearing Jessica's story, Robin realized that even though she didn't currently see others like her in tech, she had all the tools she needed to blaze the trail and help her community flourish. "I want people excited about tech, and I want to see more Natives in tech! So I can't get complacent—this is something I want other people to know and experience."

You don't have to wait for anyone to give you permission to dream. You don't need to see your perfect role model out in the world or in the pages of this book—**you** can be that person. It can be uncomfortable, Sisyphean-feeling work sometimes! But ultimately, when you take up the task of pushing forward, you can become the person you once needed to see.

YOU DON'T HAVE TO GO IT ALONE

Start-up founder Clarence Bethea* told us his advice for succeeding in business is the same as his advice for life: Staying vulnerable and vocal about when you need help is always more valuable than trying to push the tough stuff down. And he knows because he's come up against some pretty tough stuff.

Growing up around drugs, alcohol, and domestic abuse, Clarence was sucked into his environment, and started selling drugs himself at the age of fourteen. His life could've spiraled down a very different path from there, had it not been for the support he found along the way.

"Find somebody you can lean on, whether it's a significant other, a really good friend, or a teacher, find somebody you can feel vulnerable with . . . if you keep all that pushed inside of you and you think you're gonna figure out how to get that stuff out, it just won't happen."

*   ▶ **roadtripnation.com/leader/clarence-bethea**

For Clarence, help first came from his high school basketball teammates and coaches, who helped him realize he didn't need the validation of selling drugs when he had the support of a team. Later in life, he found further support in the form of therapy and counseling sessions. "Most of the time, things are baggage because you haven't verbalized [them] to someone else. Through therapy, I figured out that I don't have to carry these things."

If **you're** looking for someone to lean on, you have tons of options. We've talked to Leaders who swear by support groups like Alcoholics or Narcotics Anonymous, formerly incarcerated Leaders who got their footing at rehabilitation programs like Homeboy Industries, Leaders with learning and attention issues who found a community in organizations like Eye to Eye, even military veterans who found comfort in their workout groups.

Today, Clarence is running his own business with tens of thousands of customers, but it was only after he found the help he needed and realized how much he was carrying that he was able to let go of his heavier baggage and freely pursue his dream.

Remember that when things get heavy past the point of what you can support, more help is always out there. Even if you're tackling emotional issues that feel lonely, you never, ever have to go it alone.

YOUR EXPERIENCES ARE YOUR FUEL

Dropping some baggage will make it easier for you to move forward—but what does it really mean to "let go"? Does it require radically changing your environment or completely forgetting your past? Or can you use your obstacles to push you further, rather than letting them hold you back?

Growing up, user experience (UX) designer Pete Denman* always thought his biggest challenge in life would be his dyslexia. After struggling with reading for years, he knew something was seriously wrong after he failed third grade. It was years before he was properly diagnosed, but by then, he was tired of letting everyone down. "I had zero self-confidence. I went into high school and basically began a career of being that charming kid who liked to party."

Then everything changed. While diving outside of Portland, he was thrown into a sandbar, broke his neck, and became paralyzed in all four limbs and his torso. He was only twenty years old.

Yet, even in one of the most tragic experiences imaginable, he found an unexpected silver lining: "I basically was starting over again at that point. The only thing that anybody expected from me was to breathe. All I could do was go higher."

Still, recovering from his injury was a slow, grueling process. After nearly three years of "just breathing," his mom decided it was time for him to give school another chance and enrolled in a local art history class with him. His discomfort crept back in, but this time, he had all the accommodations he needed—not just for his quadriplegia, but for his dyslexia, too. He started excelling, passing class after class until he'd earned his bachelor's degree in design.

* ▶ **roadtripnation.com/leader/pete-denman**

After graduation, he took a job at Intel, and it was there that someone else's story started to shape the rest of his life. After hearing a mentor talk about his own dyslexia, Pete slowly worked up the courage to open up about his struggles. "Why aren't you telling people this?" his coworker asked. Pete answered, "Because it's my biggest shame in life!"

His mentor invited him to a retreat specifically for people with learning and attention issues, and introduced him to artists, actors, industry leaders, community organizers, and everyone in between. Hearing everyday success stories from a support group of peers radically changed Pete's viewpoint. "Since then, I've thought, this is not a disability—this is a different way of thinking."

As he started opening up about his dyslexia, his bosses realized his unique point of view made him perfectly suited to tackle their next big project: redesigning the user interface of theoretical physicist and author Stephen Hawking's computer. Pete's work ultimately contributed to an open-source software kit that helps drastically raise the quality of life for people with motor neuron diseases.

All of his accomplishments might not have been possible had Pete not sought the support he needed, found inspiration in the stories of others, and ultimately used the challenges from his past to positively change the lives of others for the better.

"Don't think that when you get to a certain point, it's all gonna be all better and magical. It's still tough. But keep pushing, because you *can* do it. Everybody thinks differently, and dyslexia is just one way that somebody thinks differently. **I think it's a power, not a curse."**

Letting go doesn't mean forgetting who you are. Chris Gardner, Jessica Santana, Pete Denman—none of these Leaders would've found success without their unique experiences and the identities they forged during the difficult times. Their "powers," as Pete would call them.

No, letting go simply means releasing everything that's holding you back or trying to define you, your happiness, where you want to end up, or what you dream about. It means that rather than letting your hurdles box you in, you do whatever it takes to use the things that've been stacked against you to reach even greater heights. Elaine Del Valle puts it perfectly: "Don't jump over and look past the things that have hurt you in your life. **Stand on your obstacle."**

Understand that where you come from, your circumstances, your environment, your family life, your struggles—these things are going to shape you. But none of those things have the power to define where you end up, or what you accomplish—only you can do that.

65

"Use what's happened in your past as your fuel. Own it, but don't let it define you. It's an awesome power cell that's going to propel you in whatever direction you want to go."

—Antonio French, former alderman, St. Louis's 21st ward

"The road that's taken me to where I am was so hard. But those trials were, in actuality, paving the way to greatness."

—Scout Bassett, Paralympian

"I [came] all the way [from] Colombia; I had no family in the U.S., I didn't speak the language, we didn't have the money to pay for my education—if I was all the way there and I was able to come here and work super hard . . . if I was able to do all that, you can do it, too."

—Catalina Laverde, engineer, Spotify

"If you don't transform your pain, you'll just keep transmitting it. You want to get people to a place where they can stand in awe at what you've had to carry, rather than stand in judgment of how you've carried it."

—Father Greg Boyle, founder of Homeboy Industries, the largest gang intervention, rehab, and reentry program in the world

"If you feel like right now you are stagnant, then something's holding you back. Find what that barrier is, and find a way to work around it. Then you can find a way to open more doors for other people than you ever would've imagined."

—Kyle Maynard, *first person with quadruple amputation to climb Mount Kilimanjaro without prosthetics*

"I call it the art of struggling: Students who come from the inner-city, who come from the hood, who come from nothing, whatever you do is going to be ten times harder than the next person. But because of what you went through, you're ten times more capable. Iron sharpens iron."

—Tristan Love, *former gang member turned high school vice-principal*

"You have to be a courageous person to ask for a helping hand, to change that life."

—David Andrade, *Homeboy Industries graduate and solar panel program coordinator*

"It's not where you are, but how far you've come to get there. We're all a little broken, but I've never seen a broken crayon you couldn't color with."

—Lisa Legohn, *master welder and cancer survivor*

CHAPTER 4

BUILD A LIFE, NOT A RÉSUMÉ

What defines you as a person? What have you done, what do you do now, and what will you do that makes you who you are?

When you think about these questions, we'd wager that the last thing that comes to mind is the résumé you're tinkering with. Yet the world we're brought up in has taught us to focus on that list of accomplishments as the most important indicator of who we are. "Will this look good on my résumé?" we ask ourselves when faced with crucial life decisions.

Where, on the balance sheet of skills, accomplishments, and career history, can we codify our actions in a way that will impress the next hiring manager who happens to quickly scan the record of all our accumulated work? Or worse, the hiring robot or algorithm that scans for the "right" keywords before a human ever gets to it? Such is the dilemma facing the modern résumé builder. How do you play a game where the board keeps shifting and the rules feel hidden? So we continue to go through the motions as we've been taught. We dutifully seek life paths that have very little to do with who we are—and a lot to do with what appears to be successful.

"On your tombstone at the end of the day, they're gonna see three things: your birth date, that dash, and your death date. The thing that has the most importance to me is that dash. . . . What happened in your life during the time you were born to the time you passed away? What defines you as a person?"

—GREGORY CARROLL, *CEO, American Jazz Museum*

Gregory's question gets to the core of any act of self-construction. A résumé will never be the answer to "What defines you as a person?" It won't stand in as the dash that separates your birth date and your death date. Résumé building that is divorced from any exploration of what truly fulfills and excites you will lead to unhappy consequences. Maybe it's a high-paying rat-race job that finds you working seventy-two-hour weeks for no particularly good reason, or maybe it's an unfulfilling "stepping stone" job that doesn't seem to be doing much stepping toward anything meaningful. When that winning job is neither stimulating, nourishing, nor in line with our interests, we can get stuck in the working-for-the-weekend, *Office Space* mentality. There's a reason that situation is so justly satirized: because it sucks.

Obviously nobody sets out to find a job they hate, but in accepting the Noise and following the Assembly Line, many of us inadvertently end up there, living in service of a résumé—which is crazy. Think about it in terms of pure hours. A third of your life will be spent at work (and much of the rest of it will be spent sleeping). Which comes out to eight hours a day, five days a week, fifty-two weeks a year (minus two weeks' vacation, if you're one of the lucky ones), and if you keep it up, you'll be doing it for roughly forty-five years. So that's . . .

90,

hours of your life wasted at

a job that you can't stand

All in the service of what? Paying the bills. Which of course has to get done, but if we've learned anything in our two decades on the road, it's that there is truly more than one way to get there. Financial security and an engaging, satisfying work life are not mutually exclusive. In fact, our experience shows that they go hand in hand.

So let's flip that narrative. The best résumés aren't the ones that showcase all the "right" steps and benchmarks. The best résumés tell the story of someone who is engaged and excited by the world and actively pursuing their interests. And if you're busy doing that, you're probably not, well, just focusing on building a résumé. You're building your life.

The funny thing is, when building your life is the focus, you'll build a great résumé.

RÉSUMÉ VS. REALITY

Instead of trying to craft a résumé that showcases you as an ambitious, hard-working problem-solver, go out there and be ambitious, solve problems, and work hard, all in the name of what interests and excites you. Don't wait to do what you really want to. You have to go out and find it, and it doesn't always match what you imagined. Those expectations of a neat list of accomplishments you should have by a certain time can work against you.

Gabrielle Lee* knows more than most the effects of putting this pressure on yourself. She works at NASA, but her path there, and the work she does, might not be what you expect.

In college, Gabrielle studied dance. "It's so funny to me when people are asking, 'Oh, well, what's your major and what are you going to do with that?'" she says. "I feel like the people who ask those questions were sold on this lie—when you

*   ▶ **roadtripnation.com/leader/gabrielle-lee**

pick a major in college you're definitely going to go along a specific career path. I started off with dance choreography and then somehow made it to contract management in government aerospace." Gabrielle's the one who makes sure everything's in order for NASA's earth science missions at the Jet Propulsion Laboratory.

Wait a minute, though, there must have been some stuff connecting the dots between a dance degree and NASA, right? Something . . . science-related? Well, no—the thing in between was an MFA in creative writing. After deciding against pursuing professional dancing, she followed her other love: writing. But once out of grad school, she couldn't find a writing job that paid a living wage for the kind of life she wanted to lead—in California, with a family someday. On paper, to be the writer she wanted to be, it seemed like she should be teaching or working in publishing. But those jobs were hard to come by where she lived, so she applied to, and won, a really competitive spot at JPL as an entry-level assistant working with NASA. If you put it on a résumé—entry-level assistant, even at a place like NASA—it might seem like a step down when you have two degrees.

"I was devastated. I was like, what am I doing? I have a master's degree and I'm being an assistant—which was a very egotistical thing for me to think, but I was just disappointed that I wasn't in publishing."

What she didn't anticipate was that being on the ground floor of such a dynamic organization meant that she could explore and experience everything. "Ultimately," she says, "it ended up helping me find my place here. It took me a while to find contracts"—the department where she works now—"but I couldn't even imagine having this job. It wasn't on my list. It wasn't on my radar. I didn't even know contracts administrators existed until I applied for this job, and I'm so thrilled with it. I get to be the most nitpicky grammar nerd ever."

"[I had these] perfect, clean expectations that I'd set for myself, and that my parents set for me, and that I thought people expected of me. And I just sort of embraced imperfectness—and it was really hard, it's still hard, it doesn't end. But I stopped thinking of things as end products and I started thinking of them as practice."

"Ultimately, the things that you get excited about workwise, they're going to find you," she says. "Follow a place where you can find your own sense of stability and also be happy, and you might be surprised by what that looks like."

Being open to a job that didn't look exactly like what she imagined would show up on her résumé led to an unexpected career that fulfills her love of language, grammar, and process—all the same things that drew her to writing in the first place. The point is, don't live your life waiting and doing what people say you're supposed to do in the order they say you should do it. Go build the life you want now, and don't be afraid to look outside of what's expected.

THE DEFERRED LIFE PLAN

We all know people who adhere to the "suffer now, enjoy later" concept; a kind of deferred life plan. It certainly hits close to home for us at Roadtrip Nation. We don't mean just when we're out talking to Leaders who once lived that life— we're talking about our experience with the RV culture in the United States. Don't get us wrong; we're not judging RVers. They're our people! But to say we stand out among them would be an understatement. Every road we take, every campsite, truck stop, rest stop we sleep at, we get sideways looks.

The point is, not only do we stand out visibly; there's something else subtly going on here. There's a palpable air among many of the RVers we encounter that silently communicates: "You kids shouldn't be out here. You haven't earned this yet." And viewed in the context of the deferred-life plan, it seems like their attitude is part of the whole Noise message, the defensive societal struggle to keep the world the same.

We can sympathize. They've spent years working toward retirement. Postponing. And it was all for this moment, this trip! And here we are, appearing like a ragtag group of wayward youth, green to the "real world." Bet they wouldn't be too impressed with our résumés, either. But this is a perfect example of the residual effects of the old way of thinking. The traditional career template, which is increasingly obsolete, still dictates the way we act, dress, format our accomplishments, and chase the job that makes the most amount of money so someday, decades from now, we can afford to retire, buy an RV, and do the very thing we're actually doing at the moment . . . living our lives the way we want. Remember, there is no guarantee of a certain future waiting for you, even if you do everything right.

FORGET WORK-LIFE BALANCE. INTEGRATE!

There is a paradigm shift happening in the way we think about work and life. Well-meaning social scientists have been bandying about terms like "work-life balance" as a solution for people stuck on the Assembly Line, and CEOs have been lapping it up and dispensing it in their memos and all-hands meetings like it's gospel. But we think work-life balance is a sham. Work-life balance implies two separate and opposing points that orbit about each other. *A sacrifice must be made somewhere. Either follow what truly motivates you or put food*

77

on the table. In order to balance the two, we toil away at jobs that don't fulfill us, and then, if we have the energy, we cram a few hours of pursuing our genuine interests into our evenings while we juggle cooking dinner, getting our clothes into the washer, and maintaining some semblance of a normal relationship with partners, friends, or family. Hardly a balance, right?

But "real living" doesn't have to be like that. With the right intention and mindset, you can feed and clothe yourself *by* pursuing work you believe in. What we're talking about is not work-life balance, but work-life integration—the incorporation of your interests into your work. "I say my work is my hobby, my hobby's my work," says entrepreneur Cindy Eckert. "It's not about some work-life balance. I love to work, but it's because I have always done those things that really rip the sheets off in the morning for me. If you find yourself in an environment in which you have put up the wall of 'This is my work. I'm punching the clock. I have to show up this many hours and then I get to go have fun in my real life,' you're in the wrong job."

Imagine waking up every day energized to be doing what you're doing at work that day. It doesn't mean you won't still want to ignore your alarm and go back to bed, but when you do stop hitting the snooze button, you're not filled with dread as you start your day. We've seen this demonstrated over and over with the people we've interviewed. Sometimes they did it from the get-go, sometimes it was a midlife shift, and sometimes they struggled throughout their entire careers to figure it out. But we wouldn't be writing this book if we didn't have proof that it is in fact possible to live with integrity and authenticity in the pursuit of meaningful work built on deep personal interests while still paying the bills.

Mountaineer and Academy Award–winning filmmaker Jimmy Chin* is an extreme example, but in his story, we see how intentional decisions motivated by interest can get you to fantastic places. As a professional climber and an expedition photographer who snaps photos for clients like *National Geographic*, The North Face, Patagonia, and the *New York Times*, Jimmy has the kind of gig people envy—explore the world and get paid. But what is powerful in Jimmy's story is that he didn't come from a background that empowered him to take the risks he did to build his career.

He just took them. Before beginning a traditional post-college path toward business or law school, he convinced his parents he needed a year to explore the world and himself. In Europe, the notion of a "gap year" (often between high school and college) is common for just this sort of exploration. Here in the States, Jimmy had to force his own gap year. And that gap year became seven years of living in the back of a beat-up Subaru. Jimmy did odd jobs that others wouldn't dare waste valuable "résumé space" on, as he skied, climbed mountains, and took photos. He wasn't living in a car because he had to, but because he wanted to intentionally pursue what was important to him on his own terms, devoting his limited resources to his interests. "When you do something like that," he says, "it goes against the grain of everything you've been brought up to think."

But those intentional choices started to work in Jimmy's favor in unexpected ways. One gorgeous photo taken on a friend's camera and sold to a magazine led to another, and another, and then in a few years, Jimmy was leading some of the most daunting photography expeditions ever attempted, capturing breathtaking moments, from the sandstone towers of Mali to the peak of Mount Kilimanjaro.

* ▶ **roadtripnation.com/leader/jimmy-chin**

For Jimmy, once he found what he loved most, one thing led to the next. "All these little stepping stones kind of just led me to all these different places. In some ways, I don't feel like I ever had control of my life. But I would throw myself at climbing. And climbing produced photography. And also out of climbing, I put together complex expeditions to really remote places. And I couldn't have done that without my education. You pick up skills that you don't even know you have in college. And then all of a sudden you begin to apply different things that you've picked up."

Like Gabrielle (and like so many of the other Leaders we've met), Jimmy used what he had already learned, integrated it into his interests, and built a life that translated into a stellar résumé. But the life was the goal, not the piece of paper.

It all comes down to how you spend your limited time on Earth—to that dash on the tombstone between your birth and death dates. How will you define yourself as a person, how do you add genuine meaning to the space between the two dates on your tombstone?

The best advice: Start now and act with intention. If you're young, explore and pursue your interests while you're likely more free of overarching responsibilities like family and finances. If you're older, you can still do it, you just might need to be a little more strategic. Regardless of where you are or where you start, the skills, experiences, and expertise you gain along the way will give you much more pride in the "dash" that is your life . . . and what ultimately shows up on your résumé.

Spend some time thinking about how you can begin the integration of your work and interests, and how they each exist in your life now. Will your time be spent working on something that gives you meaning? Building skills so you can do more of what you love?

What will fill the "dash" on your tombstone?

Jot down anything and everything you envision for a life well lived according to *you*.

WHAT DEFINES YOU AS A PERSON?

RIGHT OR LEFT?

By Zachariah Cowan

IT WAS AN UNHOLY 115°F/46°C AS WE CAME BUSTING THROUGH
THE DESERT, SWEATING THROUGH OUR SHIRTS, STARING STRAIGHT
INTO THE WHITE HEAT AHEAD ON OUR WAY TO OUR NEXT INTER-
VIEW. WHILE IDLING AT A ROADSIDE GAS STATION WE WERE GREETED
BY A TARANTULA THE SIZE OF MY HAND, SLINKING PAST THE PUMPS
AS IF TO SIMULTANEOUSLY WELCOME ALL THE PASSERSBY TO HIS
TERRITORY AND REMIND THEM THAT THEY'RE NOT HOME ANYMORE.

WELCOME TO ARIZONA.

OUR PLANNED ROUTE WOULD TAKE US FARTHER SOUTH, CROSS-
ING THE RIO GRANDE AND INTO EL PASO, BUT I KNEW THERE'D BE
NO RESPITE FROM THE HEAT. SO IN A WAY I WAS THANKFUL THAT
OUR NEXT INTERVIEW WAS PLANNED FOR EARLY THE FOLLOWING
MORNING, AT WHAT I HOPED WOULD BE A SLIGHTLY LESS BLISTER-
ING 7:00 A.M.

OUR INTERVIEW WAS WITH DEON CLARK, AND WE WERE TO
MEET HIM AT THE PALO VERDE NUCLEAR GENERATING STATION,
THE LARGEST NUCLEAR ENERGY FACILITY IN THE UNITED STATES,
GENERATING ELECTRICITY FOR FOUR MILLION PEOPLE IN THE

Zachariah Cowan is a bundle of inquisitive energy from Columbus,
Ohio. Captivated by everything from sustainable agriculture
to blacksmithing, he followed his love of sciences to a major in
geology at Ohio State University. But even with that direction,
Zachariah had difficulty funneling his varied interests into one
concrete pursuit. He joined two other roadtrippers in our green
RV on a cross-country search for ways to turn his interests into
a meaningful livelihood.

SOUTHWEST. WAKING UP AT THE LOCAL TRUCK STOP WHERE WE
HAD SLEPT THE NIGHT BEFORE, I COULD SEE THE STEAM RISING
FROM THE SPACE STATION-LIKE STRUCTURE ON THE HORIZON.
AFTER A BIRDBATH IN THE GAS STATION SINK, I GRABBED A CUP
OF COFFEE FOR DEON AND WE HEADED TO MEET HIM.

DEON IS A BIG GUY WHO GREW UP ON THE SOUTH SIDE OF
CHICAGO. HE HAS THAT EX-MILITARY LOOK, ALL POSTURE AND
MUSCLE, BUT TEMPERED WITH A GENEROUS DEMEANOR AND A
WELCOMING SMILE. WE SPENT THE MORNING WITH DEON AS HE
TOLD US ABOUT HIS HARDSCRABBLE YOUTH, WITH A FATHER WHO
WAS MORE OR LESS MIA HIS WHOLE LIFE AND FAMILY MEMBERS
FLOATING IN AND OUT OF JAIL—AN ALL TOO COMMON STORY LINE
IN HIS NEIGHBORHOOD.

HE HAD GOTTEN OUT OF THE SOUTH SIDE BY JOINING THE
NAVY. "I WAS SEVENTEEN WHEN I WENT IN," DEON TOLD US.
"FRESH OUT OF HIGH SCHOOL, AND THE NAVY'S PROGRAM WAS SET
UP THAT IN EIGHTEEN MONTHS YOU WENT FROM KNOW-NOTHING
TO QUALIFIED TO OPERATE A NAVAL NUCLEAR POWER PLANT.
EIGHTEEN MONTHS! FIFTEEN HOURS A DAY, MONDAY THROUGH
MONDAY. NO WEEKENDS, NO BREAKS."

BY AGE NINETEEN, DEON WAS LEADING A CREW OF FORTY-
TWO TECHNICIANS ON A NUCLEAR AIRCRAFT CARRIER. "THAT'S THE
PART THAT I LOVED ABOUT IT. YOU BECOME A VALUABLE ASSET

TO ANYONE IN ANY INSTITUTION BECAUSE OF THAT KNOWLEDGE."
HIS NAVAL EXPERIENCE LED TO LUCRATIVE WORK IN THE CORPORATE
SECTOR OF NUCLEAR ENGINEERING.

THAT UP-BY-THE-BOOTSTRAPS STORY ALONE PROBABLY WOULD'VE
BEEN ENOUGH TO BRING US OUT TO THE DESERT TO VISIT HIM, BUT
DEON'S TALE GETS EVEN MORE COMPELLING. IT BEGAN WHEN THE
ADULT DEON WENT BACK TO THE SOUTH SIDE ON A VISIT TO HIS MOM.
"IT WAS SEEING THIS SENSE OF HOPELESSNESS. SO I STARTED VOLUN-
TEERING A LOT OF MY TIME WHERE I WOULD GO TO DIFFERENT HIGH
SCHOOLS AND JUST TALK TO STUDENTS AND SHARE MY STORY. I WOULD
FIND THAT THESE YOUNG PEOPLE WANTED TO KNOW: HOW DID I DO IT?"

DEON USED HIS LIFE SAVINGS TO FOUND THE LEGACY INITIATIVE,
A NONPROFIT WHOSE GOAL IS TO FOSTER OPPORTUNITIES IN UNDER-
SERVED COMMUNITIES. THIS WAS POSSIBLE BECAUSE OF HIS FOCUSED
DETERMINATION TO MASTER A SKILL. WHEN YOU GROW UP AS DEON
DID, THE IDEA OF SECURITY AND SAFETY TAKES ON A DEEPER
MEANING. HIS ADVICE TO US:

"THE MILITARY'S TRAINING CAUSED ME TO BECOME VERY, VERY
USEFUL IN THE CORPORATE NUCLEAR WORLD. MY ADVICE IS TO LOCK
IN ON A SKILL, AND MASTER IT, SUCH THAT NOW YOU'VE GOT SOME-
THING TO FALL BACK ON."

I'D HEARD THIS KIND OF THING BEFORE. THE OLD FALLBACK
PLAN THAT MANY PARENTS AND COUNSELORS USE TO CHECK OUR
DREAMS. THAT KIND OF STATEMENT IS VERY OFTEN AND VERY EASILY
TRANSMUTED INTO THE NOISE. BUT COMING FROM DEON, IT FELT
DIFFERENT, REAL IN A POWERFUL WAY—DEON HAD LIVED IT AND
EARNED IT. DEON'S FALLBACK WAS AN INTENTIONALLY DEVELOPED
SET OF SPECIALIZED SKILLS THAT SPOKE TO HIS NATURAL TALENTS.
IT MEANS HE HAS A SIX-FIGURE SALARY WITHIN HIS GRASP WHENEVER
HE NEEDS IT. AND IT GAVE HIM THE FREEDOM TO FUND HIS NON-
PROFIT AND MAKE A POSITIVE IMPACT ON OTHER PEOPLE'S LIVES.

WE SAID OUR GOODBYES AND CLIMBED BACK INTO THE RV. WE
DROVE EAST IN SILENCE, EACH OF US LOST IN THOUGHT AS WE WRES-
TLED WITH THE IMPLICATIONS OF DEON'S STORY. DID I HAVE, IN MY
OWN LIFE, SOMETHING LIKE WHAT DEON HAD? A PURPOSEFUL FALL-
BACK? DID I HAVE THE GUTS AND DRIVE TO LIVE LIKE DEON? AND IF
I DID, WHAT WOULD I DO WITH IT?

Our next stop was Columbus, New Mexico, population 1,664, but with our RV camped out on Columbus's deserted main drag, we would've guessed it to be more like 25. Maybe 50, tops. With its row of low-slung storefronts silent under the moonlight, it felt like a town out of *The Last Picture Show*. With no picture show of any kind to divert us, we kicked rocks around on the street to pass the time until we killed the lights and settled into the creaks and sways that come with sleeping in an RV.

We were there to meet Paul Salopek. Paul is a two-time Pulitzer Prize–winning journalist who has written for *National Geographic* magazine and the *Chicago Tribune*, among many other publications. How had this globe-trotting reporter ended up in what seemed like the middle of nowhere, a stone's throw from the Mexican border? By choice? By accident? What led him to this tiny corner of the country?

Paul was a rambler in his youth, and in many ways he still is. One summer, after graduating with a biology degree, Paul was crossing the country on a motorcycle, with the end goal of shipping out on a shrimp boat in the Gulf. But then, in sleepy sunbaked Roswell, Paul's motorcycle gave up the ghost. With only sixty bucks in his pocket, Paul had to stick around and earn enough money to get the bike back on the road.

Through a random recommendation, and on the strength of having a college degree, he scored a job writing police reports for the local paper. Almost immediately he discovered both his skill for writing and his joy in the process. Suddenly, he was a journalist. And he loved it. That love, and the work he became immersed in, carried him around the globe. Roswell was where Paul discovered his Open Road.

"I got to where I am by no sort of preplotted line," Paul told us. "No career-oriented, well-thought-out plan. I was going where the story was.

"It's easy to say 'find your passion,' but people don't appreciate as much the power of serendipity in their lives. I hear a lot about the word passion. It's a popular word these days, especially in the United States. I think it's overused. It's been devalued. It's like a coin that's been rubbed too much. But what about when something happens and it knocks you off-kilter; what's your reaction? It might be irritation, or frustration, but when you look back on it ten years from now you might say, 'I'm really glad that happened because I've accumulated this since then.' So, you have to be open to these 'Ys' in your road, and open to being moved by new experiences."

Straight lines versus tangents. Credentials versus experiences. Fallbacks versus whims. Planning versus serendipity. In the course of two days in the desert, we'd met two successful people who couldn't have had more contrasting worldviews and starkly different lessons to share with us. Were they both right? Could one be wrong?

After leaving Paul, I spent the rest of the day debating in my head. The advice of each of them had seemed bulletproof in the moment. And they had both led the lives to back up every one of their words. Yet they were such contradictions!

We pulled into White Sands National Monument. Happy to be free of the RV and our round-robin discussion, we sprinted out into the vast void of the evening desert. Once we were atop the dunes, ankle-deep in sand, the true lesson of these two contrasting stories became clear.

We shouldn't model our lives after anyone else's. Neither is right, and neither is wrong. To blindly follow an example, no matter how well-conceived, puts us right back on the Assembly Line. Deon and Paul each discovered a set of values to guide their decisions, and so must we. Each one of us on our own Open Road.

CHAPTER 5

LIFE IS LINEAR ONLY IN THE REARVIEW MIRROR

We've left something out of this book so far. A word, to be precise. One that, since we're in the life-figuring-out business, we hear all the time. It seems to come at us in our most vulnerable moments. And if your experience is like ours, it often hits when you're feeling especially lost.

Passion.

"Just follow your passion." It's a constant chorus these days, but you won't hear it from us. That's because as a jumping-off point, it's just plain overwhelming. What if you don't know what your passion is? If each of us could begin by pinpointing one singular passion that has enough force to magically bend our lives in the right direction and show us the best things to do, we never would have needed to write this book, and you probably wouldn't be reading it either. The reality? For most of us, expecting to know our passion at the beginning of the journey feels like learning to walk by running a marathon.

Passion isn't a starting point, it's a destination. It's a place you arrive after, in many cases, years of making small decisions aligned with the things that interest you. For most of us, it's something we build over a lifetime. And sometimes, it's only apparent once you've given yourself the space to explore and try things.

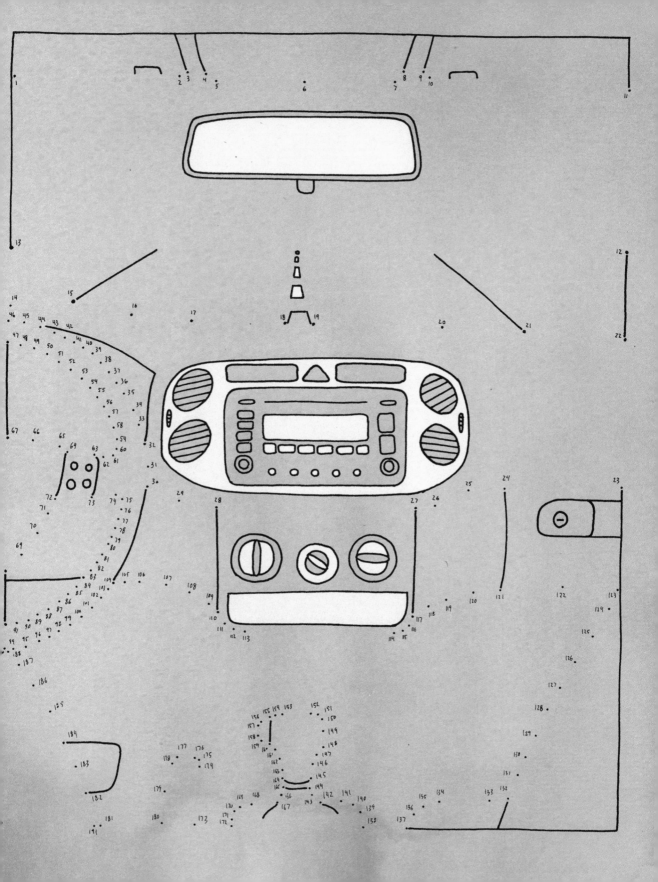

It's easy to assume that our role models always knew what their passion was, that they had some kind of genius master plan, a straight and secure path that led them to the top. In a haze of fear about our own choices, we assume successful people didn't face our same fears or ever take a step that led them astray. But they did. Often.

"The quest for knowing what it is you're here for—you may never really know," Beverly Robertson* told us when we visited her at the National Civil Rights Museum, where she's the president. "But guess what? Do something! And then decide if that's what you want to do. **Don't feel that if you're still seeking, or you're not really sure, that you've got to know right now. It's a quest, and for some of us, it's a lifelong quest.**"

DON'T LOOK FOR THE FINISH LINE

It's pretty much impossible at age twenty-one (or at any age) to know what will make you happy for the rest of your life. Even more difficult is planning an error-free, linear route with a clear idea of where you'll end up, and it leaves out all of the beautiful, serendipitous discovery that can happen. But if the successful people we've met didn't have a clear sense of where they were going, how did they get where they are today? Well, through years of missteps, failures, epiphanies, and course corrections. Their "direction" was more of a compass heading. A loosely guided approach informed by intention and interest (and plenty of hard work), not by some preplotted plan. The key is to give ourselves the flexibility to make adjustments along the way. This calls for an elastic approach to life that is adaptable, evolving, and builds on itself. Who wants to stay trapped in a situation they've outgrown, just because they've already "made it this far"?

This mindset of adaptability doesn't mean you should throw caution to the wind and cease all life planning. While we've found that the happiest people didn't

* ▶ **roadtripnation.com/leader/beverly-robertson**

follow a fixed formula, they did follow their interests and values, and made decisions accordingly. Instead of clinging to rigid, premeditated ideas of where they would end up, they let their paths be informed by experience, so they could respond to new information and alter course when necessary.

This approach to life won't make sense in the moment. The uncertainty is unnerving, and right now, you're probably thinking, "But can't I just go to law/medical/business/whatever school and wake up a happy, well-adjusted grown-up who owns nice things?" Well, sure you can. Just know that the future you try to orchestrate can still change dramatically with time and experience.

PASSION IS A PROCESS

When United Nations Development Programme director of communications Mila Rosenthal* was a kid in a steel town in northeastern Ohio, she never could have guessed what her passion would be or where she'd end up. All she knew was that she was looking for excitement. "It wasn't very coherent," she says. "I wanted to have adventures and I wanted to do something good."

She couldn't have imagined how this would take shape. It took experience and adventure to do that. It was in the trying that things started to gel. In retrospect, the connection is more clear: from a kid obsessed with movies, to a reporter in postwar Cambodia, to an anthropologist trying to understand people's lived experiences, to running the UN department that's sparking change by telling stories from around the world. Adventure, yes. Doing good, sure. But also, the key to it all that she didn't recognize when she started: storytelling.

We've seen this play out again and again. Life is only linear in the rearview mirror. In the thick of your day-to-day experience, you may feel derailed, but if you're living a life guided by your interests, all those twists and turns, doubts and misfires, will look like a clear path in retrospect.

＊ ▶ **roadtripnation.com/leader/mila-rosenthal**

"There are two ways you can think about your career. One is a paint-by-numbers approach. In that way you're trying to create this picture, you have this toolbox of all the different colors, and you go about it systematically knowing all along what the picture is going to be. That's the path of least resistance. I like the other way. The 'connect the dots' approach, where you start off with one idea, or a conviction, something that really grabs you. Then you take the next logical step. You learn more about it, you learn more about yourself, and then you take the next logical step. You're not sure what the picture is going to look like when you're in the beginning phases, but as you proceed, you gain speed and you see suddenly that it's a circus seal with a ball. You may not know where you're ending up, but you're confident that it's a good place, and that the final picture will be beautiful."

—BRITTAN HELLER, *Human Rights and Special Prosecutions Section, Criminal Division, U.S. Department of Justice*

"The advice that people say—just follow what you're passionate about—I think that's true, but I also think that's a pretty high bar for a lot of people," Mila says. "There may be just something you like, or that you're interested in. Don't demand so much of yourself that you think, I need to do something that's grand, or I need to reach for something that seems impossible. Instead of figuring out the whole path, figure out your next step on it."

If passion is a destination—one that only becomes clear when you zoom out on the map—your interests are the guideposts along the way. Each one is a clue to follow—a hint to change direction, turn down a new path, or continue what you're doing. The danger is ignoring the interests that you think might strike others as silly or frivolous. Explore them! See where they lead. When you don't take what matters to you seriously, you could miss out on something truly great.

When it came time for CakeLove founder Warren Brown* to figure out his career, he decided he wanted something where he could effect change. Law school seemed like the right answer. But once he was practicing law, it was clear that it wasn't for him. Looking for joy, he started baking in his spare time, and people responded in a big way. On one trip, he brought a cake wrapped up on a plate, and all through the airport, people commented on it. The cake was like a magnet. It struck him: Something is happening here that I need to pay attention to.

To someone else, it might not make sense: going from law—and leaving behind years of training—to baking. But he knew that if his heart wasn't in practicing law, there was no making a difference there. Once he realized he wanted to explore his new direction, he took his interest in baking more seriously than he'd ever taken law school. He researched, asked questions, and talked to other bakers before opening up his own bakery. He's found his passion in bringing people together and fostering connection through food—that's how he makes

93

* ▶ **roadtripnation.com/leader/warren-brown**

a difference in his community. Looking back, he can see all the hints that point to where he is now. He never would have put them together in the moment, but he's always been interested in food and cooking. (In law school, he created a study group called "Gastronomy and the Law.") His friends noticed; before baking was ever on Warren's radar, a friend who picked up on his interest in cooking gave Warren a book on desserts, telling him, "When you start baking, that's when you're really cooking."

"It matters so much just to follow that little whisper or voice that's in your head and your heart," Warren says. "That's the one. It feels like it's not. It's scary. You want to deny it. You want to say, 'No I'm going to ignore it.' I mean, we've all done it. Don't do it forever. [That voice] is your friend."

THERE IS NO SCRIPT

Often, what we hear in the idea of passion is the hope that knowing what your passion is means you'll finally have the answer to happiness and you'll never be lost again. (Finally, you can relax from all of this life-figuring-out stuff.) The real answer is, even if you know what your passion is, you're still going to face challenges, self-doubt, and uncertainty. That's why you have to stay open to what you might find along the way.

"I've never been the type that had a five-year plan," professional Porsche enthusiast Magnus Walker* told us when we met him in his garage. He discovered his passion at a car show at age ten. He immediately wrote Porsche a letter saying he wanted to design their cars, and got a nice response back that essentially said, "Call us when you're older, kid."

His path since then has been defined by being open to any opportunity, as long as it aligned with his interest in unconventional self-expression. At fifteen, he dropped out of school to get out of his hometown of Sheffield, England, and

 roadtripnation.com/leader/magnus-walker

/ / / Roadmap / / /

headed to the United States, where he started selling clothes on the Venice Boardwalk. It wasn't easy by any means; he got close to giving up and going home more than once. But he kept at it and spun his free-spirited design sense into a multimillion-dollar fashion business.

That success gave him the ability to buy his first Porsche at twenty-five, and that's when he started to channel his eccentric style into assembling and customizing one of the most insane Porsche collections in existence. Any car enthusiast with enough money could assemble a fleet of Porsches. Magnus's garageful is different: These are cars (many that he finds in rough shape) that he's reimagined, rebuilt, and customized out of pure love and a desire to recapture the thrill he got as a kid when he first saw that iconic car and felt the freedom of possibility. He's known his passion is Porsches since age ten, but his initial plan—that he could work for Porsche designing cars—would have stifled his individualistic approach and vision for custom designs.

"My life wasn't structured or scripted," he told us, "but evolved because I took risks, said yes more than I said no, and just did what felt right. And, sometimes, along the way, a little bit of luck gets thrown your way, but luck only takes you so far. Ultimately, hard work, motivation, dedication, and doing something that you love gets you places you may think you would never go."

Video game designer Vicki Smith's* story follows the same unscriptable arc. She stresses the importance of diving in first and then evaluating your happiness and satisfaction along the way. Vicki began with a dream of drawing comic books for a living. "It wasn't my parents' dream that their daughter would become a comic book artist and writer. As much as they loved me and encouraged me, they said, 'We're not going to pay for a humanities degree.' So I went and got my degree in electrical engineering. It's a really good career. But I had that

* ▶ **roadtripnation.com/leader/vicki-smith**

creative side, and essentially I got really bored. I got my master's in interactive technology. Which is a euphemism for a master's in video game design." How close is Vicki's current career to her original dream of making comic books? Surprisingly close, as she explains: "So I get to make three-dimensional, interactive comic books now. I get to build a castle and figure it out. It's my story. It's my level. So I'm not actually in comic books, but I kind of got a step up."

She started with a dream of creating worlds through comics, and ended up doing an even more punched-up version of that as a video game designer. She approached her interests from another angle, surprising herself and those around her. Sounds kind of like improv, right? (Which gives us a perfect segue. . . .)

GET FLEXIBLE

Charna Halpern,* founder of ImprovOlympic (now known as the iO Theater) in Chicago, Illinois, is a prime example of intentional but unpredictable living. Charna's path was clear to her. She was a schoolteacher. But then a chance radio interview in her hometown led to a job offer to become a radio host.

✱ ▶ roadtripnation.com/leader/charna-halpern

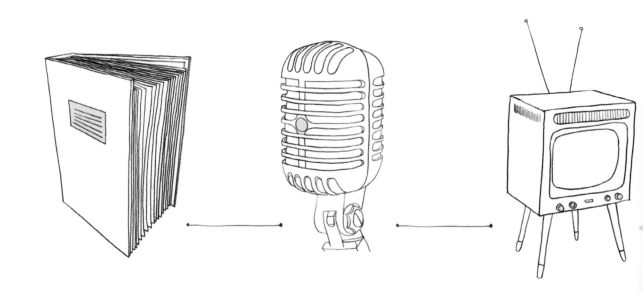

"I said, 'I don't know anything about being on the radio, I'm a schoolteacher.' But then I started thinking, 'Who said I have to be a teacher? Maybe I am a radio broadcaster!'" That spirit of grasping unexpected opportunities outside of her comfort zone led Charna to work with the influential comedy troupe The Second City and, eventually, to launching her own improv company where she trained comedic legends like Mike Myers and Chris Farley.

Flexibility is key. Just ask any biologist: Which species survive in the face of change? The adaptable ones. So be nimble and intentional with your choices. Don't think that you have to know the future. Charna's Noise was telling her to believe in only one vision of herself. Instead, she defied those expectations and stayed malleable, finding new ways to define herself. The unexpected twists and turns she followed in life put her on a path that makes total sense in hindsight. As Charna explained it, **"Life is a lot like improvisation. What happens is more interesting than what you've planned, what you planned will never happen, and if you think you know what's going to happen, you're doing it wrong."**

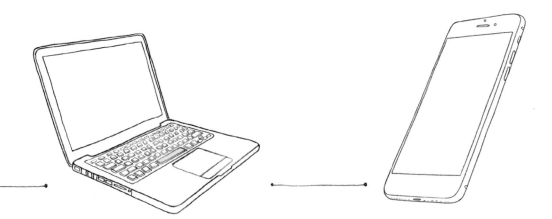

CHAPTER 6

LIVING IN BETA

- -

People will tell you to choose a path and stick to it—stay on course—look for a secure career and hold on to it like it's a life preserver on the *Titanic*. But they're ignoring the reality of how the world works—and the reality of how you can navigate it in a unique, personal way and thrive like never before.

The career as we once knew it is extinct. Not only have economic models changed, but the pace of innovation and diversification continues to accelerate. "You have no idea what field you'll be working in ten to fifteen years from now, because most of those fields don't exist yet," says Juan Enriquez,* an author and researcher who studies the intersection of science, economics, and society. Juan's personal story bears out the truth of his statement. He started out as an official in the Mexican government, and after a stint as a peace negotiator during Mexico's Zapatista rebellion, Juan grew weary of the violence and went back to academia. He studied genomics, learning about recombinant DNA and other life sciences that to outsiders may seem like straight-up sci-fi.

He founded Biotechonomy, a life sciences research and investment firm that focuses on innovative start-ups and companies. And he's gone as far as suggesting how gene editing could prepare humans for life on other planets, and, a little closer to home, how it could shape our response to diseases and help us create vaccines more quickly. Juan didn't wait for this hybridized "career" to show

* ▶ **roadtripnation.com/leader/juan-enriquez**

99

up in an occupational handbook, he went out and invented it. Just because something didn't exist twenty years ago, or even ten days ago, doesn't mean it can't exist now.

The economy, technology, and YOU are ever-evolving. So it doesn't make sense to approach life and work like they're constants. To deftly navigate the future and be able to grow and thrive amid the challenges, you have to flex your muscle for tolerating uncertainty. This isn't so much a warning as it is an invitation to approach life the way so many of the Leaders we spoke with have already been doing for years: living in beta.

LOOK FOR THE NEXT YOU

Beta testing is a concept in software development. When you beta test, you're seeing if what you've created works as planned. A beta test doesn't mean you have your final version; it means you have something developed enough to put it to the test. Putting your idea out there can show where you miscalculated or where you got it right. Often, what you discover is something you never could have predicted.

Living in beta means you are continually building better versions of yourself. It means that the current "you" is just a single iteration of what you can be, and the next "you" that you build isn't a final either—it's just one more step forward.

The nature of beta testing—trying out something that's not final—means you won't always feel completely ready. But to get the feedback that will inform where you go next, you have to release this version of yourself out into the world. Sometimes, what you learn will mean your next step is challenging—you might need more training, experience, education, or help to get to your next best version. Or you may learn that you need to scrap what you're doing and take a totally different approach.

Rolling through New Mexico on a trip that was all about adapting to change, we stopped at the ceramic studio of Theo Helmstadter. We were just there to take a pottery class, but as he started to guide us in shaping clay, we realized that the lessons he was talking about went deeper than the wheel. He's dedicated himself to an art that can never be completely controlled. Every object he makes transforms in ways that he can't predict—he's learned to master what he can and adapt to what he can't control.

But sculpting clay on a wheel is just his most recent version.

"That's not something people tell you when you're in junior high or high school," he says. "That you're going to come up with a plan, but then you're probably going to need to come up with a different plan afterward."

Going to college, moving to New Mexico, and getting a job as an English teacher was the right thing for a certain time. But then, while apprenticing in a ceramics studio in his spare time, Theo saw a new possibility—but it meant taking a risk and putting a different idea, and different version of himself, into the world. This next phase was about mastering a material and looking inward. "I knew there was a part of me that was not getting to evolve and grow, which was this contemplative, quiet, creative inner part."

When he was starting his studio, he says, "If you get into being very on-paper about it, it's easy to get stuck. At some point for me, it was a leap, and you don't have all the answers, you don't know how it's going to work out. All you know is that you've got to do it."

He stayed in that zone for a few years, hiding in his own little world and figuring things out for himself, but before long he was on to the next version: opening his studio up to be a collective and a teaching space, which is where we found him.

It's important to note that becoming the next version of yourself doesn't mean leaving who you are behind. Working with clay was something Theo had first done as a teenager, and opening a studio got him back to that place of solitary focus that he remembered. He felt that same return when he began teaching again, this time in clay. "It felt familiar, even though it was a total new beginning."

CHALLENGE VS. CHANGE

The act of self-construction is difficult, and it happens over and over, in every part of your life. But living in beta means that even when life throws you a curveball, you'll be okay because of the hard work you've been doing to strengthen who you are and what you can handle. Rather than blindly holding on to one career or version of yourself, you'll be able to move on to the next one, even when it means adjusting to something completely life-altering.

No one else we've met demonstrates the ability to iterate and make adjustments quite like Mark Inglis.* Mark, a professional mountaineer who began climbing when he was twelve years old, told us that in his field, "you have to be prepared to be scared on a regular basis, and I guess that set me up incredibly well for all the changes that have happened in my life."

Both of Mark's legs were amputated below the knee due to frostbite on Christmas Eve, 1982, after an ill-fated expedition up Mount Cook, New Zealand's highest peak. When we sat across from him twenty-six years later, the wind outside howling through the black New Zealand night, he told us:

> "The one thing I've come to understand is [that] the most exciting thing about life is change."

✻   ▶ **roadtripnation.com/leader/mark-inglis**

All we could think was, wow . . . this guy had survived some of the most difficult challenges someone could face and was still urging us to embrace the fear and uncertainty that comes with change. Mark told us about a time soon after the surgery, looking down at where his legs had been and thinking, "How can I turn this into an advantage?" Change for him meant accepting losing his legs and framing his accident not as a tragedy, but as an opportunity to take advantage of a new landscape. So dogged was he in his desire to prove to the world that he had no limitations that he went on to win a silver medal in the 2000 Paralympic Games and became the first person with a double amputation to summit Mount Everest.

No matter what obstacles we must overcome, our lives will always be in a state of flux; the only thing we can truly control about change is how we react to it. You'll have to roll with unforeseen challenges such as getting laid off, moving to a new place, dealing with death and loss, or seeing the industry you're in begin to require new skills, or even disappear when a new technology gets introduced. These are all moments where you can hold on to the past and try to deny change, or push forward into new territory to build a new version of yourself.

AVOID CERTAINTY

But living in beta doesn't mean you're wildly moving from job to job for the rest of your life, never committing to one thing. We're all subject to the disruptions that come with change. Even if you're a doctor who wants to stay in the same job for your entire life, you still need to evolve and embrace the changes and advances in your field. Adopting the living in beta mindset allows us to ride the changing tides, acquire new skills, be open to new experiences, try things out, and let go of the idea that who we are now is all we'll ever be.

Whether you're twenty-two and starting out, forty-seven and deep into a career you don't like, or fifty-six and happy with where you're at, how do you keep constructing who you are?

It's difficult to accept, but possibility actually exists *within* ambiguity and confusion. As Jad Abumrad,* the host of WNYC's award-winning program *Radiolab,* says, "Premature certainty is the enemy."

"I was pretty sure that I was going to be a musician. Specifically, writing music for films. That didn't really work out. I mean, I just wasn't very good at it. And so at a certain point I just kind of gave it up. You know, I'm clearly not a good musician. I'm not a good film scorer. That was what I was thinking at that time. And so I thought I had failed. I thought that my plan was wrong."

Looking back, Jad remembers the frustration of losing what he thought would be his central force in life. But his girlfriend (and now wife) helped push him to take a different perspective on his setback.

"She said, 'You kind of like to write. You kind of like to make music. You're not really good at either on their own terms, but maybe you could somehow find the middle ground. Try out radio.' So I went and I volunteered for a year making

* ▶ **roadtripnation.com/leader/jad-abumrad**

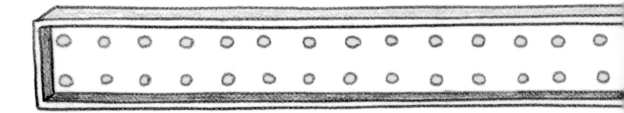

no money, working odd jobs when I could to sort of support myself. It somehow turned out to be more interesting than I expected. It was like this little arrow that pointed me in a direction."

"Composer Jad" was an earlier, not-quite-right iteration of the person Jad was capable of becoming. So the next version of Jad was born. Following those arrows led Jad to create and cohost *Radiolab*, a show that combines storytelling, philosophy, and science through sound.

But even though *Radiolab* has since earned a loyal following, and Jad has since won a MacArthur Genius Grant, Jad's version of living in beta didn't end there. Almost two decades into his show, he's still constantly searching for new ways to shake up the formula. This has meant creating a live *Radiolab* experience, opening up his Pro Tools sessions so listeners can remix the show, and launching a new podcast that delves into the history of the Supreme Court.

"I sort of see it as like your future self is leading you in some sense. It's dropping little hints. I would never have known that this is actually the job I was imagining. I didn't have the skills to imagine forward far enough."

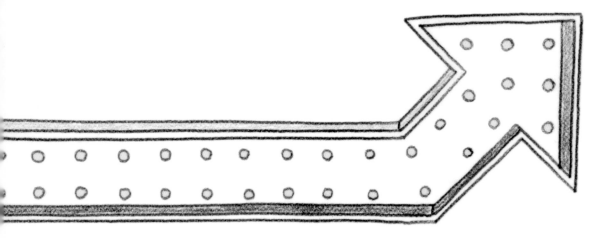

Jad encouraged us to reframe discomfort and fear, to treat feelings of dread, anxiety, and inadequacy as signposts that we must *run at* to push our ever-expanding borders. "You might be at the margins of something great. And things always get tense at the margins. It's like the physics of a liquid changing to a gas: The molecules start to vibrate, and they get very agitated, and then they change to a gas. So things are never happy at the moment of change. Things are always unhappy. And sometimes that unhappiness just means that you're doing something worth doing."

To live in beta, you have to teach yourself to crave the tension that comes from being on the razor's edge. It is in this place of discomfort that we evolve into a new beta self we didn't know was within us. We get up the nerve to be honest with someone in a way that scares us. We watch ourselves cope with stress we thought would crush us. We come up with a brilliant idea in the eleventh hour. All of these moments help us break into a new, stronger version of ourselves. When one of the roadtrippers asked Jad how to know when it's time to change, he responded, "You should be panicking a certain percentage of the time, because then you're right at the edge of what you can do. You need a little bit of 'uh-oh' in your life. Just enough."

Instead of shriveling on the vine, we have to engineer those uh-oh moments that shake up our lives. It is only in creating version upon version that we construct a life that's surprising, fulfilling, and ultimately better than we thought possible.

"At *Radiolab*, we're trying anything and everything we can think of to shock us out of our comfort zone, because that's going to lead you to the next version of yourself. Who you are next year and the year after that, that's unknown. I want to get to that person, and I want to be surprised when I meet him. I don't want to just look into the future and see the person I thought I was going to be. That's the worst thing in the world. I just want to be surprised by who I become."

—**JAD ABUMRAD**, *host of WNYC's award-winning program* Radiolab

CHAPTER 7

WHAT IS SUCCESS?

What is success? It's different for everybody. The real question is: What is success to you? Not to your parents, boss, or friends. What is it to *you*?

This is a question we've asked almost everyone we've met on the road over the years. As it turns out, no other question gives us such a wide range of answers.

For some, like record mogul Damon Dash,* success is based around a pure desire to make money. "All I knew my entire life was that I was gonna be rich. . . . We have this attitude in Harlem, you gotta have the best clothes, the best cars, the best jewelry. You have to make money to get those things, so everyone's always trying to get money." And even as that financial success came to fruition for him, that drive to make more has remained the same. "I used to hang out on a stoop, now I hang out in an office. This is my stoop now. . . . And there's no doubt in my mind I'm gonna be a billionaire. It's just a matter of how long it's gonna take."

Even for the 99 percent of us who can barely wrap our heads around making a billion dollars, some degree of financial security is often part of our definition of success. For Peter Page, the founder of a small renewable energy company in New Mexico, success is simple. "Staying in business, especially in a competitive market. That's success to me." When we posed the success question to cybersecurity expert Michael Echols,** he also acknowledged money as an essential part of the equation. "There's always the basic idea of financial success, because you have to eat. You have to pay the mortgage, right?"

* ▶ **roadtripnation.com/leader/damon-dash**

** ▶ **roadtripnation.com/leader/michael-echols**

But he took it even further and surprised us with the rest of his answer. He was raised "dirt poor" in Birmingham, Alabama, and went on to hold prominent positions in the U.S. Department of Homeland Security, working closely with President Barack Obama. Throughout his childhood he'd seen his parents fight through the civil rights movement. So for him, "Success is being able to take my grandmother to tour the White House. That's something she never thought she'd see in her lifetime. That is success to me."

The idea of success as a one-size-fits-all destination is—to borrow a phrase from the lovably cephalopodic Admiral Ackbar—a trap! The chief fallacy of success is the presumption that we all agree on what it is. Beyond that, we've seen that your own idea of success will also shift throughout your life. "I don't think that success is something you reach at one point when you're eighty-eight or ninety-two," explains interior designer Eiko Okura. "It's an every day, every moment practice."

That lesson spurred a major perception shift for one of our youngest roadtrippers ever, Sophia, a sixteen-year-old high school junior from Texas. "I guess I've always thought that you become successful," she told us, "then you never change again—that success is a point at which you plateau." After meeting various "successful" people on the road, she began to see a bigger picture. "They showed me that you can be successful and still be moving and changing. It's not a fixed point that you reach in your life. Success is something that keeps on changing throughout all your jobs and different stages of life. It's fluid. It's a state of being, not necessarily a place that you reach."

SUCCESS: WINNING OR LIVING?

To get a bit more concrete, let's look at a profession where success *should* be clear, a profession where you either win or you lose. We're talking about professional athletes; in particular, two athletes we've spoken with who, despite having so much in common, provided us with drastically different perspectives on success.

We'll start with one of the greatest competitive surfers of all time, seven-time world champion Layne Beachley.* As a child, she had a goal and focused on it unwaveringly. Layne recalls: "When I was eight years old, I decided I was going to be the best in the world at something." She began competing in every sport she could, but found surfing to be her common denominator; in it she found both success and joy.

Layne became the only surfer in history to win six consecutive world titles, and several years later won her seventh title. This took an enormous amount of drive and single-minded focus. For Layne, adhering to that kind of ambition "wasn't a sacrifice, it was a commitment." She adds, "Ultimately, to become successful in anything, you have to be relatively selfish."

It paid off, according to her definition of success. She'll forever go down in history as one of the all-time best.

Switching from one board sport to another, we spoke with legendary pro skateboarder Rodney Mullen.** Legendary? Let's rephrase that. The man is basically both the Buddha and the Albert Einstein of the skating world. Even if you didn't grow up skating and couldn't care less about the countless tricks he invented, or that in eleven years he won thirty-five out of the thirty-six contests he entered, the fact remains that the image in your mind of what skaters do exists because of Rodney. In his heyday, he was truly unbeatable. But in the midst of that outward success, it turns out he wasn't happy.

"Having a career in skateboarding almost robbed me of the joy I have in skateboarding," Rodney remembers. The Rodney Mullen storyline of unending success that every fan followed in the skating mags was in fact a sort of prison for the man on the board winning those competitions.

* ▶ **roadtripnation.com/leader/layne-beachley**

** ▶ **roadtripnation.com/leader/rodney-mullen**

/// What Is Success? ///

"I defended that title. They call it a 'title.' It's so corny. . . . All those years, I only lost one contest in eleven years. All that did was make me crazy. . . . What am I without contests? To be number one, is that important? No, it's not important. Because I just skate. I just love to skate."

So what was his answer when we asked him how he defines success?

"Peace," Rodney says. "It's just peace."

For Layne, giving up her adolescence—forgoing spending her free time social-izing and watching TV while munching delicious snacks—was worth it, because for her, coming out on top is the pinnacle of living. It's that Rocky-at-the-top-of-the-steps, arms-triumphantly-raised moment that drives her in everything she does. Her vision of success is a complete 180 from Rodney's. Rodney's idea of success would never have worked for Layne, and vice versa.

Now, remove the skateboard and surfboard from all this, and what do you have? Two opposing definitions of success. Most likely, neither is right for you, but what both of these definitions share is that they are wholly self-defined. Layne didn't become a world champion because someone told her to; she did it

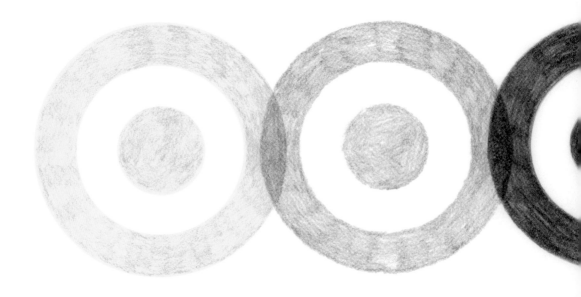

because she, through sheer force of will, wanted to be the best in the world at something, and surfing was what felt right to her. Rodney's view of success was different from the accomplishments that thrilled his fans. His success was inner peace. For him, success came through enjoying the sport for the sake of sport, and changing it from a win-or-lose equation to a lifestyle. No external influence could have told either of them what true success was for them as individuals.

To envision your own definition of success, begin by letting go of the big picture. If you cast the net too wide, you'll come back with a vague answer like "Success is being happy." But what does that mean, really? Success shifts from person to person and even within yourself as you age and gain experience.

"Success is elusive. Look within."

—**RODNEY MULLEN,** *professional skateboarder and entrepreneur*

How do you define success?

To help you get started, spend some time reflecting on others' definitions of success (your friends', family's, society's). Then think about how you would define it for yourself. How is your definition similar? How is it different? What do you want in your life that might be different than what others want?

Write, draw, or collage your thoughts. This space is yours to help you create a vision of what success means to you.

OTHERS' VISION OF SUCCESS

MY VISION OF SUCCESS

When you look at your broad vision of success, it might be overwhelming to think about how to turn big goals (such as "I just want to be happy") into actionable steps.

The more specific you are about what's important in your life, the clearer you'll see what success means to you. Success at work is different from success as a father, which is different from success on a volunteer project, which is different from . . . you get the idea.

So start to break down your broad vision of success:

In my family life, success is _____.

    In my friendships, success is _____.

        Success in a relationship is _____.

          Success at work is _____.

        Financial success means _____.

    Success in _____ is _____.

Success in _____ is _____.

Think about the different parts of your life in terms of their contribution to your idea of success. Is there a common thread that connects these different elements? Instead of a generalization like "I just want to be happy," can you sum up your vision of success so that it encompasses all of those smaller parts of your life?

Give it a try:

To me, success is _____

_____

_____

_____

_____

Wherever we fall on the spectrum, our conception of success has to go deeper than the standard vision. Once we define success for ourselves, based on what satisfies and excites us, we can work toward it. It won't come easy, and when it does arrive, it may not look like the cover of *Travel & Leisure* (or then again, it totally might), but what it will be is genuine, authentic, and deeply true to who we are.

CHAPTER 8
THE BLANK CANVAS

Life is not a to-do list. This is a difficult concept to accept when we're slogging through a long string of daily responsibilities. Emails to answer, meetings to attend, family to call, bills to pay, supermarket aisles to aimlessly wander as we debate the difference between nonfat and sugar-free. None of that ever stops, and it never will. And if we're not careful, our life becomes that to-do list. We may be having fun or we may be totally stressed out and miserable, but either way we are immersed in distraction. The Assembly Line, the Noise, skewed ideas about work-life balance, and preconceived notions about your life's path and success keep you distracted from what's underneath, which is . . . you.

Letting go of everything that society and others have decided you should be is the first step of your journey—defining who you are and what you care about can only happen when you finally clear away everything that's not you. The work of creating your own vision for yourself can only begin when you've made it to the Blank Canvas. But odds are, right now you have a canvas filled with markings that are not your own.

To clear away the paint-by-numbers picture that's been determined for you and start fresh, you need perspective and distance. That's what the first road trip did for us—it put some space between us and the everyday; it gave us room to see and ask the questions we normally avoided.

When we sat with Roy Remer* in the main room of the hospice center where he works, he had the calm and considered air of someone who is living his life in

✳ ▶ **roadtripnation.com/leader/roy-remer**

full alignment. But it wasn't always that way. When Roy was in his late thirties, he had been working in publishing and doing fairly well on paper, but he fell in love with the work he was doing as a volunteer at Zen Hospice Project. "There was this little voice in the back of my head, reminding me that there was something else I should be dedicating my life to, and it's this," he explains.

As we know, it's easy to simply ignore that little voice in the name of taking care of business. "It can be a difficult thing to give up a career and make a shift like that. It was very challenging in my relationship, I had a lot of fears around it. I was used to making a certain income; now I was going to go work for a nonprofit?"

For a while, Roy straddled both worlds. His publishing job kept the lights on, but, as he recalls, "The hospice work became what was nourishing me spiritually." Roy explained that he needed to create space from his routine to get to his version of the Blank Canvas. "I had to say goodbye to Roy who was the publishing rep so that I could fully embody this new way of living my life."

Roy's final advice to us was to mark our thresholds; that is, to recognize and honor the different phases in our lives, and let them go when it's time. That's the headspace of the Blank Canvas: creating room to become who we are now, not holding on to who we were yesterday or last year. Getting to our Blank Canvas means giving ourselves permission to change.

Roy was an active searcher, which makes his finding of his path look easy (from the outside, anyway). But many of us, depending on how immersed we are in the Noise, can find the road to the Blank Canvas filled with ideas that can be difficult to wash away.

"Our minds can be so busy. At any given moment there can be so much happening, so many distractions, so many stories we're caught up in, so many fixations on what's going on around us, and within us. . . . As human beings we often get stuck in a place; I see it all the time. People are really stuck with this concrete idea of who they are."

—ROY REMER, *volunteer manager, Zen Hospice Project*

The first step is understanding that there may be marks on your canvas that have nothing to do with who you truly are—but they can still be difficult to erase. We encountered one of the most extreme examples of this in the incredible story of Julissa Arce.*

Before she climbed the ranks to vice president at Goldman Sachs and became a bestselling author and advocate, she was a kid growing up in Texas just like any other kid. The key difference was, as American as she felt, she was an undocumented immigrant—a fact she learned at age fourteen—and that difference was all that she saw. After an internship at Goldman Sachs led to a job offer, she was faced with a decision: take the risk with forged papers, or give up everything she'd worked for. She took the risk. "Once I got in the door, I really had to compartmentalize everything: The Julissa that was laser-focused on building a career and making a ton of money. And a Julissa who was constantly afraid she was going to get caught. A Julissa that had to lie to her friends—even her closest friends—because I couldn't possibly tell them I was undocumented."

Her Blank Canvas moment came when she was finally able to break away from a word that had defined her for so long. "For me, having papers and not having papers—that doesn't define who I am as a person. I made a decision in the workplace that I wasn't going to let that define me either. The thing that was going to define me at my job was going to be my work." Once she became a citizen, she was tired of hiding. She'd achieved the American Dream in spite of the stress and panic of fifteen years living in constant fear that, at any moment, the life she'd built could be wiped away. It was time to clear away all of the misconceptions of what an undocumented person looks like—that they couldn't exist in the highest echelons of finance—and share her story. Yes, she

* ▶ roadtripnation.com/leader/julissa-arce

had been undocumented, and yes, she had also worked her way to the top of one of the most prestigious firms on Wall Street.

For Julissa, it took making her way to the center of the financial world in New York City to create a space where she could reclaim who she was. For Christina Heyniger,* getting to the Blank Canvas meant leaving the buzz of the city so that she could begin to hear herself. She was so deeply immersed in society's vision of success that she had to summon all her will and drive in order to break free.

She began, like most of us, a bit adrift, but when her friends began to climb the ladder toward bigger paydays, she panicked. To keep up, she got a master's degree and an MBA and a job as a business consultant. She soon embodied society's vision of success. Cut to eight years later: Christina was still chugging along on the Assembly Line. Successful, but . . . empty. "The biggest problem was not knowing what inspired me. What I realize now is that I had not created space from my routine to think more broadly. I was doing alright, but I wasn't energized."

There was nowhere to look beyond the din of her life and the expectations she'd created for herself. "When I thought about different jobs I wanted, I was only thinking in terms of money. It took me a long time to start questioning the whole foundation of that. Maybe I don't need to make this much money, and this house and these responsibilities—maybe I don't have to have them. Whoa. Suddenly there were crazy options."

The real turning point for her was a trip to the Grand Canyon. Rafting through the canyon reawakened old joys she'd since put aside. That distance allowed her to reevaluate and take stock of her life. What truly made her happy? What

* ▶ **roadtripnation.com/leader/christina-heyniger**

/// The Blank Canvas ///

was she missing, and how could she get it back? This was her Blank Canvas moment.

Not long after that, she left New York for good, became a river guide, and then combined her business acumen and love of travel and nature to start her own consulting firm for sustainable adventure tourism.

"I define my success by my joy. Even when I'm sad, I'm still so joyful. I'm so alive, and I feel so creative and generally thrilled. I'm the most successful I could ever imagine being because I'm so stinking happy."

Don't get us wrong, we're not advocating that everyone quit their jobs and become bearded backwoods artisanal soapmakers. Getting to the Blank Canvas requires space, but it doesn't have to be the space around a moonlit campfire. It can just be a switch-up, something to rattle and challenge you.

LET CHANGE HAPPEN

Black Girls Code founder and CEO (and former engineer) Kimberly Bryant* always knew she wanted to be her own boss. Starting something of her own began with creating the space to find a problem to solve, so she started going to meet-ups and conferences to talk to people. It was seeing the inequality in tech through her daughter's experience that spurred her to start Black Girls Code, an organization that gives girls of color opportunities to learn coding and computer science.

"The pivotal turning point for me was my daughter having an interest in computer science and sharing the same thing that I'd experienced [in engineering]. She was in class learning how to build video games, and there were just a few girls there, and she felt alone. Seeing it through my daughter's eyes, it planted a seed that this was a problem. I really didn't have an idea that I was going to

* ▶ **roadtripnation.com/leader/kimberly-bryant**

create this organization to address it. It was just this gnawing issue in the back of my mind, and I started to talk to friends who said maybe you can create something similar to that camp to prepare girls for this experience."

It can be scary to start something of your own or make a big change. But it's a good kind of scary. Knowing that this work would help girls like her daughter is what kept Kimberly going. These moments of change are often when we feel most alive. And change, of course, is life's only constant. In a way, envisioning your Blank Canvas is a tool to take control of the inevitability of change.

Roy, the Zen Hospice volunteer director, calls this process of facing change a dress rehearsal for death. He talked about sitting with the dying, and the fear and regret he witnesses in those last moments. "When I am sitting with someone who is unprepared because they've lived a life so attached to this idea of who they are, and they haven't allowed that idea to really shift in big ways, it can be really, really painful for them."

Roy warns that we can become so attached to an idea of who we are that we refuse to grow and let the past be gone. We should practice letting go of phases of our lives. "It's a radical concept," Roy acknowledges, "but [it helps] to practice dying while you're healthy. This allows us to honor who we've been, make peace with it, and move into who we are now."

That's what this book has been about so far: getting rid of the old notions of yourself to get to who you are now.

You've already been priming yourself to let go of all those layers of artifice. Getting to the Blank Canvas isn't like going to the store and picking up a new one. You get only one canvas, and the only way to get down to that clean slate is to erase all the marks that don't represent your vision. It is time to let go of all the things that aren't you.

What are the things you need to let go of? See if you can fill in a few blanks:

The Noise I used to accept was _____, but now

I know how to shed it.

I used to think success was _____, but now my

own definition of success is _____.

I used to call myself a _____, but that really

has nothing to do with who I really am.

I was a _____, but I no longer am.

When people asked _____, I would tell them

_____ even though I knew it wasn't true.

I was thinking I would be _____, but does this

really reflect what I want for myself?

I was a _____, but I've learned all I can,

and it is time I move on.

We'll admit this kind of transformation can feel difficult, maybe even terrifying. Does wiping the slate clean invalidate all the work you've put in? Are you disappointing your family? Your friends? Yourself?

Whatever those nagging voices are, ignore them. Open yourself to the possibility of new versions of yourself. Reject the idea that you already know what you're capable of. Silence the voices that question your skills and stop you from exploring your untapped talents.

Now, just look forward. As Roy explained, "Whether it be graduation, a divorce, a death, a change in career, or whatever . . . we're watching each moment as it passes away, and each moment anew as it comes up for us. ***This is who I was yesterday. That's gone. This is who I am today.***"

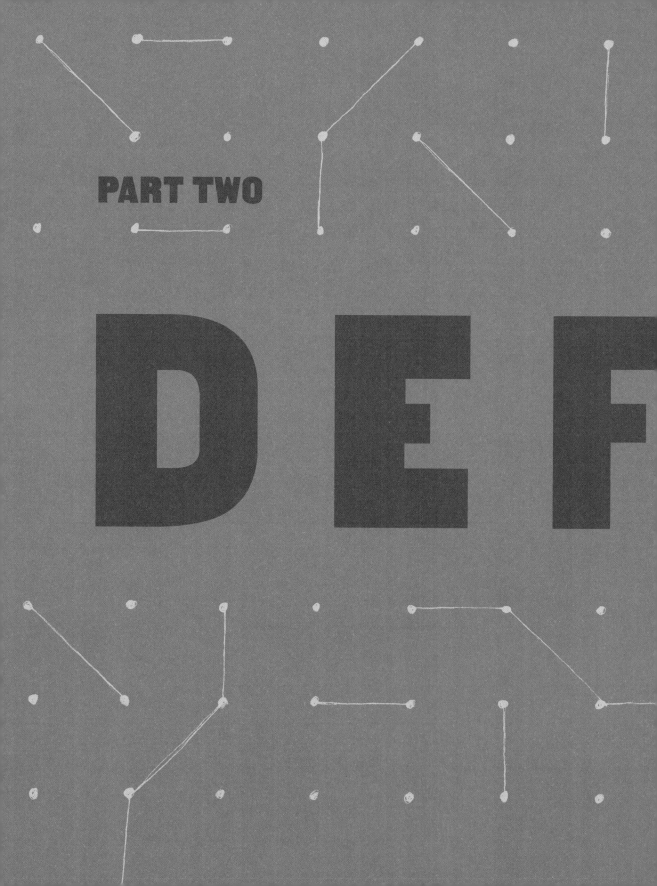

PART TWO

DEF

CHAPTER 9

PURSUE YOUR INTERESTS—NOT AN OCCUPATION

Letting go is about cutting through the messages swirling all around you. Now it's time to start asking yourself more direct questions about the kind of life you want to live. The answers will help you build a framework for pursuing your own vision for yourself. By the time you've filled out the activities in this section, you'll be ready for action.

But the approach we're proposing isn't the one you were taught in school. It's the one we've learned by talking to the people who found a way to create authentic lives in line with their own vision.

When we were first starting out, we were struck by the disconnect between the way we'd been told to plan for our careers, and the way the truly happy people we met on the road approached their own career planning. The going career wisdom seemed to be: Choose a career, then reverse-engineer yourself into it, and cross your fingers that you like it once you get there.

It felt so . . . limiting. It also felt short-sighted. On the road, almost everyone we met with studied something totally unrelated to what they ended up doing, and nearly everyone said it was impossible to perfectly plan your career trajectory. So what were we to do?

We were seeking an approach that was more flexible—that mirrored real life, that grew and changed as we did—and as the world did. We craved forward direction that expanded what was possible, instead of pushing us further and further into a corner.

Choosing a career before we'd experienced and explored would force us to make decisions without all the information. And what about all the ways of working that weren't captured in those single-career categories?

The more time we spent on the road, the more we saw a pattern in the stories of the people we met. Their stories offered proof of an alternative to what we'd been told. These Leaders didn't start with a fixed endpoint, and by trying things and listening to themselves, they stayed open to change. It took them in new directions they would have never conceived of at the beginning of their journey. It led them down paths that offered exciting, unexpected ways to connect personal satisfaction to financial stability and success.

So how did they do it? How will you do it?

You start with your interests.

This idea sounds simple, but it's more radical than it seems. We're reminded of that fact every time we talk to people whose worlds are rocked by the concept. *You mean I can try to find a career based on what I like?*

132

"Give yourself permission to explore, and try different things, and listen to yourself. I know it may feel stressful if you haven't found out what your thing is, but you should listen to that voice inside you, and cultivate that, so that you develop a self-awareness of what interests you, and then throw yourself in wholeheartedly."

—KATHERINE KUCHENBECKER,
associate professor of mechanical engineering and applied mechanics, computer and information science, University of Pennsylvania

What this interest-first approach taught us was to stop looking for a certain guaranteed output (our final career destination), and focus on a more important input (our interests!). No longer were we asking: What do I want to do with my life? Instead we started to ask: What am I interested in?

If you're among the harried readers looking for a distillation of this book, here it is. To build a life that's true to who you are, start with your interests. Everything else flows from this basic idea. The people who are the most fulfilled use what excites and engages them as the starting point for every decision they make.

But what if you don't know what you're interested in? Check out what you're already doing. We have a tendency to sneak the things we love into overlooked corners of our life—you just have to look from a different vantage point to see them. You might discover that you're already engaged in your interests in some way every day.

Sometimes, we're engaged in an activity, and time simply vanishes. We get lost in the doing. It's in those moments we might consider trivial that we can discover our interests. Maybe you're making YouTube videos on your day off, or hiking in the woods, or volunteering for a political campaign, or building an architectural masterpiece out of toothpicks—whatever it is, it's a clue.

Exploring those interests, finding ways to fold them into your work, and letting them guide your choices and commitments is the best way to break free from the standard career mindset.

If you're not truly interested in medicine, don't listen to the Noise and convince yourself you are because it sounds like an impressive and lucrative profession. And don't be afraid if the interests you uncover don't seem legitimately serious. Especially in today's fractured and diverse marketplace, there are countless surprising ways to integrate your interests into your work. You can take a love of whales all the way to being the superintendent of a marine sanctuary for humpback whales, as Malia Chow did, or you could take a simple fascination with volcanoes all the way to building volcano-exploring robots at NASA's Jet Propulsion Laboratory, as Carolyn Parcheta did. The point is, **don't silo yourself.**

Doctors work only in medical offices. Teachers work only in classrooms. All scientists wear lab coats. Programmers only make websites. When we zoom out, it becomes clear that none of those statements are true, but when confronted with trying to forge a new path for ourselves, we can have a failure of imagination in thinking about what it means to work in a certain field or follow a particular interest. The Noise drowns out creative thinking in this moment, confining us. You need to instead question your assumptions and explore to get to the truth.

Take Leila Hokulani Kaaekuahiwi Pousima,* a lawyer at the National Oceanic & Atmospheric Administration (NOAA) in Honolulu, Hawai'i. Many of us have ideas of what it's like to be a lawyer: long exhausting days of reading and research, debating and cross-examining in the middle of a cutthroat courtroom scene. But Leila was drawn to the world of law for a different reason.

"I really wanted to give back to my community, try to make a difference," she says. Leila explained that she took an uncommon approach to law by focusing on what mattered to her most: her Hawaiian heritage. "I volunteered for environmental programs, worked to become fluent in the Hawaiian language, and took classes on Hawaiian politics and natural resource management from a Hawaiian perspective." She's since become one of only eighty-nine people in

✳ ▶ **roadtripnation.com/leader/leila-hokulani-kaaekuahiwi-pousima**

/ / / Pursue Your Interests—Not an Occupation / / /

135

the world to hold a certificate in Native Hawaiian law. And her role in protecting the natural resources of Hawai'i entails much more than sitting behind a desk or arguing in a courtroom. She often travels on NOAA research vessels to remote islands, observing wildlife and performing cultural protocols.

"I would never have imagined this would be the outcome of going to law school or having the specific experiences that I do. But being able to visit the places you work to protect every day is really important to me. Being able to be in Hawai'i, in my home, doing what I love and also benefiting my community and my people is everything. I can't imagine wanting anything more."

Let's start getting into what your interests might be so that you can start to imagine possibilities for where they might lead.

"There are all of these hybrid approaches and all of these interdisciplinary possibilities, so you might as well see what's out there as much as you can and then figure out how to integrate all those things into whatever it is you want to do. That's where we're headed, into rethinking the way that we isolate: the way we isolate ourselves in the world, the way we isolate our ideas, the way we isolate our studies. Things are merging in different ways now."

—**ROBIN CONRAD,** *choreographer and lecturer in dance at Cal Poly, San Luis Obispo*

Don't silo

Yourself

Below are some Core Interests we've identified from meeting with Leaders. Mark the ones that speak to you. We've left a few blank ones for you to fill in if you think of more.

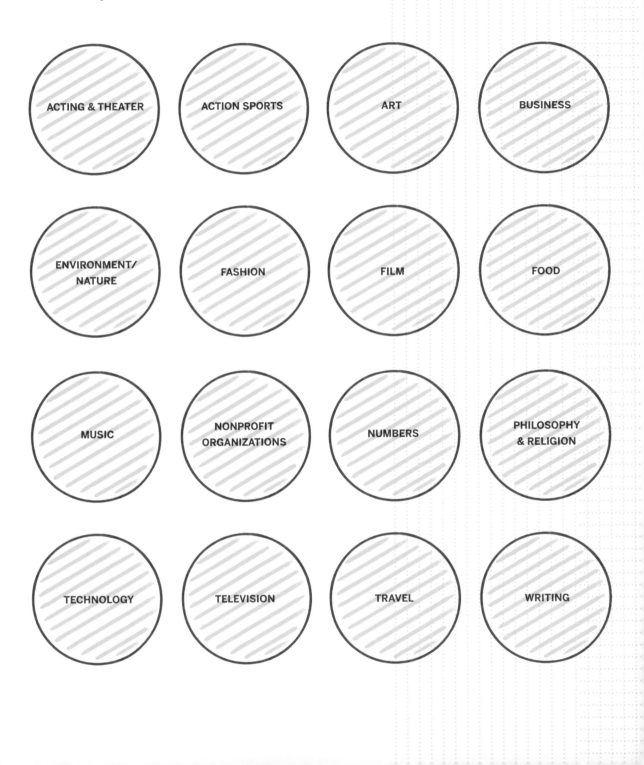

ACTING & THEATER	ACTION SPORTS	ART	BUSINESS
ENVIRONMENT/ NATURE	FASHION	FILM	FOOD
MUSIC	NONPROFIT ORGANIZATIONS	NUMBERS	PHILOSOPHY & RELIGION
TECHNOLOGY	TELEVISION	TRAVEL	WRITING

To get you into imagining how these interests translate into all kinds of careers and ways of living, it helps to see how other people turned these interests into fulfilling work. Experience all the stories of the hundreds of people we've talked to, all filtered by interest, at rtn.is/interests.

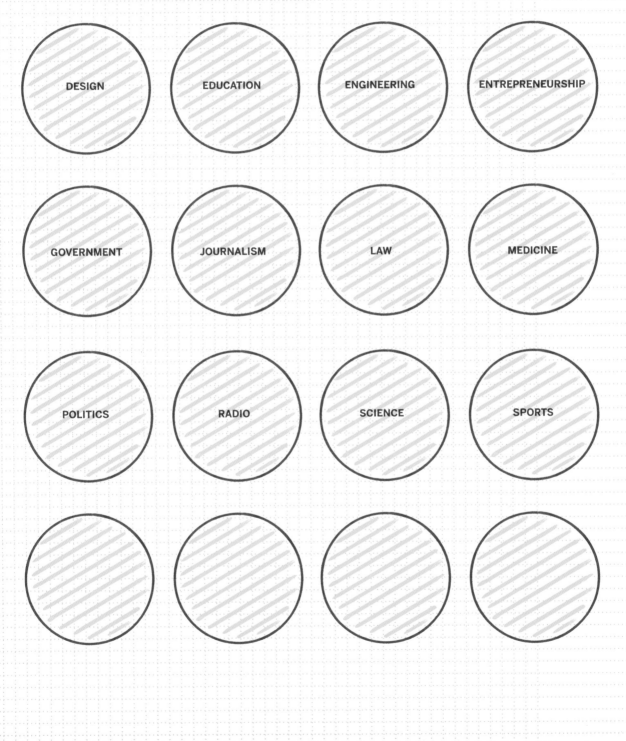

DESIGN

EDUCATION

ENGINEERING

ENTREPRENEURSHIP

GOVERNMENT

JOURNALISM

LAW

MEDICINE

POLITICS

RADIO

SCIENCE

SPORTS

EXPLORE AROUND YOUR INTERESTS

Transforming an interest into a career takes imagination and courage. Billy King,* the president of the Philadelphia 76ers, understands that sometimes that means taking leaps, taking risks, and simply trying. Billy began with a simple interest: basketball.

"I just wanted to play pro basketball," he told us. "Once I got to school I realized there's more to life than basketball." Just because he loved the sport didn't mean his only options were to play point guard for an NBA team or abandon his interest entirely. After graduating from Duke (and between bartending gigs), Billy did color commentary for ESPN and landed a job as a sports analyst at a local TV station. He explored the surprising variety of interests that surround playing basketball, developing his talents, testing options, and always growing. Starting out thinking he wanted to *play* pro ball, Billy developed a lifestyle where basketball is still the driving force—just in ways he never expected. He may not be playing, but he used that drive to work his way up to the top running a team.

It's that flexibility, creativity, and willingness to pursue an interest when the road ahead is unclear (and maybe a bit scary) that has helped people like Billy find ways to make a living from their interests.

EXPLORE BEYOND THE OBVIOUS

For Andrea Weatherhead,** following one interest led to all kinds of moves she never could have imagined. She was a singer and guitarist, so she started with her interest in music. Right out of college, while she was looking for a job, she was also producing her own music festival. She laughed, telling us that around

* ▶ roadtripnation.com/leader/billy-king

** ▶ roadtripnation.com/leader/andrea-weatherhead

142

the time she was running all over town getting advertisers for her festival, she was still preoccupied with ideas of what it took to find a "real" job, and how her slow typing speed would hold her back from getting one.

"It's so clear I was going to be involved with media and producing and collaborating and getting people together to do something," Andrea says. "But I didn't know it. It was just something I was kind of doing on the side—because it wasn't real, I wasn't going to make money at that.

"That's why I encourage you guys to do the things that don't make money . . . because those are things that do actually transform into what you end up doing—because it's who you are."

Next, Andrea decided to try out being a recording engineer. She sat in on a class about the basic physics of sound. The head of the physics department spotted her and told her they had funding and needed more women in the department. That little nudge took her deep into the mechanics of sound. She earned her master's in audio technology and acoustics and worked for years as an audio engineer.

But then she took another leap, fueled by the growth of the internet (remember that unpredictable change thing we mentioned at the beginning of this chapter?), and followed her fascination with music in a totally different direction: creating interactive music projects for Microsoft.

Her next shift took her even deeper into musical experiences, while taking her further from what she might have expected at the beginning of her journey. When we met her, she was leading huge teams and creating exhibitions at the Experience Music Project in Seattle (now known as the Museum of Pop Culture).

And though her path has taken her all over, her interest in music and music-making is still core, and she encouraged us to see how our interests shaped everything we'd go on to do, too. "That part of you is inevitably going to be a major part of whatever you do. And I just want to give you courage and confidence—just because you're not following the same path as people who go a more conventional route, that's not an invalid way of moving through life in the least—it may be more valid."

Seeing how just one interest had led her toward so many opportunities and possibilities left us completely inspired. But she'd had such a strong interest from the beginning—what if we still weren't sure what to even explore?

"What is it that really makes you mad?" she asked. "If you're not really sure what path to take, if there's something that kind of makes you mad about the world, then you can look inside and say, that's something I can do something about. That can help you look at where your values are and where you might want to think about focusing some of your attention."

Once you've begun to think creatively about building your life around your interests, don't become static in your thinking. Billy King and Andrea Weatherhead both built incredible and varied careers around one interest, and they did it by looking beyond the expected. But if you look closely, you'll see all the other interests they incorporated along the way. Many of the people we've talked to didn't just integrate one interest into their work and daily lives. They pursued multiple interests and created a career trajectory that encompasses all the different parts of who they are. So how did they connect it all together? It starts with defining your Foundation.

"Really think about what you're interested in, and if you think that will be where you want to be for a long time. And things change, you may apply your skills in a different manner, and that's okay, too. But what are you really interested in? What do you think is going to make you happy? And for some people, that definition varies."

—ROSA OBREGON, *mechanical test operations engineer, NASA's Stennis Space Center*

CHAPTER 10

DEFINING YOUR FOUNDATION

Understanding what's truly important to you starts with exploring your interests. But what are your interests built on? The more people we've talked to, the more we've seen that there is a core motivation at the center of everything they do—a driving force or goal that ties it all together. We've come to call this core motivation your Foundation.

Simply put, your Foundation is at the heart of what you enjoy doing. Your Foundation is what energizes you, and your interests are how you manifest that Foundation.

Entrepreneur Paola Santana is a prime example. Paola's Foundation is helping people, and she's been on a journey to find work that connects her to that core drive for most of her life. The obvious way to do that, she thought, was to go to law school and get into politics. But in Washington, D.C., she became totally discouraged by the slow pace of change. "If politics is not the system to create change, which system is?" she wondered.

"And that's when I decided to shift . . . I understood then my commitment was not to being a politician; my commitment was creating massive positive change for the world." Pinpointing that objective—that Foundation—is what allowed her to get outside of career categories and create her first company, Matternet, a drone delivery company that delivers goods to people in disconnected places. "With Matternet, I was doing what I was hoping politics would do," Paola says.

"Suddenly what they are thinking about doing, what they are discussing in Congress—I was able to build a system and I went and did it."

Finding that central connection can be the key to finding your road forward. For example, let's say you love food. That's useful information you can use to start exploring your road. But dig deeper and get to the core Foundation that drives that interest. What is the fundamental element that draws you to food? Do you enjoy experimenting with recipes and *being creative*? Do you get satisfaction from *working with your hands* and raw ingredients? Do you love *learning* about the stories and culture that come through in a meaningful dish? Do you find yourself *writing* detailed reviews of every restaurant you visit? Do you come alive when you *teach* your nephew how to bake cookies? Figuring out what attracts you to your interests at a deeper level can give you greater insight into what drives you and what paths will best align with what you care about.

 Working with others/ building relationships

 Teaching/mentoring

 Building things

Communicating/sharing stories

 Helping people

 Learning/challenging myself mentally

Working independently

 Upholding a cause I believe in

 Being creative

 Being physically active

 Accomplishing my goals

Problem-solving

Think of your Foundation as a "need" instead of a "would-like-to."

Try filling in the blanks below. For ideas to get you thinking, see the examples on the facing page and circle those that resonate most.

"As long as I'm _____ I'll be happy."

"As long as I'm _____ I'll be happy."

"As long as I'm _____ I'll be happy."

Maybe you're still unclear about what your Foundation is. Like we said earlier, self-doubt and confusion can easily follow the Blank Canvas stage. That's okay. To move beyond that, the following idea can help.

THINK BIG AND THINK BACK

Window Snyder* is the cybersecurity heavyweight who shaped what user privacy looked like on iOS 10 at Apple. And her path to building technologies that keep our information secure and malware at bay is a tale about how your Foundation can drive your interests.

Window grew up with software engineer parents. Her mom would debug lines of code by hand, on paper, in their living room; meanwhile Window was more interested in playing with the stack of continuous computer paper. It wasn't until college that she discovered the big question that drives her work—What's keeping our data safe?—and started digging into solving it. Computers, science, math, and technology are all interests she's found, but the thing that truly drives her work, and those interests, is problem-solving.

When we talked to her at Fastly, a start-up where she's chief security officer, she didn't talk about her love of coding or computers; she talked about her drive to solve problems. That drive brought Window, very naturally, to computer science, but there were countless other ways that drive could have manifested, from engineering to architecture to management to rocket science. Your own Foundation doesn't close doors, it simply helps you see which doors you want to open and which interests can bring your Foundation to life.

Think of your Foundation as an anchor that can keep you grounded in times of confusion. Your interests may change, your desire to do a certain kind of work may shift, or your financial requirements may evolve, but your Foundation will most likely stay constant.

Cartoonist Jorge Cham** (of the mega-popular PHD Comics) is an extreme example. He left academia, where he was studying mechanical engineering and

*   ▶ roadtripnation.com/leader/window-snyder

**   ▶ roadtripnation.com/leader/jorge-cham

robotics, to embrace a full-time career drawing comics. But here's the thing that blew us away: He told us that the core pursuit of academia and art, for him, is the same.

"I see the process of making these comics or making art in general as similar to academia in that you're always searching for truth," he says. "A comic strip or a piece of art really wouldn't get much of a reaction if it didn't have a core of truth to it. In academia, you have to be creative and you have to be analytical, but it's just a longer process. On the comics side, it's a daily cycle. But to me it was still very similar—you're searching for things that people will react to and find interesting, that expand our knowledge or our understanding of where we are."

Whether Jorge's making a running robot inspired by a cockroach (true story) or drawing a comic about what getting your PhD is like, he's still pursuing that core Foundation, searching for truth and sharing what he finds.

But while your Foundation can connect two seemingly opposite pursuits, it's also the course-corrector that can get you back on track when you start drifting.

Such was the case with Washington, D.C.–based artist Cheryl Foster,* who took twenty years to rediscover her Foundation. Although Cheryl always had an affinity for the arts, and even tried a stint in art school, in the name of security she put away her art supplies and became a real estate appraiser. Cue the long march of years (decades!) on the Assembly Line.

Day by day, a deep sense of resentment and frustration began to consume Cheryl. When we're divorced so deeply from our Foundation, that sense of separation from our true identity is gnawing. But no matter how off track we get, we all have the power to reconnect with our Foundation. For Cheryl, this meant looking back to find a memory of what being fulfilled felt like. "My

* ▶ **roadtripnation.com/leader/cheryl-foster**

/ / / Defining Your Foundation / / /

parents had introduced me to doing things with my hands," recalls Cheryl. "At church, they had hat contests. My mother would create these Josephine Baker–style hats, and we'd win every time!" Resurrecting that source of satisfaction put her on the road to a life immersed in the arts. "This is not a hobby for me; this is me. Turpentine, oil, hot glue guns, that's what's running through my veins!"

Ignoring your Foundation, or not digging deep enough to discover it, is a sure way to amplify your dissatisfactions and frustrations. Seeing the energy and joy that Cheryl's Foundation—being creative—brings her, it's hard to imagine her living any other way. It might take years to discover, or it might surface tomorrow morning, but as we've seen with so many Leaders, truly understanding what drives you creates a sense of urgency to act on it.

152

"**Find that thing deep inside you that you're so hungry for that you cannot live without it. Whatever you're hungry for, that is your purpose.**"

—**ARTINA McCAIN**, *assistant professor of piano, Rudi E. Scheidt School of Music at the University of Memphis*

CHAPTER 11
ROADMAP

The process of self-construction is ever-evolving and requires constant self-examination of who you are and who you want to be. It's about asking yourself tough questions and recalibrating if things aren't feeling quite right—and it entails a heck of a lot of trust that the exploration you're doing will lead you where you want to go.

When you're building your life around your interests, there are going to be times when you feel confident in your decisions, and times when doubt, fear, and anxiety leave you feeling lost again. In those dark moments, when you're frustrated and confused and aren't sure what the next step is—when your head is spinning with the question "What am I doing with my life?"—it can be comforting to have something tangible to hold on to.

For us, that tangible thing is what we call the Roadmap—a tool for mixing and matching Foundations and Core Interests in order to see possibilities that we might not have otherwise considered.

This Roadmap is not a set of turn-by-turn directions; we left that approach on the Assembly Line. It's a framework for you to fill in and reference as you navigate your life. Only you know the nuances of your Foundation and Core Interests, and only you know how and in what ways they align with your values and vision.

Once you've begun to think creatively about building your life around your interests, don't become static in your thinking. We've discovered that some of the most interesting pathways are found at the intersection of our Core Interests and Foundation. When you think beyond the ordinary and mash your interests together, you'll have a better chance at fulfillment. When we look at the people we've talked to, they followed their interests, but most of them didn't just integrate one interest into their work and daily lives. They took multiple interests and created a mashed-up work life that encompasses all the different parts of who they are. Indira Phukan is a teacher who makes Yosemite National Park her classroom. Before this, though, she was a teacher in a more traditional classroom, but felt limited by the standardized tests and the standardized curriculum. As a field science educator with NatureBridge, she helps her students engage with science by taking them on hikes and showing them the natural world. Her Core Interests are education and environment/nature. The magic happens in that interest mashup.

EMBRACE THE MASHUP

We like to think that the first step in creating your own Roadmap is imagining yourself as a DJ. You're the DJ of your own life, mixing, merging, and layering all the things you care about to make your own one-of-a-kind mix. A DJ doesn't work from a single record. It's when they combine sounds and songs together that things get interesting.

So it's time to create your own unique-to-you masterpiece. It's in the overlap that you'll find your own rhythm. And you can always mix in new interests to create an endlessly evolving anthem of your own that will see you through all the challenge and change in the years ahead.

"When you start out pursuing everything, getting a taste of all the things you know you love, you'll start to figure out how to combine them and integrate them."

—**ZARIA FORMAN**, *artist and climate change activist*

No story embodies the power of mixing and mashing up interests more than that of the cofounders of Two Bit Circus, Brent Bushnell* and Eric Gradman.** After studying electrical engineering and computer science, respectively, they collected an incredibly eclectic series of experiences between the two of them. While Brent pursued the world of tech entrepreneurship, he worked as everything from a furniture salesman to a sushi chef. Meanwhile, Eric became a touring circus performer, working as a fire dancer, a clown, an aerialist, and an acrobat.

So what could possibly bring these two, and their variety of interests, together? Creating a truly unique, technologically driven modern circus. Collecting a band of what they describe as "mad scientists, roboticists, visual artists, and storytellers," they engineer interactive entertainment experiences. "I think there's a lot of creativity to be found at the intersection of domains," Brent explained to us. "I love computer science, and I love circuses. What sort of weird things can come out of those two things combined?" That is the essence of the mashup: taking seemingly disparate interests—in this case, circus, engineering, and technology—and merging them in unexpected ways through ingenuity and exploration.

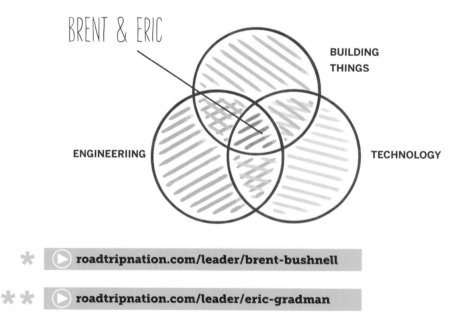

BRENT & ERIC

BUILDING THINGS

ENGINEERIING

TECHNOLOGY

* ▶ roadtripnation.com/leader/brent-bushnell

** ▶ roadtripnation.com/leader/eric-gradman

158

That's what's wild about all this mixology, and what continually amazes us: the unexpected quality of it all. Like Brent and Eric, many other people we've interviewed had no idea where their interests would lead them. But in following them, they arrived somewhere deeply satisfying. Here are just a few of the interesting, diverse places that following your Roadmap can lead you.

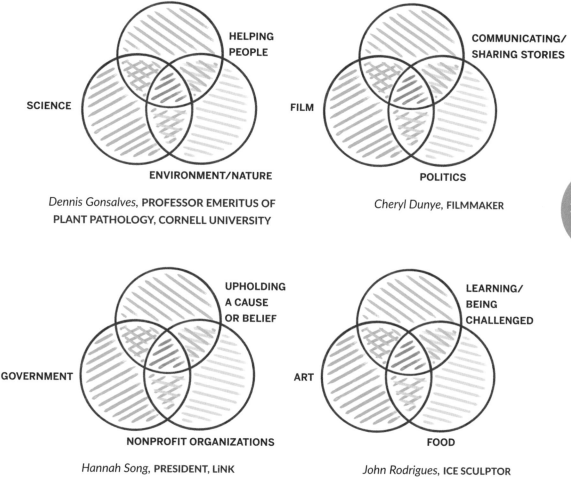

Dennis Gonsalves, **PROFESSOR EMERITUS OF PLANT PATHOLOGY, CORNELL UNIVERSITY**

Cheryl Dunye, **FILMMAKER**

Hannah Song, **PRESIDENT, LiNK (LIBERTY IN NORTH KOREA)**

John Rodrigues, **ICE SCULPTOR**

And keep in mind, like any good DJ, you won't play the same track forever. If you get tired of the song you're playing, swap a record out. Reflect, reassess, and, through trial and error, create a new mix that sounds right.

Consider Pixar's Danielle Feinberg;* the power of the mashup is integral to her story. She's the director of photography for lighting for films like *Brave* and *Coco*. She showed up at Pixar right out of undergrad with her computer science degree, started in an entry-level technical position, and then found her way into the art department. "It's this perfect combination for me of art and technology," she says. "There's some coding, a lot of problem-solving and getting the computer to do what you want it to do, but the end result is the visuals, which to me is so magical; you're doing this very left- and right-brain thing, and that's kind of my happy place."

Just as Danielle has experienced, when we look beyond the common examples, we can find connective tissue that brings our interests together. It's that connective tissue that holds the inspiration.

How do you put these ideas into action in your own life, with your own circumstances and challenges?

One way to start is to go fill out the Roadmap for yourself at rtn.is/roadmap and explore the Leader stories that connect to your Foundation and Core Interests. Swap out one Core Interest for another and watch how the results change. Each time you make a change to a Core Interest or Foundation, you're looking at a different way to approach your life. Which combination sounds right to you?

* ▶ **roadtripnation.com/leader/danielle-feinberg**

Look how many possibilities there are in just one Roadmap.

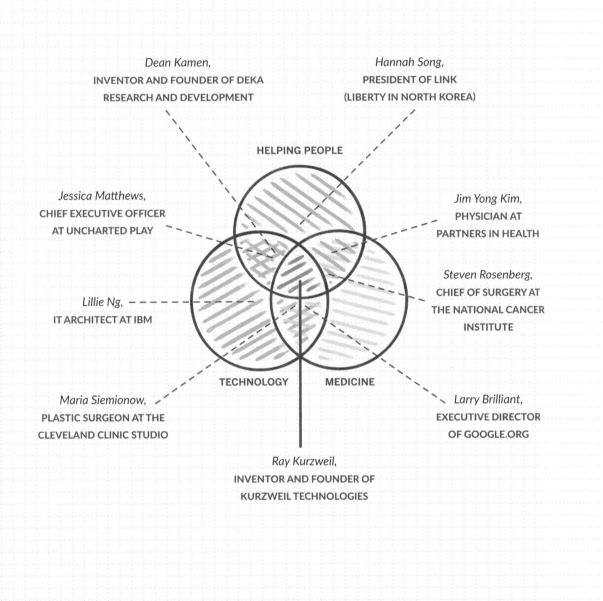

Dean Kamen,
INVENTOR AND FOUNDER OF DEKA
RESEARCH AND DEVELOPMENT

Hannah Song,
PRESIDENT OF LINK
(LIBERTY IN NORTH KOREA)

HELPING PEOPLE

Jessica Matthews,
CHIEF EXECUTIVE OFFICER
AT UNCHARTED PLAY

Jim Yong Kim,
PHYSICIAN AT
PARTNERS IN HEALTH

Steven Rosenberg,
CHIEF OF SURGERY AT
THE NATIONAL CANCER
INSTITUTE

Lillie Ng,
IT ARCHITECT AT IBM

TECHNOLOGY   MEDICINE

Maria Siemionow,
PLASTIC SURGEON AT THE
CLEVELAND CLINIC STUDIO

Larry Brilliant,
EXECUTIVE DIRECTOR
OF GOOGLE.ORG

Ray Kurzweil,
INVENTOR AND FOUNDER OF
KURZWEIL TECHNOLOGIES

Now it's time for you to practice for yourself in the context of your own life.

In the spaces below, jot down as many combinations as you can of Foundations and Core Interests that speak to who you are and where you want to go (or go to rtn.is/roadmap to try out combinations online and record your favorites here!). You can revisit the Foundations on page 148 and the Core Interests on pages 140 and 141 and choose the ones that excite you most. You don't have to commit to any one direction now; the goal is to identify all the combinations that you find compelling.

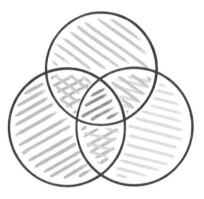

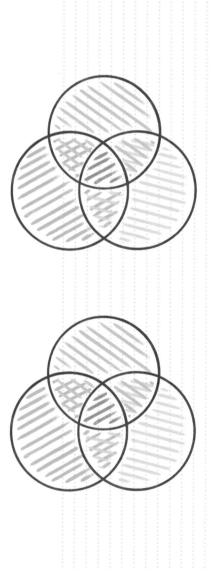

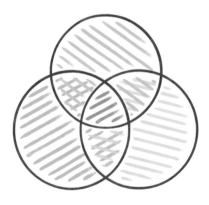

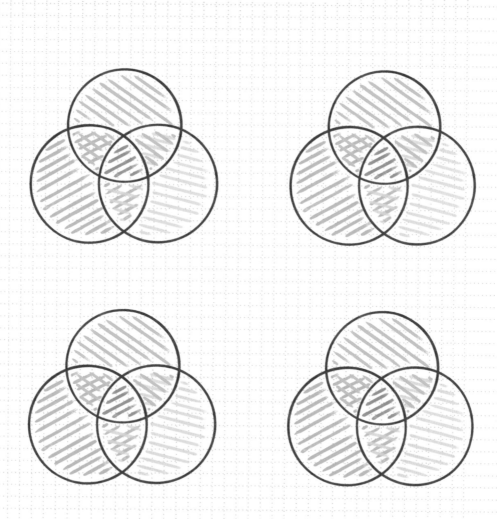

The goal here isn't to make any kind of final decision—we've got more thinking and exploring to do first. Right now, your goal is to get as many ideas down on paper to take with you for the next few chapters, where we'll start to put these ideas through a few tests to see if they're in line with the kind of life you want to build.

CHAPTER 12

YOU MIGHT NOT BE CRAZY, BUT MAYBE YOU SHOULD BE

The summer that roadtripper Brooklyn Smith joined us on the green RV started as one of exasperation for her. "I'm not sure how people do anything other than be a lawyer or a banker, which is what my parents sent me to college to be," she said.

Her parents had given her a pretty standard blueprint: "Just do something conventional. Make money. That's all you really need." The options she'd seen growing up in her Ohio hometown hadn't inspired her either. All she knew was she didn't want to follow the Assembly Line, but everything else just seemed . . . unknowable or unrealistic.

She hit the road with us with an eye on a goal: find those truly inspiring role models her life so far had sheltered her from. Were they out there? Were they successful? Were they happy? That summer Brooklyn did indeed find them, all over the country. People like the owners of a studio that crafts bikes from bamboo, the inventors of a soccer ball that generates electricity when it's kicked, the creators of a mobile film school, robotics engineers, civil rights lawyers, sculptors, brewers, kung fu masters, and monks.

Brooklyn was astounded. "You're the people that I've been told don't exist!"

Those people, each of whom had a work life that was unheard-of or seemingly unrealistic, were thriving. Brooklyn's world opened up.

EMBRACE PLAUSIBILITY

When we aspire to live a life fueled by our interests, the first hurdle we face is accepting that it's even possible. Embracing the plausibility of our vision for ourselves can be enormously difficult in the face of everyday pressures and expectations, to say nothing of our own hampered worldviews. We are the sum of our experiences, and if our experiences haven't presented us with alternative paths, we tend to believe in only the path we can see. This is true no matter who you are. If your worldview never included the idea of becoming a lawyer or an engineer or a street artist or an organic coffee roaster, those are going to seem like crazy options.

Think about blinders on a horse, like the cab horse teams in New York's Central Park. The blinders keep them on their path, ferrying gawking tourists from one corner of the park to the next, but they also act as insulation. If you take the blinders off the horse, the influx of stimuli could be frightening and confusing. So many choices! So many different directions to canter off to: the entirety of Manhattan, and the bridges and all that leads beyond them. That's what can happen to us when we take our own blinders off. At first it can feel overwhelming and intimidating.

Thanks to the myopic view we develop from the Assembly Line, we resist the very real possibility of doing things differently.

If, however, you can learn to question your own ideas about what is possible despite perceived limitations, you can start to see what's Noise and what really is within your grasp.

Shamayim "Mama Shu" Harris,* a former school administrator, showed mastery of this perspective-altering approach when we met her in Highland Park, a small, struggling city inside Detroit. Mama Shu is the founder of Avalon Village, a sustainable eco-friendly village that she's created to transform her neighborhood into a safe and beautiful space for the entire community. Mama Shu had no experience as an architect or an urban planner, but she held on to the dream and the teaching of previous generations. "You fix up your neighborhood," she recalls. "You make it beautiful and serve in any way that you can."

When Mama Shu's two-year-old son Jakobi RA was killed in a hit-and-run car accident, even in her sorrow, she says, she also felt a wave of invincibility. The worst thing had already happened—she had nothing else to lose. That feeling helped her muster the courage to "step into the bigness" of her crazy dream to transform an entire neighborhood.

But even crazy-sounding dreams can be accomplished if you just start and then begin knocking out the steps of your plan. "It was a pure vision, something that I saw. And because I am organized, I can plan. I can see what will come next." She adds, "And that's the thing. You've got to start the thing." Mama Shu just approached it as fixing up her own backyard and the neighborhood. She wasn't a wealthy real estate developer or urban planner, but she made it happen.

No matter what is happening in our lives, believing in the idea of multiple possibilities for ourselves can be difficult. We look at the rent due in a week, the endless bills, the plans for an upcoming vacation, the growing family, or whatever the realities of our situation, and we freeze. Combining your Foundation and your Core Interests into a dream job might sound great, but it's all too easy to return to the notion that it's too crazy, too risky, too much.

We're here to remind you it's not a pipe dream.

/// You Might Not Be Crazy, but Maybe You Should Be ///

Be crazy.

Because it's not as crazy as you think.

THE BALLAD OF THE TURTLE WALKER

We often host events at schools, and one of our staple activities when we present to students involves getting them to think more broadly about where their futures might take them. We start by asking them to think of their dream jobs. We get back some sincere answers, and some joke answers from the meatballs in the back. Little do they know, the jokesters are actually playing right into our hands.

Once, we heard **"I wanna be a turtle walker!"** followed by an eruption of laughter from the group.

One of us replied, "What do you mean by turtle walker?" while another one of us hopped online, searching "turtle walker."

"You know, I want to be someone who takes people's turtles on walks, and makes sure they're getting enough exercise and stuff," the funny guy answered.

"Come on up here."

He came to the mic, loving the attention. He didn't love it so much when we handed him a phone with the number for a turtle rehabilitation center we'd looked up and implored him to call and ask about turtle exercise.

He turned beet red, but was good enough to play along, like the ham he was, and have an informative conversation about the ins and outs of turtle rehab with a real-life turtle walker at the Hidden Harbor Marine Environmental Project in Florida.

We've conducted this "You make up a job, we'll find you a phone number" exercise over and over again. It's a tried-and-true experiment that never fails to yield interesting and legitimate occupations.

IF YOU CAN DREAM IT UP,
SOMEBODY IS PROBABLY GETTING
A PAYCHECK FOR IT.

The point is, what you might think is a ridiculous option is very likely work that puts food on somebody's table. In the face of the utterly bizarre and unexpected, how "crazy," really, are your own dreams?

Skeptical friends and family besieged Peter Lynn* when he decided to devote his engineering skills to making kites. On the surface, kite making can seem trifling, but it's based on real skills and real-world demand for entertainment, beauty, surprise, and play—all of which people will pay for. Now the owner of a beloved worldwide kite brand based in New Zealand, and one of the premier creators and suppliers of innovative designs for kites and kiteboards, Peter's success is a perfect example of how crazy becomes feasible when we follow our interests.

There's nothing wrong with following a traditional path, but you'll find deeper satisfaction when you tweak the expected to support your unique self. Take Elise Benstein.** She's a scientist. You can't get more traditional than that, but Elise took her science background and became a real-life Willy Wonka, veering from the norm by working for the candy manufacturer Jelly Belly to create new flavors. "I'm at the forefront of developing new candy products and . . . I never thought I would be doing that." Elise combined her love of science and food and now creates such wacky confections as the vomit-flavored jelly beans in the company's Harry Potter Bertie Bott's Every Flavour Beans. Elise advised us to be open to capturing those opportunities when they present themselves and embracing new concepts.

* ▶ **roadtripnation.com/leader/peter-lynn**

** ▶ **roadtripnation.com/leader/elise-benstein**

"You can make a living and still follow your hobbies, even if you do the smallest thing. If you don't do anything else, and you just concentrate on it, and you do it forever, there will be a place in the world for it. It doesn't matter how small a thing it is. The world is big enough for these small niches to be a life."

—**PETER LYNN**, *kite maker, engineer, and inventor*

Here are a few more custom-tailored livelihoods we've come across:

ENGINEERING + TOY DESIGN = *Debbie Sterling,*
FOUNDER/CEO OF GOLDIEBLOX, *which makes engineering toys for young girls*

PRIMATES + GERIATRICS = *Raven Jackson,*
RESIDENT VETERINARIAN AT CHIMP HAVEN, *a retirement community
for chimpanzees*

FOOD + POLITICS = *Andy Shallal,*
OWNER OF BUSBOYS AND POETS, *a restaurant, bookstore,
and community gathering place that encourages diversity
in the discussion of art, politics, and culture*

HORSES + PHYSICAL THERAPY = *Maya Arlington,*
HIPPOTHERAPIST, *using horseback riding to promote focus and
fine-motor skills for people with learning and attention issues*

When we first met artist and activist Zaria Forman,* we were blown away by her energy for tackling the big and the seemingly impossible. She's a prime example of how far you can go when you combine all the things you love—for her, that's art and environment/nature. Her otherworldly yet hyper-realistic pastels are an elegy for landscapes that are disappearing, and a call to action to protect them.

"Climate change is such a distant concept for most of us, because it's not happening in our everyday lives," Zaria says. "It's like this slow train wreck, and it disengages us. You get scared and shocked, and overwhelmed, and then you don't know what to do."

* ▶ **roadtripnation.com/leader/zaria-forman**

But tackling big ideas is nothing new to Zaria. You'll frequently find her on all kinds of adventures, such as flying on Antarctic expeditions with NASA to measure polar ice. And it all started with a wild idea for an arctic trek up the coast of Greenland. Zaria's mother, a photographer of the most remote regions on earth, hatched the idea for an arts expedition, but she didn't get to see it happen. Zaria planned and led it in her honor, and bringing together such a big, complex, and personally meaningful journey has given her the energy to keep taking on the big, crazy ideas. "Executing that kind of expedition really empowered me and gave me confidence to move forward and continue."

As you look at your own life, don't limit yourself in imagining the ways that your interests can manifest. William Morris, a renowned glassblower and successful niche builder, challenged us with this hypothetical: "Would you rather have one year of utter vitality or ten years of just ho-hum mediocrity? You know, either choice is fine! But just be the choice that you make. Be it! Don't make the choice of vitality and live mediocrity." In other words, once you've realized you want to live true to your interests, don't hold back. Take a moment right now and look back at the combinations of Foundation and Core Interests you drafted on pages 162–63. Did you really set yourself free to imagine? Did you cast your net wide enough to capture all the wild opportunities available to you, like Elise did, using a science degree to dream up zany candy flavors? For a moment, just let the external and internal naysayers fade away and ask yourself:

What's the craziest thing I can imagine?

THE INTERNAL GPS

By Willie Witte

THE WORD "LOST" WAS TAKING ON A NEW MEANING FOR ME. I FOUND MYSELF WAKING UP REGULARLY IN THE MIDDLE OF THE NIGHT, SQUINTING INTO THE DARKNESS, AND WONDERING, "WHERE AM I?" I WOULD SLOWLY REGAIN CONSCIOUSNESS, THE DIMLY LIT WALLS COMING INTO FOCUS AND RESTORING A VAGUE SENSE OF FAMILIARITY. I WAS, OF COURSE, IN MY TEMPORARY HOME ON WHEELS, A BIG GREEN RV.

ONE MORNING, NOT LONG AFTER I'D FINALLY SETTLED BACK INTO SLEEP, MY CELL PHONE ALARM STARTED TO BUZZ, WAKING ME FOR ANOTHER LEG OF OUR JOURNEY. I FISHED THROUGH THE COUCH CUSHIONS TO FIND MY PHONE AND GLANCED AT THE DATE ON ITS SCREEN: JULY 21. WE'D BEEN OUT ON THE ROAD TWENTY-EIGHT DAYS.

HOW PEOPLE SURVIVED BEFORE GPS IS BEYOND ME. BY THIS STAGE OF OUR TRIP I'D REACHED A SPECIAL LEVEL OF DISORIENTATION, A KIND OF LAND-BORNE JET LAG I'D DEVELOPED BY HAVING TO

Willie Witte's business card reads "Professional Roadtripper." Seriously, it does. With more than sixty thousand miles clocked in Roadtrip Nation's green RV, he has set foot in forty-nine of the fifty United States (someday he'll make it to North Dakota!). More important, as a camera operator and now the creative director of Roadtrip Nation, he has been behind the lens for more than two hundred interviews with inspiring people from all walks of life. When Willie was on the road trip he describes here, he had recently left his small hometown of Sandpoint, Idaho, and was filming a team of roadtrippers from the similarly small town of Stevensville, Montana. Ten years later, Willie still regards this experience as one of the most impactful in his life.

NAVIGATE THE STREETS OF A NEW LOCATION EVERY TWO OR THREE DAYS. THE MAMMOTH CAVE IN KENTUCKY. IT HAD BEEN KNOXVILLE BEFORE THAT, AND BEFORE THAT ATLANTA, NEW ORLEANS, AUSTIN, SANTA FE, ROSWELL, SEDONA, AND LOS ANGELES. ON JULY 21 IT WAS CLEVELAND, AND WE WERE, ONCE AGAIN, LOST.

"OH, WAIT," I STUTTERED FROM THE PASSENGER SEAT, "THIS THING IS TELLING US WE'RE GOING THE WRONG WAY. HOLD ON." IT'S NO SURPRISE WE WERE OFF TRACK, CONSIDERING MOST OF US IN THE RV HAD NEVER BEEN EAST OF THE MISSISSIPPI BEFORE. I WATCHED AS THE GPS RECALIBRATED.

"YEAH, UM . . . SORRY, WE NEED TO TURN AROUND."

MY FATIGUE, HOWEVER, WENT DEEPER THAN THE GRIND OF THE ROAD. AFTER WEEKS ON THE ROAD, THE MENTAL BURNOUT FACTOR IS REAL, BUT THERE WAS A SIDE TO IT THAT WAS THE BEST KIND OF EXHAUSTION POSSIBLE. IT GREW FROM THE SATURATION OF STORIES AND WISDOM WE'D BEEN SOAKING UP AT EACH STOP. LIKE EVERYONE ELSE ON THE TRIP, I'D GROWN UP IN MY OWN BUBBLE THAT WAS SLOWLY STARTING TO BURST. RAISED IN A RURAL COUNTRY TOWN, MY ROADMAP HAD BEEN CLEARLY DEFINED BY THE NOISE, BOLDLY MARKED WITH PLENTY OF "DO NOT CROSS" LINES THAT TOLD ME WHERE I DIDN'T BELONG, WHAT I WAS NOT CAPABLE OF, AND WHAT I SHOULD BE AFRAID OF TRYING. MY OWN FEVERED MIND HAD DRAWN A FEW OF THOSE LINES ITSELF.

BUT OUT HERE ON THE ROAD, ABSORBING STORY AFTER STORY, THOSE LINES WERE STARTING TO DIMINISH. THE BIG QUESTION EMERGING NOW WAS: WITHOUT ALL THESE BORDERS, HOW AM I SUPPOSED TO KNOW WHERE TO GO NEXT?

THE MAN WE WERE EN ROUTE TO MEET THIS OVERCAST CLEVELAND MORNING PROMISED TO BE A WELCOME ADDITION TO THIS CHOIR OF NEW VOICES IN MY HEAD. UP TO THIS POINT, OUR ONLY KNOWLEDGE OF HIM CAME FROM A MAGAZINE ARTICLE ABOUT THE MOST INTERESTING PEOPLE IN CLEVELAND. THE SHORT BIO WENT LIKE THIS: VAN TAYLOR MONROE IS A CUSTOM SHOE ARTIST. HE HAND-PAINTS TENNIS SHOES. FOR MONEY. HIS CLIENTS INCLUDE WILL.I.AM, T.I., AND P. DIDDY. ONE OF HIS WORKS, A PAIR OF NIKE AIR FORCE 1S FEATURING AN ICONIC

IMAGE OF BARACK OBAMA, WILL BE ON DISPLAY AT THE SMITHSONIAN NATIONAL MUSEUM OF AFRICAN-AMERICAN HISTORY AND CULTURE IN WASHINGTON, D.C. WHERE DID THIS GUY COME FROM? HOW EXACTLY DOES ONE CREATE A SUSTAINABLE LIFE IN THE TENNIS SHOE-PAINTING BUSINESS?

VAN WAS WAITING FOR US IN THE COURTYARD OF THE TOWER CITY CENTER, A MALL IN DOWNTOWN CLEVELAND. HE HANDED ME A PAIR OF AIR JORDANS WITH AN IMMACULATE RENDERING OF LEBRON JAMES ON THEM. MY FIRST REACTION WAS THAT I COULDN'T BELIEVE THE SHOES WERE HAND-PAINTED, AND AFTER VAN ASSURED ME THEY WERE, MY SECOND REACTION WAS TO SET THEM DOWN FOR FEAR OF SMUDGING HIS MASTERPIECES.

"I WAS BORN AN ARTIST," HE TOLD US. BUT WHEN COLLEGE CAME AROUND, VAN PURSUED A BUSINESS DEGREE INSTEAD, LANDING HIM, POST COLLEGE, AS AN UPWARDLY MOBILE ACCOUNT EXEC FOR A LOGISTICS FIRM IN CINCINNATI.

"MY PASSION WASN'T THERE, BUT THAT WAS WHERE THE MONEY WAS AT," VAN SAID. "AND I'M THINKING THIS IS HOW I'LL PAY THE BILLS AND HAVE A FAMILY. I'M JUST GOING TO PAINT ON THE SIDE." IT WAS, UP TO THIS POINT, A FAMILIAR STORY. THAT BALANCE BETWEEN OUR AUTHENTIC INTERESTS AND A NEED TO PAY THE BILLS IS A CONSTANT STRUGGLE—AND WE ALL KNOW THAT SOCIETY TAKES THE "EITHER/OR" APPROACH, USUALLY FAVORING THE OR SIDE. AT THE FIRM, VAN COULDN'T FOCUS. HE COULDN'T EVEN PICK UP THE PHONE TO FOLLOW

UP ON A MAJOR ACCOUNT BECAUSE OF HOW LOUDLY THE VOICE IN HIS HEAD WAS TELLING HIM HE WAS ON THE WRONG TRACK. "MY HEART WAS SPEAKING TO ME, 'QUIT YOUR JOB, QUIT YOUR JOB.'"

WHEN HE FINALLY DECIDED TO QUIT, NOBODY UNDERSTOOD HIS MOTIVATION, BUT HE COULDN'T IGNORE HIS GUT. FREAKING OUT, HIS SUPERVISOR COUNTERED WITH, "YOU CAN MAKE TWO HUNDRED THOUSAND DOLLARS A YEAR HERE, AND YOU ARE GOING TO QUIT TO BECOME AN ARTIST?" BUT THAT'S WHAT VAN DID. I FELT A CHILL RUN DOWN MY ARMS. I REMEMBER LOOKING ACROSS THE TABLE AND THINKING, IS THIS GUY FOR REAL? $200K IS NO JOKE! I ASKED MYSELF THE DIFFICULT QUESTION: COULD I LEAVE THAT KIND OF MONEY ON THE TABLE AND JUMP WITHOUT A SAFETY NET? MY ANSWER (NO WAY) GAVE ME A NEW LEVEL OF RESPECT FOR THE CONVICTIONS OF THE ARTIST SITTING IN FRONT OF ME.

"BUT I NEVER THOUGHT IT WOULD GET AS BAD AS IT GOT," VAN CONTINUED. HE WAS PAINTING CANVAS, PAINTING ANYTHING HE COULD, BUT WAS UNABLE TO MAKE A VIABLE LIVING. THINGS WERE LOOKING GRIM, BUT WITH YOUNGER SIBLINGS AND LITTLE COUSINS LOOKING UP TO HIM, HE DECIDED NOT TO LET ANYONE KNOW WHAT HE WAS FACING.

"IDEAS ARE LIKE BABIES," HE TOLD US. "THEY NEED TIME TO DEVELOP IN SECRET, IN THE WOMB, BEFORE THEY CAN SURVIVE OUT IN THE WORLD." I CONSIDERED THE LIST OF "IDEA BABIES" I WAS HARBORING IN MY OWN MIND.

"January comes around, and I got an eviction notice on my door," said Van. But Van wasn't ready to throw in the towel. Again, he thought of the example he needed to set for his family. "If I was homeless for a while, I was gonna get back on my feet, and I was gonna make this a success story." This was 2008, a tough year for anyone to find work, let alone an artist. It helped that Barack Obama's voice and encouraging message were infiltrating psyches. One night, Van woke from a dream with a rush of inspiration, and decided to paint the president-to-be a pair of Nikes he had lying around. He took a picture and posted it online, saying he didn't think much of it.

The shoe went viral. First it sprawled across the blogosphere, and then appeared on the news networks.

Smiling at the irony, Van told us of the rush of recognition the shoe brought. "I was in the *Wall Street Journal*. The *Wall Street Journal*! With a painted tennis shoe!" I imagined the faces of Van's former coworkers at the logistics firm, opening their journals at their cubicles, seeing Van and his shoe. Triumph!

From there, Van's name gained notice and the celebrities began wearing his shoes to high-profile events. Even President Obama owns two pairs of Van's custom shoes. Van had, indeed, made it a success story. But how? What did it take? Before the rappers and basketball players were blowing up his phone, before the media and the museums were tracking him down, when he was quitting his steady job and, later, preparing to be evicted, how did he know this would happen? How did he know it would work out?

Van explained, "Your heart is like a GPS system. A GPS system in your car will tell you where to go, but it won't turn your car for you. You're going somewhere you don't know, looking around saying, 'Alright! I hope this knows what it's talking about!'" Now he was speaking my language. I must have been nodding my head like an idiot because all I could think was "I've been there!" How many countless times had I deferred to that little blue blip on my phone over the course of this trip alone?

Van continued, "And sometimes, like a GPS system, your heart will recalibrate. . . . You might not listen, just like I didn't listen at first . . . You don't know where you're going, and that's the scary part about it. And I think a lot of people are afraid of pursuing their dream because they don't know what's behind the next door, they don't know what's around the corner." At this point something changed in the way he spoke. He leaned in closer. "You can make a lot of wrong turns, and it will continue to recalibrate. But if you continue to go down the wrong path, just like if you were going to the movies, by the time you make it to that movie it's gonna be over." He paused on that note and stared me dead in the eye, adding, "I think a lot of people wait too long to listen to their heart. So I say listen to it while you can because you never know when your show is going to be over. Listen to it. Follow it."

CHAPTER 13

WHAT ARE YOUR SUBJECTIVE TRUTHS?

Most of us agree on the big truths in life: Murder is wrong, you shouldn't steal, it's good to help old ladies cross the street, you should never microwave fish in an open office. Those are easy, but what about the things that are true to you and only you? We each have a set of defining parameters that speak to the core of who we are—these are our subjective truths. And the way they interact with our Foundation and our Core Interests is important.

TRUTHS	SUBJECTIVE TRUTHS
– Without water, we will die.	– I want to make a lot of money.
– Camels have three eyelids.	– Starting a family and spending time with them is of paramount importance.
– Economic bubbles will burst; job markets are cyclical.	– I thrive best in the structure and security of the business world.
– Karaoke means "empty orchestra" in Japanese.	– I work best when I'm my own boss.
– The Ms in M&Ms stand for "Mars and Murrie," the last names of the company's founders.	– I hate big cities.
– There are multiple ways to build a life around your interests.	– I need to live in a city.
– The term "jorts" is a portmanteau of the words "jeans" and "shorts."	– Jorts are both a gift and a plague to the human race.

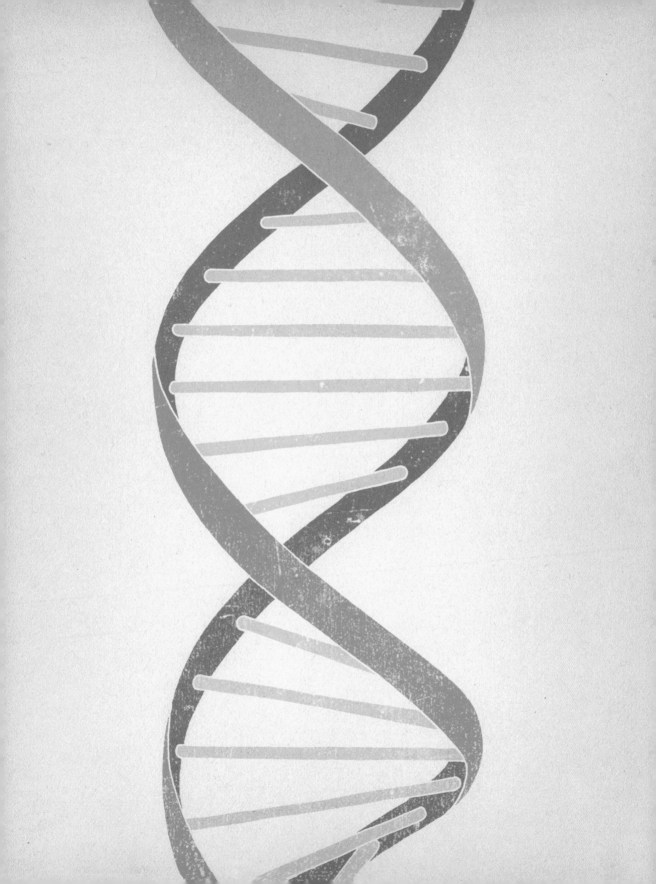

Subjective truths are like a gold miner's sifting pan. As you shake the possibilities around, the ideas that don't matter as much to you fall through, leaving you with the gold—the possibilities that feel right because they agree with who you are.

Some of your subjective truths will be evident immediately, but others may not be revealed until you're staring them in the face. Such was the case for Nathan, one of the original roadtrippers and a cofounder of Roadtrip Nation. "My freak-out," Nathan remembers, "began at a career fair at college." After listening to the Noise and shelving an early dream of being an artist, Nathan had done a stint at a local junior college, taken some business courses, and transferred over to a four-year university to earn his degree as a business major. "I was too passive, not asking myself the important questions. I just accepted that business students become business consultants. That was the path." And Nathan was on it.

At the job fair, Nathan met the people who were at the other end of his Assembly Line. "It was all these super well-dressed career people representing the top-tier consulting companies. I passed around my résumé, even though I really had no clue what this job was I was applying for. So I asked one of the consultants if I could take him out to lunch and learn a little about what he did."

While they ate and talked, Nathan asked a question: "So, do you have to wear a suit every day?"

"Well, yeah," the consultant responded. "But I love wearing suits—wearing nice clothes. We even get a clothing budget, so it's pretty great."

"My response," recalls Nathan, "and I don't even know if I could call it a response as much as a gut reaction, was, 'This is not me. I am not a suit-and-tie guy. Weddings and funerals. That's where I draw the line.'"

Once he had claimed that subjective truth as his own, Nathan's path instantly changed. A huge portion of the jobs that a business major would aspire to immediately dropped from his range of possibilities. The subjective truth-sifter washed away the ill-suited choices (pun intended), leaving Nathan with opportunities more in tune with his values.

YOUR SUBJECTIVE TRUTHS ARE CALLING

The point isn't "suits bad, T-shirts good." It's that we each have to listen to our own subjective truths, because every subjective truth matters, and making choices against them will result in dissatisfaction and frustration down the line. It also gives us perspective on other people's choices and motivations: We all place things differently on the subjective truth spectrum. Understanding whether we're happiest working in a large corporation with lots of structure or figuring things out for ourselves in a small business is part of living a life guided by our own truths.

"I went through hell trying to retain my own life," remembers the wonderfully nutty Barry Brickell,* a potter, author, artist, and (believe it or not) railway conductor, who operates a pottery studio and popular narrow-gauge railroad that winds through a gorgeous patch of land in the rural mountains of New Zealand. "I started making pottery at age fourteen, right through university. I was not a good academic, but I was told by my mother and father I had to get a degree from a university so that I could have a successful career. But I wanted to be a potter and make pots. My father was horrified and shocked and said, 'You'll never be able to bring up a family and have a nice wife and give me lots of grandchildren if you're going to be a potter.'"

✱　▶ **roadtripnation.com/leader/barry-brickell**

With a tinge of mock rage Barry replied, "But I don't want a nice wife. I don't want to make lots of grandchildren for you. I want to make pots!" Barry, from his studio in the dense forests of New Zealand, laughed at the memory, but his story holds something special. Barry's subjective truths were clear, and although he did get his degree and tried his hand at a "normal" profession, he quickly gave it up. Life with a spouse and children and a picket-fenced yard was out the window for Barry, for better or worse. He was, no other way to put it, a potter. Barry's subjective truths informed his vision and guided his road forward. This led him down curious paths, including native forest restoration and, along with his pottery, founding the Driving Creek Railway—a personally operated railway that is part playground, part scenic tour, and part art installation. All of it is a lasting testament to his resolve to stay true to himself.

"I wasted as much money as I could, buying rails and timber and steel beams for bridges," he recalls of the enormous amount of work it took to create the railway that runs through the pristine mountainside forest and is now one of the most well-known tourist attractions in New Zealand. "I've got four drivers now, and that means I can stay in my 'asylum,' my studio, and make pots, which is what I've always wanted to do. My father, if he could see this setup now, he would do a double take, wouldn't he?"

As we know, the Noise is pernicious. It sneaks in, and it has a way of implanting ideas in our brain that might actually conflict with our subjective truths. No matter how we were raised—rich, poor, religious, hippie commune–style—we'll be exposed to values and ideas that, if we take the time to think about them, might not actually be ours. These ideas can even sneak in later in life, at our jobs or schools, or even in our own families. Differentiating between what's authentically your truth and what's societal Noise takes some digging, and some good old-fashioned resistance.

John Passacantando,* the executive director of Greenpeace USA, deeply understands this. It began at an early age, when John's parents gave him a great gift by telling him, "We don't care what you do, just so long as you do your best at it." Simple words, but they hold a remarkable power.

* ▶ roadtripnation.com/leader/john-passacantando

187

"Try to drop the dogma that you get, even from your own peers," John urges. "That stuff is always somebody else's agenda, and it won't help you, and it will never speak to your heart. Whether something is good or bad to do should be based on how it feels to you and your own sense of ethics, not somebody else's rule book. If you feel passionately about doing conservative political work, you should do that. If you feel passionately about working for the companies that I think are pillaging the earth, you should do that, and you should do the best job you can for them. And you shouldn't let somebody else judge you, as you follow your own path; that dogma can get you off course, but your own heart will never set you astray."

Subjective truths are just that: subjective. We can't judge them, or pretend to understand what they mean outside of our own experience, but if we respect our own truths, we move in a direction that is in line with what we need. My Harrison, a section chief in the FBI, went from poverty to the halls of government by following her own need for stability, something her childhood lacked. "I grew up very poor in the housing projects in Tampa," My says. "I knew I wanted to get out of the projects. That was my ultimate goal. I knew that everything I did was for a purpose—a specific purpose. Growing up in the conditions I grew up in, you learn that drive. Nothing stands in your way."

YOUR SUBJECTIVE TRUTHS ARE YOUR VALUE SYSTEM

Respecting your subjective truths is about creating a life you want to live without compromising your values. Your subjective truths all add up to a unique value system that will inform your important decisions. For some of us, a strong sense of moral rectitude might bar us from working for a company whose practices we disagree with. Others might be completely content at that same company for the great pay, health insurance, and company parties. It might even be something visceral, like hating the feeling of being in a hospital (Mike, another original roadtripper and cofounder of Roadtrip Nation, who was studying to be a doctor, luckily realized this before he went too far down that path). Either way, it's up to us to determine what we value. There will always be someone out there who disagrees, but the point is: Who cares? You're the one who has to live your life.

You'll find that some subjective truths outweigh the power of others. Knowing that spending extra time with your family is a louder subjective truth than the $10K more per year you'd earn at a more demanding job will help you say "Thanks, but no thanks," when the wrong offer pops up (and "Yes, please!" when the right one does). Your task is to listen to your own value system and weigh what works best for you. Money might be the most obvious factor in balancing your subjective truths. How much money do you need?

Consider our ragtag fleet of green RVs. Most companies would trick theirs out with slick paint jobs—but we weren't trying to show off a corporate brand or advertise some trashy product, so we found old RVs and covered them in cheap bright-green house paint. Our priority of saving money kept gas in our tanks and allowed us to have more of the conversations and experiences that we valued in those early days. "Experiences over fancy RVs" is one of our subjective truths, and while it might not be right for everyone, it's right for us.

For subjective truths to be useful, you need to examine and understand them so you can make decisions in tune with your values. Those values will influence the people you have surrounding and supporting you.

189

Kimberly Bryant, founder of Black Girls Code, an organization that gives girls of color opportunities to learn coding and computer science, says to let authenticity guide the work you want to do so that the right people will help support your vision. "Be okay with showing a little bit of yourself to the world," she says. "They need to see you. Because that's what allows people to connect to you in a really strong and deep way.

"You need those people that are going to see you, you know? Not some made-up vision of who you're trying to be. No, they need to see you. Because those people that see you, and they connect to that, will ride or die with you—no matter what."

Take a look at how the life paths of the Leaders we've talked to were guided by the values and vision derived from their subjective truths.

DEON CLARK
was a nuclear engineer

Is it important that your work has a social impact?

 YES NO

Founded a nonprofit to help underserved youth.

VAN TAYLOR MONROE

was an account executive

Is it important to make a lot of money?

 YES NO

Quit his job to find a way to paint for a living.

JES WARD

was working in nonprofit management at PeaceJam Foundation

Do you want to work directly with students?

 YES NO

Took a job at cityWILD, taking students on outdoor excursions to teach them self-empowerment and leadership.

JEWEL BURKS

was working at Google in Silicon Valley

Do I need to live close to my family?

 YES NO

Took a less prestigious job closer to home, and discovered a market need she could solve by founding her own start-up.

What are some of your subjective truths?

Do I want to work
independently?

YES   NO

Do I need to be in touch
with nature?

YES   NO

Do I need to make a lot
of money?

YES   NO

Does financial security drive
my decisions?

YES   NO

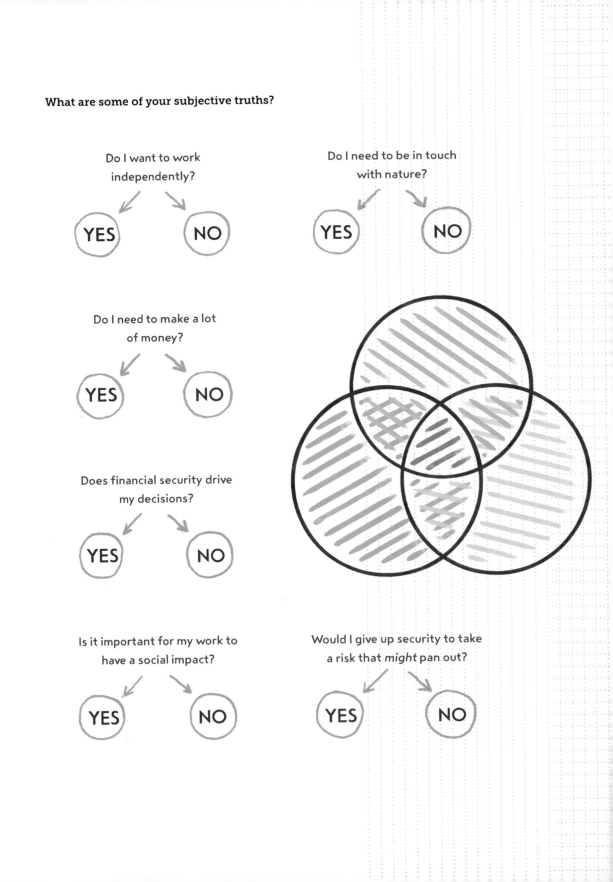

Is it important for my work to
have a social impact?

YES   NO

Would I give up security to take
a risk that *might* pan out?

YES   NO

Would I rather dress casually
at work?

YES   NO

Do I need a lot of
structure?

YES   NO

Does what I do in my career have
to match my personal beliefs?

YES   NO

Do I want to stay near
my hometown?

YES   NO

Do I care about having a
long commute?

YES   NO

Do I need to be physically
active in my job?

YES   NO

Do I want a job that allows me to
spend a lot of time with family?

YES   NO

Would I rather live in
a city?

YES   NO

CHAPTER 14

SKILLS PAY BILLS

Let's not forget the nitty-gritty: Unless you're continually finding bags full of money on the street, you will need to get paid. It's easy for us to say "define your own road," and "do what you love," but we know you can't simply forget all your responsibilities. You have to keep the lights on and pay off your credit cards. Life's necessities generally cost money, and there's no way around it. It's this cold, hard fact that keeps many of us on the Assembly Line.

But there are sustainable ways to marry what you like to do with what you have to do and build a sustainable work life. If you think about it, your economic viability is like an engine in a car. But it's only the engine—not the *entire car*. The car won't go anywhere without an engine, of course, but an engine isn't going to hurtle forward on its own, either.

The best cars—those sleek automobiles we see hugging a winding mountain road in a car commercial—are not just about the engine. From the wheels and the suspension to the door handles, it is all these parts working in harmony that make the magic of the automobile. And the same is true about our lives. Making a ton of money with no meaning is like having a Lamborghini engine inside a Pinto with no working air-conditioning and windows that roll down only half-way. Conversely, "following your passion" with no way to feed yourself is akin to a car without an engine—which leaves you broken down on the side of the road. The trick to keeping the car rolling comfortably is finding a way to build the right engine that will keep you moving toward what you love. And that's where skills come in.

LOVE + MAKING MONEY = POSSIBLE

Mixing what you love with how you make money is a process that can seem daunting—and starting it *now* can seem frighteningly mistimed, especially when you have rent to pay. But the important thing to remember is, it can be done, and not just by the lucky few. You can build a career aligned with who you are as an individual, and you can make money doing it.

There are, however, a few hurdles on that path. The first is probably obvious: to get paid for something, it helps to be skilled at it.

When we talk about skills, we don't mean magical abilities. If your Foundation is your skeleton, the structure that creates stability, and your Core Interests are the nervous system, the messengers that send impulses that get you moving, your skills are the muscles, the heavy lifters that cause locomotion. And like muscles, skills need to be exercised and developed. Your skills are built by activities and challenges that feed into your Foundation and Core Interests, but all of these things have to work together. You could be inherently skilled at logical, ordered thinking, but if you have zero interest in JavaScript or spending hours plotting out code, your skills would be wasted as a web developer.

So, how do you get "good" at something? How do you develop skills in line with your Core Interests? You need to be engaged by something that interests you enough to put in the initial work. This isn't the end by any means, but it's the start. Before you know whether you're (potentially) good at something, you have to try it.

Artist Janet Echelman* doesn't have a background in science, and yet to create billowing architectural sculptures that seem to float above the cities where they're installed, she had to learn about analytical models. "I didn't have all the skills in engineering or in computer science," she says. "I have no background in STEM. I'm not even good at it. But I'm curious.

"If you're going to achieve something, it's going to take a lot of just sticking with it. I don't ever tell anybody, 'Just follow your dreams.' Find a dream that you are interested in, that makes you want to work hard."

EXPERIENCE PERPETUAL MOTION

We might know what we're good at, but to Janet's point, it's more likely that we develop what we're good at as we genuinely explore what we're interested in. It's a perpetual-motion situation—your interest in something drives you to develop your skills in it, not the other way around. It's important to start with what you're interested in so that as you layer on your skills the two will come together in the right way. Just because you're skilled in math doesn't mean you need to learn to love crunching numbers at an accounting firm. Better to start with your interest in sports and then layer on your skill in math to end up running the stats for the Lakers. You start with your interests, develop skills, and then see what happens.

It's all about self-driven growth. "Even the stuff you're really good at, you're not necessarily really good at right away," says Ira Glass,** the host of *This American Life*. His show has been on the air for more than twenty years and reaches

* ▶ **roadtripnation.com/leader/janet-echelman**

** ▶ **roadtripnation.com/leader/ira-glass**

almost five million listeners every week, but more importantly, it ushered in a new wave of journalistic storytelling that's influenced most of the radio and podcasts we all listen to now. Ira himself is, of course, a master storyteller and—as befitting a good interviewer—a great listener. But was he always? Was that how he started out? Did he have the skills and just follow them? When we asked this, he paused for a moment, looking around in his recording booth, and then out of his archives he pulled up one of his first broadcasts on NPR to play for us. When one of Ira's fellow producers from *This American Life* listened to it, Ira told us, she said, "Wow. There was no sign you had any talent at all. There wasn't even a hint you'd be any good." Pay attention to that: One of the most influential voices in radio was unrecognizably bad when he first started.

Ira continued, "The key thing, I think, is to just force yourself through the work, to put yourself in the position where you have to turn out product. That's what will force the skills to come." The interest was there, and then he developed the skills.

The revolving dance between skills and interests is, as Ira says, the hardest part of the process. Your confidence will be shaken, you will fail, you will question your desire to do the work and doubt your abilities. "Fortunately," Ira says, "things happen in stages. I was a terrible reporter, but I was still perfectly good at certain parts of working on the radio. I was an especially good editor, and in a way, that's the best part of my job now." Ira's skill as an editor intersected with his interest in storytelling, and of course, the more he did it, the better he became as both an editor and a host.

198

Is there a flip side to this? What if it just seems like you can't cut it, no matter how much work you put in? Even Ira admits that there are times where you just have to cut your losses and get out. If the skills you have or the skills you are trying to develop simply cannot align with your interests (or don't pay enough) no matter how hard you try, it may be time to change.

But this doesn't mean abandoning your interests entirely; it just means changing your perspective. Just because you're ill-suited to one pathway within your interests doesn't mean that interest is a dead end: just reconfigure how your skills are best used, then find another avenue within your interest that fits better. Say you want to be an actor, but you've been slinging coffee for years to pay the bills and you've never gotten a callback. You don't have to turn your back on the entertainment realm. Think bigger and broader. Maybe you're more suited to casting, editing footage, production work, PR, event planning for premieres, a corporate position at a network, and so on and so on. The possibilities are almost endless when you view your interests through a flexible lens.

Sometimes, the way you think your skills and interests will collide is not the way in which they end up working together. Richard Woolcott,* a cofounder of the action sports lifestyle brand Volcom, is a prime example of that sort of elasticity.

A surfer almost since birth, Richard was all set to go pro—until the unexpected struck: "I grew up very active in skateboarding and surfing. . . . I was building a professional surfing career, and then I had an accident my first year in college. I broke my neck right before I was going to go on the pro tour."

✱ ▶ **roadtripnation.com/leader/richard-woolcott**

Richard faced a devastating reality. Pro surfing was over for him. He could either abandon his interest in surfing entirely, or adapt, tinker, and develop new skills to keep himself aligned with his interest. Once he recovered, he enrolled in school as a business major, worked at Quiksilver, and gained the entrepreneurial know-how needed to create one of the most prolific brands in action sports history. "Everything shifted," he recalls. "I took that focus and turned toward the action sports industry. My background is really a big part of where I'm at today." Being CEO of a major action sports company was not his original vision, but Richard made adjustments along the way, stayed true to his interests, and then developed a new skill set that allowed him to create a work life within his interest of surfing that still paid the bills.

Now you can see that the more surefire way to satisfaction is not just to develop skills for any old career, regardless of whether that career interests you. Instead, your skills *can* be propelled by the things you really enjoy; you just might have to spend some time figuring out how.

200

Visit the Roadtrip Nation Interview Archive at **rtn.is/interests** and select the Core Interest that intrigues you most (food, education, entrepreneurship, sports, and so on). Then select five different people who are each earning a living in different ways within that Core Interest. List them here and identify their "economic engines"—that is, the skills that power their work:

LEADER	ECONOMIC ENGINE

FOLLOW THAT SPARK

For Lisa Legohn,* who holds multiple Guinness World Records for her skill in welding (including making the world's largest electric guitar!), that meant opening up a catalog for ROP classes in high school and following what sparked her interest.

"If you're curious about something," she says, "you can explore without leaving your home. You can read a book and it takes you anywhere you want to be. You have this at your fingertips to explore. Call some of the numbers: Can I take a tour? Can I come see what this is about? Go and look and observe. And if it sparks you, find a class and try it."

That's what she did. "I just saw the word 'welding' and was curious. Welding, what is that?

"The instructor came out and said, 'Welding is the art of fusion,' and I was captivated. I could take something so small—an eighth of an inch—and it could hold seventy thousand pounds per square inch if I welded that electrode correctly. That captivated me."

Now she's that instructor teaching the next generation of welders how the world is built and how to get the skills to be part of it. And she left us with the same advice she gives her students.

"Go and look, but don't settle, because you're like a pond—you get stagnated. Nothing coming in, nothing going out. It's okay to be that stream; I've never seen a tree planted by a river dying of thirst, have you?"

✶ ▶ **roadtripnation.com/leader/lisa-legohn**

"Put as much effort into school, accomplishing your goals and your dreams as you do into your favorite sport. Do the work. If you don't put it in, it's just like that bank account: If you never make any deposits, what's going to be in your bank account? Zero—empty hands. Zero—empty heart. Zero—no money. Zero + zero + zero is what? ZERO. Why should society invest in you if you want to be zero? You can do that all by yourself."

—LISA LEGOHN, *master welder*

But building your skills isn't about learning something once and being set for life, as Kimberly Leser reminded us. You have to be open to learning and feedback, even when you're at the top of your game. Kimberly is the curator of behavioral husbandry and animal welfare at the Oklahoma Zoo, where she oversees more than fourteen hundred animals.

"Every person finds their own path in this career," she says. "Many go to college, many don't.

"Even when you go to college, with this job there's a huge apprenticeship. I have been doing animal behavior for twenty years; I will continue to learn for twenty years."

BE UP FOR THE CHALLENGE

Above all, don't let the challenge of learning something new get you down. Some skills and subjects are just challenging. Don't think that one failure or taking a little extra time to get something means that you're not cut out for it. NASA construction project manager Katie Carr Kopcso reminded us, "School's hard. It's supposed to be."

Spotify software engineer Catalina Laverde spent high school thinking she'd be a journalist. But when it came time to choose what to study in college, she decided she wanted a new challenge, and she definitely got it when she chose systems engineering. "That's when I took my first programming class," she says, and realized, "Oh god, what did I get myself into?"

Developing skills won't always be easy, and it won't be immediate. For some, like Ira Glass, it's about developing your craft over a lifetime. And sometimes, it's a steep hill upward to get fluent in what you're trying to do before it finally clicks into place.

For Catalina, it was about reframing the challenge—this was no different than learning a language, the way she'd learned English when she came from Colombia. "This is a skill—coding," she says. "And every skill can be acquired."

"Don't confuse not liking something with it being challenging," Catalina says. At first, coding seemed impenetrable, but now she loves it and it's the basis of her work. It's all built on that one skill that she put in the time to learn.

"If you're going to tell me, 'No I'm not going to pursue that, I don't like it,' that's fair," Catalina says. "But if you're going to say, 'No I'm not going to do it because I'm afraid that I won't make it'—that is not a valid excuse. You're so much better than that. You're so much stronger and you know so much more than you think you know. And most importantly, whatever you don't know you can learn. Just put one foot in front of the other and keep going. If I want something badly enough, I can get it done."

So what dream are you willing to work at?

205

PART THREE

BEC

MY ROADMAP

We've spent almost two-thirds of this book talking up all the possibilities and options that are available to you. Now it's time to choose a direction. We're not saying pick your one career—that would be the old-school approach—but now is the time to pick the Roadmap you'll refer back to for the last part of this book.

Look over all the Roadmap combinations that you put together on pages 162–63. But this time, look at those combinations through the lens of what we've talked about since you first put them down—the need to be (at least somewhat) crazy; your subjective truths; and the skills you'd be willing to invest time to develop. With this new perspective, some combinations will make more sense, and others will fail to connect as well as they did when you first wrote them down. Look for the combination that you think has the best likelihood of generating a whole, unique, and fulfilling work life, and fill that in on the diagram on the following spread. So this is your Roadmap. At least for today.

+ What feels a little bit crazy? + My subjective truths + The skills I have or want to build

_____

= Where I want to grow and explore

Use your Roadmap as a guide. From choosing a major or part-time job, to changing careers, or even down to the simple things like choosing how to spend your free time, this framework will keep you on course.

Hang your Roadmap on your wall, fold it up and keep it in your wallet, or fill it out with our online tool at **rtn.is/roadmap** to find Leaders who've built careers guided by a Roadmap similar to yours.

It won't tell you exactly what your next destination will be or what next step you need to take, but it will give you comfort that the direction you are heading in is one that is most true to who you are. And if it doesn't, do it again . . . and again . . . and again.

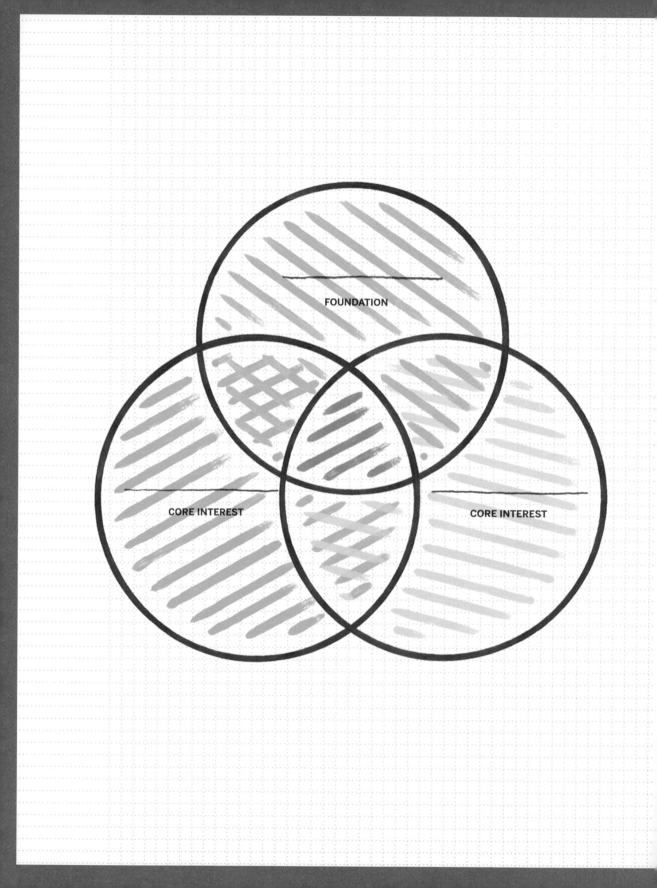

"I DON'T THINK THAT YOU 'DISCOVER' WHO YOU ARE; I THINK YOU CREATE WHO YOU ARE." —**SXIP SHIREY**, *musician*

CHAPTER 15

DRIP. DRIP. SPLASH.

Plotting out your Roadmap is a major triumph. It can make you feel like you've just climbed the Matterhorn. *Finally, direction! Satisfaction is achievable!* And trust us, it truly is. But then you start to think, "What now?" And all of a sudden, you're back at the bottom of the summit. In the face of the daunting path from who you are today to the person you want to be tomorrow, paralysis sets in.

The goal can seem so far away and impossible to achieve. Movement of any kind can be difficult to start. It's easy to get lost in debating the exact "right" next step. But what if, instead of being frozen in indecision, you simply moved?

Vicki Smith, the video game designer we mentioned earlier, summed it up this way: "I knew a priest, when I was in college and drifting, who told me that it's impossible to steer a bike that's standing still." She told us, "Just go for things. If you move forward, you'll find your way because your way will be informed by who you are. **At some point, you need to stop wondering what you are going to do with your life and just go out and do something.**"

When you're guided by your Roadmap, sometimes the specifics of your decision aren't nearly as important as making a decision itself. The small choices you make today will lead to new relationships and new opportunities, all more in line with your interests and values than where you were when you began. Leap. Or hop. Or skip. Or stroll. Or even crawl. Take that as your starting point. And just move. And then move again. Every body of water, no matter how big, starts with a single drop. And then another.

What
possibilities
are within
my reach?

When we met with Jad Abumrad from *Radiolab* (see page 104), he introduced us to the idea of the Adjacent Possible, a powerful concept culled from the study of evolution. Jad told us, "If you imagine the primordial soup, it was full of all these chemicals; like, arsenic was in there, there's amino acids floating around. Those things aren't going to suddenly bump into each other and create a human being, you know? Or even a flower. It's not part of the possibility of that space to create the flower."

So, how did we get flowers and human beings from that stew of inhospitable chemicals?

"You can take an amino acid, and you can take a fat cell, and you can slam them together; suddenly you've got a [new] cell. And that cell has more possibilities. It can become a two-celled organism, and eventually an amoeba," Jad explained. And so it goes, on down the line of Adjacent Possibilities, until we get to people building skyscrapers and decoding genomes and writing TV show recaps.

215

"You have to ask yourself," Jad continued, "what is your Adjacent Possible? In some sense, right now you're in your own primordial soup of dreams. But you have to think of your possibilities in their most expansive and their most constrained [forms]. Like, okay, I can't be Michael Jordan, but maybe I could go play in a pickup game or work on my jump shot, or something like that. You have to ask yourself, what is possible right outside my border?"

In order to cultivate the virtue of humility, Benjamin Franklin said we should "imitate Jesus and Socrates." Whether or not you agree with his sentiment, the key word here is "imitate." Franklin understood that in order to succeed at something, you basically have to start out pretending to be able to do it and figure it out along the way. Franklin championed a fake-it-till-you-make-it approach for the eighteenth century: Imitate what you want to be until you actually become it. If you've spent time identifying your Foundation and exploring your Core Interests, you will know roughly what you want. So start walking toward it.

You may feel a little bit like a huckster when you're in the process of faking it till you make it, but if you really go for it with intention, you'll find yourself on the way to your Roadmap. Take Jakob Laggner,* the cofounder of Treks and Tracks, a firm that leads outdoor education courses. An immigrant from Austria to America, Jakob was working in a call center and bored out of his mind. During his downtime at the office, he started building a website for his dream company.

Describing the services of his not-yet-formed business, Jakob listed skiing, rock climbing, trips to New Zealand, and other expeditions he and his friends had undertaken. He listed his site on a community website called Bay Area Kid Fun, and suddenly started getting sign-ups for his excursions. He remembers thinking, "Oh my God! I don't have insurance. I don't have a permit. I just made this up." But that forced him to enlist a buddy who had experience with camps, and together they made it happen. Cut to now, years later: leading outdoor tours and climbing adventures for Treks and Tracks is Jakob's full-time job—just like what he had proposed in his "fake" business.

* ▶ **roadtripnation.com/leader/jakob-laggner**

HOW TO GET TO MARS IN TEN MILLION TINY STEPS OR LESS

Adam Steltzner,* the lead mechanical engineer of NASA's Mars *Curiosity* rover landing, is not entirely sure that he graduated from high school. Did he ever get that pesky C-minus in a long-forgotten class that was required for his diploma? He's never gone back and checked. At that time, grades weren't really important to Adam, but if you trace his path, you see strong evidence of the Adjacent Possible, of the deep power of tiny actions to move a life in unexpected and exciting ways.

Looking back at Adam's post–high school life, NASA didn't really seem like it was on his list of targets. Adam worked as a cashier at a health food store and played bass in a string of rock bands. He had the directionless quality that so many of us feel when we're off the path of our Roadmap. But then late one night, while driving home after playing a show, he looked up at the sky.

"I started to notice that when I would return home from playing a show at night, the stars were in a different place in the sky," Adam recalled. "I was thinking, 'Whoa. They're moving. Why do they move?' Obviously, I really wasn't paying attention in high school. . . . And so I literally went to the local community college to take an astronomy course to teach me why the stars were moving."

* ▶ **roadtripnation.com/leader/adam-steltzner**

/ / / Drip. Drip. Splash. / / /

One class at a community college. One small, simple step.

DRIP

"Then they had a conceptual physics course, so it was physics without the math," Adam recalls.

+

DRIP

It turned out Adam loved physics.

=

SPLASH

Today, Adam Steltzner is directing spacecraft landings on planets millions of miles away. Can you imagine telling that to the twentysomething Adam who didn't even understand basic planetary systems? It would've seemed like an ocean of drips away.

The best part about taking the small steps is that it prepares you for the big ones. Everything is fractal; you're just doing the same thing on a bigger scale— following simple steps that make it easier to face the fear and the setbacks. Take Adam's thoughts on the distinct possibility that the (very expensive) *Curiosity* might not have survived its touchdown on the red planet. "If we had put a smoking hole on the surface of Mars," he reflects, "I would have definitely failed. But I think humanity is better for trying that and making a smoking hole on the surface of Mars than [for] never having tried."

"I had to surrender to the act of doing, rather than the promise of success or something at the end of it. Surrender to the process, rather than the goal."

—**ADAM STELTZNER**, *mechanical engineer, NASA*

Look back at your Roadmap. Think about the first tiny steps that you can take to align with your Foundation and Core Interests. List things that will take no more than ten minutes, such as reading a blog, subscribing to a magazine, or following someone on Twitter whose work aligns with one of your Core Interests. Then ramp it up a little bit. List things that will take a bit more time. Try visiting a museum, attending a Meetup, or signing up for a class. Keep ramping it up until you have a page full of first steps.

10 MINUTES   1 HOUR   1 DAY +

The Projects at the end of this book will help you, too. We've given you a general framework for each of them, as well as an idea about the level of engagement it will take to get started.

The cumulative effect of action is the most powerful force in defining your road.

Do something.

Then do something else.

Then do something else.

Then splash.

Put this book down for the next ten minutes and take one of the actions you just listed. Make your first move. It may seem like just a small drip, but that's okay!

CHAPTER 16

SHIFT YOUR SKILLS

In our nearly twenty years of sending people out on the road, there's one comment we get more than any other: *You should have a road trip for people older than their twenties!*

And we get this joke a lot: *When are you going to have an AARP Roadtrip?* And variations of this message: *I'm in my forties/changing jobs/retired, and you might be surprised to know that your work really helped me!*

What we hear behind each of those messages is the reality that society pays a lot of attention to the turmoil of twentysomethings, but those transitional moments, and those big questions, don't go away. We all face uncertainty, at many points in our lives—there's no doubt that even the thousand-plus Leaders we've interviewed continue to feel it. And the truth is, the more established you are, the scarier that transition or that decision to change might be.

But no matter whether you're in high school, college, at the beginning of your career, partway through, or even once you retire and have to figure out what's next, change isn't a failure, it's a feature. Industries shift, markets swing, new doors open, and stability and certainty are the collateral. The only thing you *can* control in the face of change is what you do with it.

Being in a place of transition is an opportunity to get outside of what you're used to and make sure you're living a life in line with your Roadmap. That's what we meant back at the beginning of this book when we said that you'll go through this process of self-construction again and again in your life. Something changes, or you change, and the questions come pouring back in. Building your life is a constant process.

For most of us, that process will include at least a couple of career transitions. When the time comes, how do you use your skills to build a bridge to something new? How do you measure the skills and knowledge you have? And then how do you get the new skills you need to move toward a new goal?

Your experiences, no matter how seemingly unrelated they are to what you want to do next, will help you when you get there. Charna Halpern, who told us earlier that life is a lot like improv, reminded us of this when she recounted her winding path from schoolteacher to running the legendary Chicago improv space, the iO Theater. She felt pressure to choose a career, and when she did, she thought it would define her: She was a schoolteacher, and that was that. But life throws new opportunities—or new challenges—at us, and where we've been and what we've done will always contribute to what we do next.

"What I've learned is, that's just a path," Charna says. "Perhaps it's just something you're learning for something else. Don't think that's all you can do, whatever you choose. You're going to see that all these things you do are lessons along the way." Everything you've learned and experienced stays with you; the key is in how you apply what you know to something new, and how you gain the knowledge and skills you need to tackle that next thing.

Transitioning to a new path or career will never be easy, but with the right mindset and hard work, you can do it. And you can come out the other side happier and more fulfilled. But know that the newness, the departure from what you're used to—it will be uncomfortable at first. It might feel embarrassing to be in a new area, feeling like a fish out of water, when you're used to knowing what you're doing; you might feel vulnerable and overwhelmed as you have to contend with new ideas and technologies. But you've faced challenges before, and you have it in you to overcome this one, too.

TELL YOUR SKILLS' STORY

Sometimes the skills you have will transfer seamlessly to the next thing you do. Take hacker-for-good Samy Kamkar.* From hanging around in chatrooms learning about hacking as a kid to writing and selling software in his teens and starting his own company by seventeen, his skills took him far, fast. But when he wrote a virus that spread to over a million Myspace users in less than a day, the Secret Service ended up on his doorstep. Now, as a security researcher, he uses those same skills that got him into trouble to help companies find and fix vulnerabilities in their systems.

But this kind of seamless crossover isn't always the case. Sometimes your skills and experience are harder to quantify. That was the situation U.S. Navy veteran Art delaCruz** faced. By the time he decided to leave the Navy, after more than twenty years, he'd commanded a strike-fighter squadron and made six combat deployments. With that experience, he looked at the civilian world and was at a loss. Job descriptions weren't exactly matching up with his experience, you could say. The skills he'd developed in the military were powerful ones—he just wasn't sure how to translate them to the job postings he was finding. It wasn't a one-to-one transfer of his skills and experience.

"How do you unlock that?" he asked. "How do we tell that story?"

225

* ▶ **roadtripnation.com/leader/samy-kamkar**

** ▶ **roadtripnation.com/leader/art-delacruz**

Art has seen many other veterans experience that same feeling. "It's a huge disservice if someone says, 'I drove convoys on Highway 1 in Afghanistan, so I'm going to be a truck driver,' when that person's wired to be an artist or a musician or a coder or a manager or a construction worker or a teacher," Art says. "Because every one of those jobs I listed, it takes leadership, it takes decision-making, it takes integrity, it takes intelligence, it takes training."

So how did Art connect his past, commanding a flight squadron, to his present, running operations for a nonprofit? They might seem unrelated, but as the chief operating officer of Team Rubicon, a nonprofit that coordinates military veterans to quickly respond to disasters and humanitarian crises around the world, Art leans on the skills and experiences he developed in the military—leadership, organization, quick decision-making, disaster management, and handling intense stress and pressure. Both his past and present roles connect to his interest in armed services and fulfill his need to have an impact. And both honor his Foundation: helping people.

We each have skill spikes and skill gaps. What Art had to learn to do was tell the story of how the skills he gained in the military could create impact for his current endeavor.

WHAT YOU'RE GOOD AT CAN GUIDE YOU

While your situation might not be exactly the same as Art's (how many people can say they've commanded strike squadrons?), there's no doubt that whatever your experience or education, you have skills in your arsenal that will apply to whatever it is you want to do next. They might not be immediately obvious, which is why we're going to walk you through it! Think of your skills as something that you can use alongside your interests to open up even more possibilities for what you can do.

If you're a good writer and communicator, that's a critical skill in all kinds of jobs that may seem like they have nothing to do with writing. For example, it's pretty valuable to most organizations that they feel confident their employees can write an error-free email. Or, if you're someone who's able to organize and manage complex situations, that could apply to anything from working in business or engineering, running an organization, being an activist or organizer, or working as a wedding planner.

These are what are usually referred to as common skills, which is not to say that they're easy to develop or not valuable. Common skills are the critical foundation of what you know how to do; they're the broad, transferable skills you take with you from job to job. They can be personal skills or business skills. (And don't worry, even if you don't have a ton of career experience yet, or if you've never had a job, you still have them!) As you think through your experience and identify your common skills, the key is to be creative and flexible in how you think about what you've done before or excel at, and to think beyond the obvious within the careers you're curious about.

227

EXAMPLES OF COMMON SKILLS

Problem-Solving

Customer Service

Teamwork

Hard Work

Willingness to Learn

Organization

Technology

Written and/or Verbal Communication Skills

Leadership

Time Management

Adaptability

Christine Simmons,* president and COO of the Los Angeles Sparks, walked us through her path and how she discovered her skill set through experience, and let it guide her, even as she hopped between industries.

"So what is it that you know that you're good at?" she says. "If I dropped you into this industry, in this environment? 'I'm a leader, I'll get it done,' or 'I'm a great analyst,' or 'I'm great with numbers'? What is that skill? And then from there, figure out the where and the how, and the industry.

"What I found is that I'm a scientific mind; I like to figure out problems. I'm a leader, I'm a doer. So give it to me, I'll do it. Pass me the ball. Maybe I'll make the shot, maybe I won't. But I want the ball. And diversity and advocacy—those are the things that I'm really good at. And so then, what industry does that happen in? I worked for United Technologies, which owns Otis Elevator Company. But what I did was help minority women–, LGBT-, and veteran-owned businesses get opportunities to compete. So diversity, advocacy, business, solving problems, right?

"Then I did it in the entertainment world; for Disney, for NBC. Still diversity and advocacy, still solving problems, still business. I love business and operations, but now in entertainment, I'm like, *Oh this is fun. This is better than elevators!* (No knock on elevators.) And so now I'm in this wonderful world of sports. But again, it's a women's professional team. So diversity and advocacy, but still solving the business problems of what we do."

Now try this for yourself. Ask: "What do I know I'm good at?" Then get creative with how that skill, affinity, or interest can open up different opportunities within your Roadmap.

✳ ▶ **roadtripnation.com/leader/christine-simmons**

GIVE YOURSELF PERMISSION

Speaking of different opportunities, we heard all of those requests for roadtrippers of different ages and we listened. We've since had roadtrippers in their thirties, forties, and fifties edging on sixty; they've been returning veterans, parents, grandparents, people in disappearing industries who didn't choose the change they're facing, or people who are hungry for something different. When we sent roadtripper Dana out, she was fifty-eight with no retirement plan and a fear of technology, feeling the pressure to maintain the life she'd built training horses, even if it wasn't fulfilling her anymore.

"As I've gotten older, I've found that I've been stuck," she said, "because that risk of starting something new affects more people's lives than my own. And that's where I've found myself more paralyzed: just finding the courage. Do I step away completely from what I'm doing? Or do I phase it out? Or . . . ?"

This was the first interview of the trip,* and she was sitting across from Gary Bolles, an expert on the future of work (It's the family business; his dad wrote the famous career guide *What Color Is Your Parachute?*).

"The first thing it turns out you need," he said, "is permission from yourself."

When you're moving to something new, you might hear all kinds of Noise. *You're too old to switch. You're too young to know what you want! What if you make less money? You don't even know how to add an attachment to an email! You've already come so far, do you really want to take the risk?* But you won't be open to change if that resistance is coming from within yourself. With all this Noise, giving yourself permission is the first step, whether you're looking to shift when you're in high school or in your seventies; either because you want to or because you have to.

* ▶ **Watch the documentary *Rerouting*: rtn.is/rerouting**

IT'S NEVER TOO LATE

Clinical psychologist and hypnotherapist Nancy Irwin* reinvented herself at age forty-four. She'd always been a performer up until then: She was an opera singer with a master's in opera performance and spent nine years doing stand-up comedy. Switching to psychology was a huge leap. A huge leap that also meant starting over with new training. But she loved what she was studying, so she didn't mind taking the risk. But the message from people around her was loud and clear: "Oh my gosh, you're going back to school at your age? How old are you going to be when you finish?"

"Well," she'd answer. "The same age as if I don't."

Her exposure to psychology began with volunteering at a shelter for teenagers who had experienced sexual abuse. That work gave her a new mission, and that was the spark to begin pursuing her doctorate in clinical psychology at California Southern University. Most of the careers you're exploring probably won't require a doctorate, but Nancy's return to school is inspiring for anyone who's thinking about getting back into a learning mindset to get a degree, or a certificate, or any other kind of training.

Nancy had to gain new skills and expertise—but she wasn't leaving the skills she'd developed over her career as a performer behind. "Life is long. Most people switch jobs four or five times in their career," she says. "So the main thing to learn is to be flexible and trust, and follow your heart, and there will always be a transferable skill in everything you do. With my operatic background and comedy, I get to use my stage skills. I treat a lot of creative artists, which is thrilling because I speak their language. And I use humor, when it's appropriate of course. Everything has a transferable skill—even if it seems really diverse when you're studying it."

✳ ▶ **roadtripnation.com/leader/nancy-irwin**

/ / / Roadmap / / /

BRIDGING YOUR SKILL GAPS

Assessing where you've been is the first part, but it takes something more than just telling the story of what you've done to move on to something new.

Let's jump back to roadtripper Dana for a moment—as she looked ahead, she still felt overwhelmed by how to get to that next, new thing.

"I feel like I'm more than what I am on a piece of paper," Dana said. "[I'm very passionate about] anything I do. And it may not be what's on that piece of paper that shows that. Especially when what you've done for thirty years has nothing to do with what you want to do or what you see yourself doing in the future—and that's where I am now. What I've done will get me right back where I was. But I don't want to be where I am or where I was."

As we mentioned in "Skills Pay Bills," the skills you build in support of your Foundation and Core Interests help power your economic engine. But if your Roadmap changes and you want to switch careers or directions, how do you transfer that engine to a new car and get it up and running again? Those common skills we've been talking about make up your basic engine, but you'll need some specialized upgrades to fit the needs of this new career—those custom parts are the technical or applied skills that you need to add to get the whole thing driving.

Depending on what you want to do, a four-year degree doesn't have to be the default. Woodworker and business owner Laura Zahn* used her college years to explore. But once out of school, she found herself working in climate change policy and sitting behind a desk far more than she liked. She came from a family where people worked with their hands. She missed that satisfaction of making things. So she went to a year-long furniture-making program.

✳ ▶ **roadtripnation.com/leader/laura-zahn**

That's not the only available avenue for getting into woodworking or furniture making, Laura says. Depending on your interest, you can go to a certificate program like hers, community college (just by taking a class or two, or to get a certificate). You can also get an apprenticeship and work your way up if you're looking for something less formal.

Laura had to make adjustments to how she transitioned to woodworking to accommodate her life. Her school debts limited the risks she could take in moving toward her new career. At first, she kept her regular full-time job for the income and stability, and then slowly transitioned to her new career in woodworking—first to part-time office work while she ran her fledgling woodshop, then just cushioning it with consulting gigs on the side. Now Allied Woodshop, where she teaches classes and builds furniture, is her main gig, but the financial realities and demands of her life meant it couldn't happen overnight. You can always change, but you have to figure out the pace that will work for you.

THERE ARE ALL KINDS OF WAYS TO TRANSITION TO SOMETHING NEW

▶ **Would you need to make a slower transition to a new career, like Laura Zahn?**

▶ **Could you drop everything and jump into something new right away, like Nancy Irwin did?**

▶ **Would you seek out a step in between where you are and where you want to go, like Tinker Hatfield?** The renowned Nike shoe designer started out as an architect but wanted to try product design. Instead of a total restart, he got an architecture job at Nike, the place he really wanted to be, and then found his way into the design department and worked his way to the top.

▶ **Would you build skills to level up in your current career, like master welder Lisa Legohn?** She worked by day and went to school by night to get her teaching certification so she could become a welding teacher at a technical college.

"As long as you're doing something, a door will open. And when it does, you just stick your foot right in that crack and try to get it open for yourself."

—**KEANA MCGEE**, *global creative marketing, Netflix*

THE STORY OF MY SKILLS

Learning how to tell the story of your skills is a useful activity to go through whether you're looking to make a big leap, a small jump, or even if you want to grow in what you're doing now.

The first step is brainstorming the skills you already have. Whether you're a seasoned professional or fresh out of school, you have both common and technical skills you can transfer to other lines of work. Spend some time thinking about what you already know how to do. Think back to jobs (however brief or long ago!), school, volunteer or community service, and all of your experiences (even those that aren't connected to work).

MY SKILLS

COMMON SKILLS	TECHNICAL SKILLS

Before we go any further, let's take a second to appreciate how much you already know how to do! Whether you've had only one job bussing tables in a restaurant, or you're fifteen years into a careeer, you've already built an arsenal of important skills that you carry with you. What strengths and commonalities do you see?

Now it's time to compare the skills you have to the skills needed for careers that interest you. Spend some time exploring the Leaders connected to your Roadmap at **rtn.is/roadmap**, then research job postings and general job descriptions for the careers and areas you're interested in. Fill in all the skills below that you see repeated in the careers you're drawn to, including the skills you already have. Underline the ones that you see repeated.

SKILLS NEEDED FOR THE CAREERS I'M INTERESTED IN

COMMON SKILLS	TECHNICAL SKILLS

Compare the list on the left page to the list above. On the list above, cross off any skills you already have. Circle the skills that remain (and pay extra attention to those underlined ones)! These represent your **skills gap**—the skills you'll need to develop. Gap might sound negative, but any gap is bridgeable, and a gap is just a space for growth!

There are infinite ways to acquire these skills. Here are a few places to explore:

▶ Online courses such as MasterClass, General Assembly, or Coursera

▶ Local trade certificates

▶ Community college

▶ Online technical certifications

FIND THE COURAGE TO SHIFT

Going back to Dana's road trip, one of the final, most surprising stops for her came as the team crossed into West Virginia. Up until this point on the trip, she'd talked to Leaders who had faced change—but not at the magnitude she saw here. In West Virginia, a whole industry—the basis of the economy, which had employed generations of families—was disappearing as demand for coal dwindled. For the affected coal miners, who suddenly found themselves without the work that was their history and their identity, the new reality was an existential gut punch.

"The stereotype of hillbillies or rednecks—it's deeply ingrained now," said West Virginia local Brandon Dennison. "And it's created these insecurities here. Sometimes when you're told you're something for so long you start to believe it about yourself."

Brandon founded Coalfield Development in his home state to creatively reimagine on-the-job training to help people in his community transition into new careers. "We're asking southern West Virginia to think differently and to do some things differently," Brandon said, "and that can take a lot of courage, especially when you've been one thing for so many generations. It's scary to think about being something else."

Brandon told Dana about one of those coal miners, Wilburn Jude, who had worked in the mine for twenty years. Now he was in the program, working and taking classes to get his associate's degree in applied science while he worked in a new job Brandon's company had secured for him. "Wilburn, his first few months, did not have a vehicle to get to work," Brandon said. "And so he was riding a four-wheeler over *several* mountains every morning, getting up at 5 a.m. to make it to work on time at 7 a.m. Forty-something years old, going back to community college, feeling way out of his element. And so when we talk about courage—that's what we mean by courage."

If you truly want to change your path, you'll need plenty of courage. But the thing you'll need to back that courage up? Hustle.

CHAPTER 17
HUSTLE

There is no one way to define your own road in life. It takes creativity and determination, and there are a million different ways to do it. But no matter what road you take, there will always be times when you will have to grin, bear it, and slog through some seriously thankless tasks. No matter what or how you do it, you're just going to have to get down and do the dirty work. **This place where creativity meets hard work is what we call the hustle.**

But the key to building a meaningful work life that's in line with your Roadmap is hustle with purpose. Is the hard work you're doing advancing your goals and interests? That's the essential question, and that's where your Roadmap comes in to keep you on track. Raza Ahmad,* who works in narrative creation and game design at Niantic (which made a little app called Pokémon Go), reminded us how important this convergence of purpose, hustle, and opportunity is. "Luck is wind," he says, "And then your job becomes, A) figure out where the wind is coming from, B) build the best sail possible, and C) make sure the sail is up and open when the wind comes at you."

Hustle is building that sail so when the wind comes, the boat moves. It's about relentlessly pursuing the skills and experience you need to grow. It means not stopping. It's working for free to get your foot in the door. It's taking on the grunt work and doing it well. It's making it to the finish line, regardless of failures and setbacks. It's believing that what you have to offer is worth fighting for.

✳ ▶ **roadtripnation.com/leader/raza-ahmad**

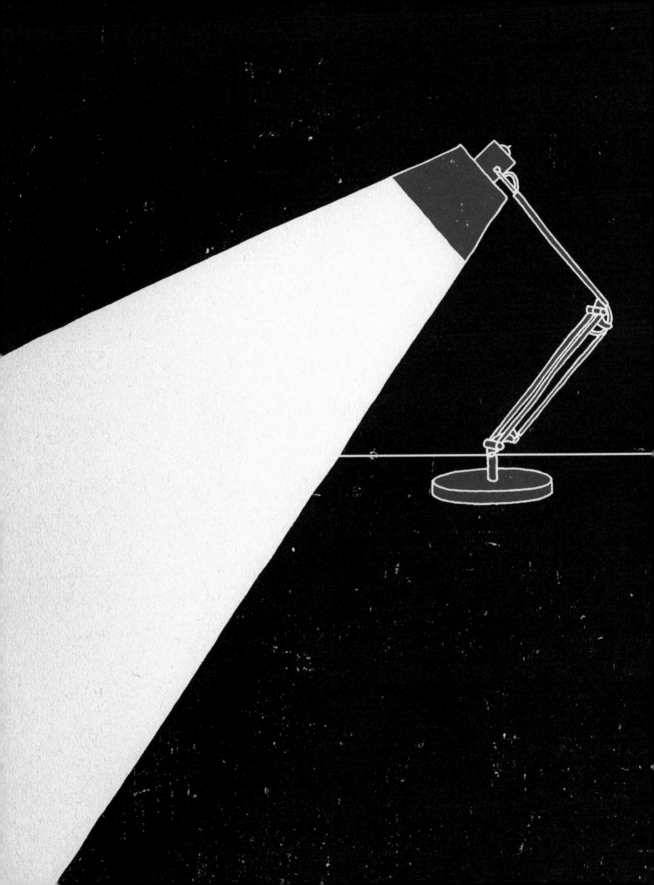

"You have to be willing to put your dream on the street."

—**KEVIN CARROLL**, *the Katalyst, Nike*

Hustle is all about, as author and Nike branding guru Kevin Carroll* told us, putting your dream out on the street.

Kevin's hustle started on the basketball court. "Little did I know that this ball was actually taking me on a journey," Kevin told us, holding a basketball in his hands. "This ball gave me courage, taught me how to deal with disappointment, taught me how to deal with things beyond my life." Kevin's potential pro career was destroyed when he blew out his knee, but this setback didn't stop his hustle.

Kevin realigned his Roadmap, studying sports medicine. He became a trainer for high school and college teams, and then later had a seven-year run as "the Katalyst" at Nike, with a mandate to bring about creative change in the company. Along the way, he also wrote a great book, *Rules of the Red Rubber Ball*.

"People told me that bouncing this ball would get me nowhere in life," Kevin recalls. "Those were the same people who asked me for tickets when I was the head trainer for the Philadelphia 76ers." Kevin was intentional about his choices and did the hard work because, for him, it was fun—it is what he loves to do— and that sense of joy motivated him to keep hustling. "When you're out there playing, you start to imagine yourself as something bigger than you are. That's how I've always done it. I see my dream in action."

Hustling is what makes the improbable the inevitable.

* ▶ **roadtripnation.com/leader/kevin-carroll**

Don't wait for an invitation to start living your life. You can hustle up the traditional corporate ladder, but these days there's just as much opportunity to hustle by inventing your own ladder. Create these opportunities instead of reacting to circumstance, even if it makes you feel foolish, even if it seems impossible.

Building an inspired work life is not a gift that falls into your lap; it has to be earned—especially if you want to keep it. Success is the payoff for effort, so get used to the effort. And if you can, find a way to enjoy it.

"It's like when you're in sports, and all you want to do is play," says Vicki Smith, the video game designer you met in "Life Is Linear Only in the Rearview Mirror." "If you don't do the push-ups, you don't get to play the game." For Vicki, the conditioning she had to do before being able to design games came in the form of learning more math and science. No matter what you want to do, there will be some form of conditioning you'll have to suffer through to get in shape enough to do it. Not only will it not be easy, you shouldn't want it to be easy. Relishing the hard work—or at least keeping a positive and intentional attitude about it—is a standout quality that will elevate you over those who won't, or can't, or don't put their all into it, and it will develop your endurance and problem-solving skills.

Naturally, the grunt work will still feel frustrating when you're in the midst of whatever menial task you're pushing through, but when it's in the service of your Roadmap, it's still a million times better than life on the Assembly Line. So when you find yourself knee-deep in work, printing a three hundred– page report on a

"I think success has a lot to do with finding something you love and putting everything you have into it."

—**JOHN LEGEND,** *singer/songwriter*

printer that jams every five minutes, remind yourself that getting through it is a key part of the hustle, an intentional act in the process of self-construction, so silence the part of your brain that thinks you're above it.

BE HUMBLE AND SACRIFICE

"I got into *MythBusters* because I was just willing to go the distance and do anything," Kari Byron,* one of the show's cohosts, says. She started out as an intern for the prop shop. "They were going out to the desert to put some JATO rockets on an old Impala and buzz it across the desert and try to make it jump into the air," she remembers. "Well, I was working two jobs so that I could have the internship. I had a job before and after my internship during the day—I didn't sleep so much. And I really wanted to see this wild creation happen, so after my waitressing job ended, I drove myself all night long into the desert, slept three hours in the parking lot until their vans pulled up, and just ran out and was like, 'I'm going with you!' I got waters, I helped out; if they needed a wrench or a bolt, I went and I got it. I just made myself important long enough to become part of it, and I think my enthusiasm and my willingness to do the hard work for no money made them say, 'Okay, she's dedicated enough that maybe we're going to bring her on.'"

In the midst of the hustle, your sacrifice might not be financial—it could be doing a job that seems beneath you, all in pursuit of the greater goal. Morris Reid,** a government lobbyist, had already run an Ohio field office for President Bill Clinton's campaign, but his real goal was to work for his idol, Secretary of Commerce Ron Brown. He asked, he hustled, a trusted colleague made some calls, and Morris was called in by Ron Brown's assistant.

* ▶ **roadtripnation.com/leader/kari-byron**

** ▶ **roadtripnation.com/leader/morris-reid**

"There are a million ways to get to success; for me, it wasn't about who I knew, it was about the hustle."

—**WENDY WILLIAMS**, *TV and radio host*

"I get there," Morris says, "and he says, 'I got something for you. Your job is to take care of Ron Brown's mother and mother-in-law.' I was on 'purse duty' with a couple of old ladies!" Morris took happy ownership of what could've been viewed as babysitting detail: getting them to places, helping them along. Morris's aplomb made him a favorite with the two women. "They talked about me nonstop," he laughs. After demonstrating his commitment through hard work and positive energy, his goodwill (and the mothers chatting him up to Secretary Brown) moved him up to exactly where he wanted to be, as Brown's protégé.

JUST SAY YES

The James Beard Award–winning pastry chef and Food Network host Gale Gand* related a story to us about the time she got the opportunity that launched her as a professional baker. Early in her career, Gale got a call from a previous boss who had a pastry position available. Gale had only worked a couple of kitchen jobs; pastries were not yet in her repertoire, but she said yes anyway. When faced with learning a new field, Gale advises, "You need to lie and say you're qualified, and then when you get there, you will be. One day in passing, this chef says to me, 'Do you know how to make croissants?' And the right answer to everything in the kitchen is 'Yes, chef.' So what do I do? After work, I make seven different batches of croissants from seven different books. I stay up all night, teach myself how to do it. So the next day, when the chef asks me the same question, I'm not lying." The takeaway? Just say yes.

Another key insight into Gale's hustle was actually something she learned from legendary chef and hustler Julia Child: Learn how to sell yourself. When Gale had revealed that she taught herself instead of going to culinary school, Julia exclaimed, "Oh, darling, never say you're self-taught. Always say you learned in the field!"

*   ▶ **roadtripnation.com/leader/gale-gand**

THERE'S ALWAYS ANOTHER WAY IN

Sometimes you have to find a different way into the house. When we were planning our first road trip, we fudged the truth a bit to get into a particularly intimidating house: the, ahem—cough, cough—highest court in the nation.

We wanted to interview U.S. Supreme Court Justice Sandra Day O'Connor—the first woman on the Supreme Court, and a cowgirl at heart, who had ruled on some of the most important cases in recent history. We had to hear her story.

"I looked everywhere for phone numbers to the Supreme Court, and all I could find was a random number for booking tours on its website," remembers Nathan, one of the original roadtrippers. "I called up and asked for Sandra. 'You mean Justice O'Connor?' the guy on the line corrected me. 'Uh, yeah, Justice Sandra Day O'Connor,' I answered."

The guy at the tour office told Nathan that directly speaking to O'Connor was out of the question. "You can come take a tour if you want, or you can write a letter to Justice O'Connor."

Nathan kept writing letters, kept calling, kept getting the same response month after month. Finally, Nathan tried a bold (crazy?) move. "This was in the days before caller ID. I called up the tour number one last time, but I used a deep, stern, business-guy voice. 'Sir!' I said testily, 'I was just speaking with Justice O'Connor and was transferred here. Please transfer me back right away!'

"Meanwhile, my mom was downstairs making lunch, while I was sweating through my shirt, thinking NSA agents just might bust through the door. But my creative approach worked. The official stammered out an apology and transferred me over to Justice O'Connor's office."

Justice O'Connor's assistant graciously listened to Nate's frazzled story about the green RV and the roadtrippers' mission. A month later, the assistant called back to say that Justice O'Connor would meet with them.

The point here isn't to lie to Supreme Court justices (or anyone else, for that matter). The point is to get creative. It's often said that the definition of an insane person is someone who keeps doing the same action but expects a different result. If what you're doing isn't working, try a new approach; there's always a way in.

WORK HARDER

Ahmir "Questlove" Thompson, drummer of The Roots, told us about his personal drive: "Average day, I do eighteen-, twenty-hour days. It's a constant mission to stay ahead."

CNN anchor Soledad O'Brien said to us, "The really good stories are not the ones where eighteen satellite trucks are parked. They're the ones where you drive a little extra distance, you ask the little extra questions, you dig a little bit harder." This vision of journalism is a reflection of the hard work Soledad has

put in. "I worked my way up. I was a production assistant, went on to become a writer trainee, then went to NBC, and then I got a job at the NBC affiliate in San Francisco, where I made about a third of what everybody else made. I was a terrible reporter, no experience. But I knew I could outwork people. I might have had no clue about what I'd been assigned to do, but I knew that I would outwork everybody, and I would stay until midnight if I had to figure it out."

Every one of the stories in this chapter underscores that there are two kinds of hard work: There's hamster-like hard work, running furiously in a plastic wheel that spins and spins and goes nowhere, and there's beaver-style hard work, damming a river to suit your needs, working step by step toward an appreciable goal.

Hustle without a Roadmap is just busywork. But when your hustle is working hand in hand with your Roadmap—when it's connected to your authentic Core Interests and speaks to your Foundation—that's when the hustle can be energizing and powerful. That's when it will get your dream on the street.

WHAT DOES YOUR HUSTLE LOOK LIKE?

WHAT DO I NEED TO **SAY YES** TO?

_____

_____

_____

WHAT **SIDE DOOR** HAVE I NOT OPENED THAT I SHOULD?

_____

_____

_____

WHAT IS WITHIN MY **REACH**?

_____

_____

WHAT DO I NEED TO **SACRIFICE**?

_____

_____

WHAT **GRUNT WORK** DO I HAVE TO DO

TO GET WHERE I WANT TO BE?

_____

_____

WHAT **BASIC RESOURCE** AM I NOT USING?

_____

_____

CHAPTER 18

RISK OR REGRET? YOU CHOOSE.

Taking risks leads to **danger**.

Taking risks leads to **rewards**.

Each of these statements is true. You just need to balance the two as you move toward the center of your Roadmap. Your job is to intentionally approach risk and determine what's at the heart of the risky decision you're considering. What are the long-term consequences of not taking a particular risk? What are the short-term dangers? What can you gain? What can you lose?

At first, you'll probably end up no less confused, mainly because the whole point of taking a risk is that you don't know what's going to happen. That's why it seems risky. (And by the way, we're all grown-ups here, and we don't have to formally define what we mean by "risk," right? We don't mean dumb decisions. We mean decisions that don't have a certain, predictable outcome but do have the potential to shape your road in unexpected ways, good or otherwise.)

In facing risk, it's necessary to remind ourselves that we are the sum of our decisions. Is taking the risk going to keep us on our Roadmap, even if we might fail and there might be consequences we didn't foresee? Will the regret in not taking a risk pile up like compound interest on an overdue loan, so that years from now, we are buried in "What ifs"?

As we've seen earlier, that accumulation of "What ifs" is what awaits us on the other side of the Assembly Line. The comfort of not taking a risk, of making a safe bet or "right" choice, may be a bigger risk down the line. Cheryl Foster, the artist we met in "Defining Your Foundation," spent two decades in that comfort zone, working as a real estate appraiser, building up a heavy load of regret and dissatisfaction. But there's a bigger risk that comes with deferring what you want to do, which Cheryl saw firsthand.

Just as Cheryl's mother was preparing to retire from a nearly thirty-year career as a teacher, she was diagnosed with terminal cancer. The reality of the deferred life plan hit Cheryl's mom hard. "As I was administering morphine," Cheryl recalled, "she was babbling out of her mind [that] she wanted to go up in a hot-air balloon," Cheryl recalled. "She wanted to go to the Bahamas! Why wasn't there any time for that when she could still make that journey?" In that moment, Cheryl got a rare glimpse into her future. She could practically hear herself on her own deathbed wishing she'd done things differently and not squandered all her time working in a field she never had any affinity for. "When she passed, that was it! I never appraised another thing," Cheryl reflects.

By the time we sat down with Cheryl she was happily doing what she loves as a multimedia artist and serving as the master artist-in-residence for the John F. Kennedy Center for the Performing Arts. It's safe to say that her experience with her mother's passing shifted her view of risk. "You wanna take the safe path? There's no joy in that. I don't want a safety net, I just want to be out there and doing it. But my happiness is a little bit different from everybody else's."

And that's a key point. When you define happiness for yourself, it usually looks different from the one-size-fits-all model that society hands us. And chances are, you'll have to be willing to take the risk to pursue your definition of happiness. Because on the other side of risk lies a life that is worth living.

If you never take a risk, you never get the reward. Simple as that.

Jonathan Poneman,* the cofounder of iconic indie rock label Sub Pop Records, deals with the risk/reward ratio by redefining what the terms mean.

"If everything in life is characterized as risk versus safety, the human instinct is to choose safety. But if you use a whole different standard for evaluating your life, like necessary versus unnecessary, happiness is necessary and love is necessary. For me, it was just changing the way I evaluate my life, and taking the whole idea of security out of the equation."

And that's the best way to view regret: to see it as the cost of not doing something, of not taking a risk because you're afraid. Afraid of failure, afraid of the unknown, afraid of—what? Many Leaders have challenged us with this simple question, so we'll do the same for you. When you feel yourself backing away from a risk, ask yourself: What's the worst that can happen?

*   ▶ **roadtripnation.com/leader/jonathan-poneman**

257

If you consider living a life that you find meaningful and engaging as a necessary act of survival, then risk, in a traditional sense, goes out the window. Like Jonathan, you will have created a new set of standards by which to judge your decisions.

~~SAFE vs. RISKY~~

NECESSARY vs. UNNECESSARY

Think about some of the risks you think you should take but haven't. Use this new set of standards to decide whether the "risky" decision is one that is necessary or unnecessary to your well-being.

RISK	NECESSARY	UNNECESSARY
_____	_____	_____
_____	_____	_____
_____	_____	_____
_____	_____	_____
_____	_____	_____

EVALUATE PERCEIVED RISK VERSUS ACTUAL RISK

What's the greater risk? Trying something with an uncertain outcome, or staying where you are, even if it's not fulfilling, because it gives you the illusion of safety and certainty?

One way to approach the decision is by borrowing an idea from economics: opportunity cost. Opportunity cost is the cost of choosing one option over another. What do you stand to gain, for example, if you make a choice to take an entry-level job to get by versus spending your time working on your own project, which might not pay you right away? The difference between the two is big, so the opportunity cost of choosing to work on your own project is high in the short-term. Your life situation will dictate whether you can take such a risk, so you have a decision to make. In the long term, you may calculate that the opportunity cost flips; putting in that time upfront may pay off in a few years, but what you choose all depends on your situation.

Cost of selected alternative

– Cost of next best alternative
_____

= Opportunity cost

When you're in the concrete world of dollars and cents, calculating opportunity cost works just fine. But in balancing alternatives on your Roadmap, there's more nuance, since the "cost" of your decisions is based on your own individual needs and values. When you're young and free of obligations, it may be more doable to take those short-term risks like choosing to spend your time on an unpaid project, even when the opportunity cost is high. If you have a family, or are supporting your aging parents, or have a mortgage, then the balance might shift. And then there are the emotional opportunity costs—will choosing comfort over risk leave you with gut-wrenching regret when you look back in your later years?

The Adjacent Possible theory from "Drip. Drip. Splash." (page 215) is the best way to balance out a risk when it does indeed seem too costly. Maybe you can't quit your job and start that small business you want to today, but what is immediately outside of your current realm of possibility? What steps can you take to get to a point where the costs balance out in your favor?

GO EXPERIENCE THE WORLD

As we started to think about risk and opportunity cost and making decisions when the outcomes are unknown, we realized that the subjects of one of our more recent road trips were particularly well suited to help us answer this question. Who better to talk about risk than the people who have to stare down the unknown every day, then try to quantify and understand it? Who better to talk about risk and danger than . . . people who work in insurance? Okay, okay, hear us out—because no one thinks more about how to calculate risk, and what the limitations of those calculations are, than these folks.

Karen Clark was one of the first people we met. The main thing you need to know about her is that she was the first person to ever build a hurricane catastrophe model, and once she did, she created the whole field of catastrophe modeling. She's been at the forefront of disaster modeling ever since. Let us slow you down there for a second and say that again: She figured out how to build models that map potential outcomes for the seemingly unpredictable, and she's still at the top of the field. Her whole career has been about using data and building models to estimate the risks of different kinds of disasters. So listen to her when she says of the big life decisions you may be facing, "You won't know, so don't try to predict."

"Don't labor over every decision that you make—is it right, is it wrong?—because you're never going to know. You can't predict. It's interesting—people say we have prediction models and I always have to correct them; our models don't predict, they basically give you the probabilities of different outcomes based on today's conditions." Not so different from what you're trying to do, right? Based on where you are right now, what are the chances of these different outcomes? And if you don't like those outcomes, what should you be doing to change the conditions to get the ones you want?

And about that decision point—the overthinking and agonizing we all do about our next step or a risk we're not sure we should take—she got pretty real with us about that, too.

"I wouldn't spend a lot of angst and mental energy over trying to labor at this point in your life whether it's the right decision or not. Chances are it's not going to be the right decision. Chances are you will not stay there forever, but you'll learn something and hopefully you'll learn more about what you like and don't like, and then you can use that." In other words, the only thing you can do is assess where you are, and then make the best choice you can and see what happens, then use it to make a better decision the next time—to take a better risk.

Economist and Harvard Business School professor Mihir Desai* echoed that sentiment and told us a story about philosopher Charles Sanders Peirce, the founder of pragmatism, which he summed up for us quite simply: "Basically, don't introspect; go out and experience the world."

"What he figured out," Mihir says, "is the problem for most human beings is the problem of an insurance company, which is, there's chaos everywhere and

＊ ▶ roadtripnation.com/leader/mihir-a-desai

you've got to make sense of it. How do insurance companies do that? Answer: They get experience. They look for the patterns in the randomness. You see all this randomness and chaos in the world. The only way to solve it is to experience it. Insurance companies survive because they get a lot of experience, right? They sample the population. They go out and figure out the regularities. And [Peirce's] point was that's what you have to do as an individual: Go out and experience the world."

As you come up against situations in life that call for either taking a risk or making a safe bet, remember that not taking a risk can be the riskiest thing to do. Taking a risk is a preemptive strike against regret.

So peer into the distant future for a second—envision yourself, as Cheryl did, taking your last breaths. Now ask yourself . . .

WHAT RISKS WILL I

REGRET **NOT** TAKING?

YOU'RE THE CENTER

By Keakealani Pacheco

IT WAS HARD TO BELIEVE IT'D ONLY BEEN TWO WEEKS SINCE I'D MET TRAVEN, TEHANI, AND THE ROADTRIP NATION CREW AND BEGAN THIS HOLOHOLO[1] AROUND THE ISLANDS. WE WERE ONLY TWO HUNDRED MILES FROM MY HOMETOWN OF HILO, HAWAI'I, BUT I WAS GETTING PROGRESSIVELY FURTHER OUTSIDE OF MY COMFORT ZONE—AND THIS DAY WAS NO EXCEPTION, AS I GOT MY FIRST EXPOSURE TO THE WORLD OF COMPETITIVE SURFING.

I'D HEARD OF PIPELINE BEFORE—I'D SEEN PICTURES AND VIDEOS OF THIS ICONIC WAVE ALL OVER THE PLACE—BUT HONESTLY, I DIDN'T KNOW WHAT TO EXPECT. THE BEACH BELOW US WAS PACKED WITH THOUSANDS OF ONLOOKERS LAID OUT ON BEACH CHAIRS AND TOWELS, CHEERING AND SNAPPING PICTURES AS SURFERS IN BRIGHTLY COLORED JERSEYS TOOK TURNS PULLING INTO DOUBLE-OVERHEAD BARRELS. TEHANI, MY FELLOW ROADTRIPPER, COMMENTED ON EACH RIDE IN LINGO I DIDN'T UNDERSTAND. SHE GREW UP HERE ON THE NORTH SHORE OF O'AHU AND THIS WAS SECOND NATURE TO HER, BUT EVERYONE SEEMED SHOCKED WHEN I SHAMEFULLY ADMITTED THAT THIS WAS THE FIRST SURF COMPETITION I'D EVER BEEN TO.

I UNDERSTOOD THEIR SURPRISE. HOW IS IT THAT A GIRL WHO HAS LIVED HER WHOLE LIFE ON THE ISLANDS HAS NEVER SEEN A

[1] Holoholo - vi. To go for a walk, ride, or sail; to go out for pleasure, stroll, promenade.

Born in Hilo, Hawai'i, **Keakealani "Kea" Pacheco** is a college student trying to charge forward while feeling pulled in several directions—by her varying interests, her family's expectations, her desire to leave Hawai'i, and her deep connection to her heritage. But even as she tacks between her options, one constant has been her love of technology. She hopes to one day use her passion for tech to build tools that will empower people all across Hawai'i. Kea and two other roadtrippers explored the islands of O'ahu, Maui, and Hawai'i by Jeep, marking our first-ever green RV–less road trip!

SURF COMPETITION? I'M EIGHTEEN YEARS OLD AND CURRENTLY IN MY FIRST SEMESTER OF COMMUNITY COLLEGE, AND AS I STEP OUT INTO THE WORLD, IT'S QUICKLY BECOMING CLEAR TO ME THAT I DON'T FIT OTHERS' EXPECTATIONS. I'D LIKE TO TAKE PRIDE IN THAT, BUT THE TRUTH IS, IT'S SCARY TO STEP OFF THE KNOWN PATH. MY FAMILY, FOR INSTANCE, COMES FROM A LONG LINE OF COMMERCIAL FISHERMEN . . . BUT I GET SEASICK AND HATE BOATS! THEY FISH, I DON'T. I'VE ALWAYS HAD AN INTEREST IN TECHNOLOGY BECAUSE I SEE POTENTIAL FOR IT AS A GREAT TOOL FOR BENEFITING MY COMMUNITY. THAT'S WHY I'M CONSIDERING STUDYING COMPUTER SCIENCE ONE DAY, BUT I GET NERVOUS BECAUSE I'VE NOTICED VERY FEW YOUNG PEOPLE IN HAWAI'I PURSUING CAREERS IN TECHNICAL PATHWAYS. I'VE LOOKED FOR ROLE MODELS OF HAWAIIAN WOMEN (OR ANY MINORITY WOMEN!) WORKING IN COMPUTER SCIENCE, AND THE LANDSCAPE IS PRETTY BLEAK.

I'M PROUD OF MY HAWAIIAN CULTURE AND ANCESTRY, AND THE LAST THING I WANT TO DO IS LEAVE MY HERITAGE BEHIND. BUT I STRUGGLE TO SEE A PATH FOR MYSELF IN TECHNOLOGY THAT WILL INCORPORATE ALL THE ASPECTS OF WHO I AM. BETWEEN MY IDENTITY, FAMILY, FRIENDS, TEACHERS, AND MY EVER-EVOLVING INTERESTS, IT FEELS LIKE THERE ARE A MILLION THINGS PUSHING AND PULLING ME IN DIFFERENT DIRECTIONS AT ANY GIVEN MOMENT. I DON'T ONLY FEEL LIKE I AM LOST AT SEA, BUT SOMETIMES I FEEL LIKE I'VE EVEN LOST TOUCH WITH MYSELF.

AFTER THE COMPETITION, WE HOPPED BACK INTO OUR JEEP AND WOVE OUT ONTO KAMEHAMEHA HIGHWAY. IT FELT GOOD TO GET OUT OF THE CONGESTION AND CHAOS OF THE COMPETITION AREA, BUT THERE WAS A PIT IN MY STOMACH KNOWING WE WERE HEADING TOWARD ANOTHER POTENTIALLY UNCOMFORTABLE EXPERIENCE FOR ME: WE WERE GOING SAILING ON A TRADITIONAL HAWAIIAN VOYAGING CANOE. I KEPT QUIET BECAUSE I DIDN'T WANT TO DRAG DOWN THE MOOD, BUT I KNEW THERE'D ONLY BE SO MUCH I COULD DO ONCE WE GOT OUT ON THE OCEAN AND I BECAME VIOLENTLY ILL.

IT WAS MIDAFTERNOON WHEN WE ARRIVED IN KĀNE'OHE BAY, AND WE WERE GREETED BY THE WARM AND WELCOMING PRESENCE OF BONNIE KAHAPE'A-TANNER, A CAPTAIN AND SAILING INSTRUCTOR

KNOWN AFFECTIONATELY IN HER COMMUNITY AS "AUNTIE KAHAZ."
SHE LED US INTO THE BACKYARD OF THE HOUSE WHERE SHE OPERATES
THE KĀNEHŪNĀMOKU VOYAGING ACADEMY, A PROGRAM THAT TRAINS
LOCAL YOUTH IN TRADITIONAL HAWAIIAN NAVIGATION TECHNIQUES.
SHE HAD A STRENGTH ABOUT HER YOU MIGHT EXPECT FROM SOMEONE
WHO'S SAILED ALL AROUND THE WORLD, BUT SHE ALSO HAD A PEACEFUL
AURA THAT, FOR THE MOMENT, CALMED MY NERVES ABOUT GETTING ON
THE CANOE. I COULD SEE IT ANCHORED OFFSHORE: KĀNEHŪNĀMOKU,
A TWENTY-NINE-FOOT DOUBLE-HULLED CANOE (OR WA'A, AS AUNTIE
KAHAZ CALLED IT), SAT THERE SLEEPING, WAITING FOR US. ITS BRIGHT
YELLOW HULLS POPPED ON THE GLASSY BLUE BAY. BUT BEFORE WE
TOOK TO THE WATER, WE CLIMBED UP ONTO A PLATFORM AT THE TOP
OF A HAU TREE SITTING PROUDLY ON THE SHORELINE TO LISTEN TO
AUNTIE KAHAZ'S STORY.

SHE'D GROWN UP LOVING THE WATER, SO WHEN SHE WENT TO
COLLEGE AT UNIVERSITY OF HAWAI'I AT HILO, SHE STARTED EXPLORING
THE OCEAN'S ROLE IN HAWAIIAN CULTURE, AND ITS IMPORTANCE TO
HER OWN IDENTITY. "THROUGH THAT PROCESS I GOT INTRODUCED
TO THE VOYAGING CANOES. PRETTY MUCH SINCE THAT FIRST TIME I
GOT ON THE CANOE, I'VE BEEN TOTALLY HOOKED, AND IT'S LIKE I'VE
NEVER REALLY LEFT THE CANOE."

EVENTUALLY SHE GOT THE OPPORTUNITY TO VOYAGE FROM
HAWAI'I TO MICRONESIA WITH LEGENDARY POLYNESIAN NAVIGATOR
"PAPA" MAU PIAILUG. "IT WAS LIKE WE WERE SAILING WITH OUR
ANCESTOR." AFTER THAT VOYAGE, SHE WANTED TO SPREAD PAPA
MAU'S KNOWLEDGE, SO SHE EARNED HER MASTER'S DEGREE IN TRANS-
FORMATIVE LEARNING AND STARTED HER OWN VOYAGING ACADEMY.

AFTER HEARING HER STORY, MY FELLOW ROADTRIPPER TRAVEN
ASKED HER A QUESTION THAT WAS ON ALL OF OUR MINDS: "HERE IN
HAWAI'I, CULTURAL IDENTITY IS ONE OF THE TOP ISSUES UNIVERSITY
STUDENTS FACE. SO WHAT ADVICE DO YOU HAVE FOR KIDS WHO ARE
TRYING TO FIND THEMSELVES?" WITH A BIG LAUGH, SHE ANSWERED
SIMPLY, "I'D TELL THEM ALL TO GO ON A VOYAGE!" AND THAT WAS
OUR CUE. IT WAS TIME TO CLIMB DOWN FROM THE TREEHOUSE AND
SET SAIL.

WE WADED OUT TO KĀNEHŪNĀMOKU. THE WARM THIGH-HIGH WATER AND SOFT BAY FLOOR WERE COMFORTING, BUT AS WE GOT CLOSER TO THE CANOE, MY NERVES WERE ON EDGE ONCE AGAIN. I EXPLAINED TO AUNTIE HOW OUT OF MY ELEMENT I WAS, THAT I'D SPENT MOST OF MY LIFE ACTIVELY AVOIDING THE WATER, WHICH MAY BE PARTIALLY WHY I'M CONSIDERING A CAREER BEHIND A COMPUTER. TO THAT, SHE OFFERED ME THESE WORDS: "A'OHE PAU KA 'IKE I KA HĀLAU HO'OKAHI." AN OLD HAWAIIAN SAYING SHE EXPLAINED TO MEAN, "ALL KNOWLEDGE IS NOT LEARNED IN JUST ONE SCHOOL." IN OTHER WORDS, YOU HAVE TO GET OUT OF YOUR COMFORT ZONE AND EXPERIENCE AS MUCH AS POSSIBLE. THAT WAS MY WHOLE INTENTION IN GOING ON THIS ROAD TRIP, SO I TOOK A DEEP BREATH AND CLIMBED ABOARD. WITH AUNTIE KAHAZ AT THE *HOE ULI*,[2] WE SET OUT.

THE WA'A SLID GRACEFULLY FORWARD WITH THE LIGHT WIND, THE SHORE RECEDING BEHIND US. WITH A MAJOR SENSE OF RELIEF, I REALIZED I WAS ACTUALLY ENJOYING MYSELF! I SAT COMFORTABLY AT AUNTIE KAHAZ'S FEET AND LOOKED OUT AT THE VAST BLUE HORIZON AHEAD, IMAGINING WHAT IT WOULD FEEL LIKE TO BE THOUSANDS OF MILES FROM LAND. STRANGELY, THE FEELING THAT AROSE IN MY GUT REMINDED ME OF THE FEELING I GET EVERY DAY WHEN TRYING TO FIGURE OUT WHAT TO DO WITH MY LIFE. IN THAT MOMENT, I REALIZED THAT THE EXPERIENCE OF NAVIGATING THE OPEN OCEAN AND NAVIGATING ONE'S LIFE PATH MIGHT BE ONE AND THE SAME. THE TIDES, CURRENTS, AND WINDS WERE LIKE THE VARIOUS PRESSURES I'D FELT PULLING MY LIFE IN DIFFERENT DIRECTIONS.

AFTER MAKING THAT CONNECTION, IT BECAME INCREASINGLY INTERESTING TO LISTEN TO AUNTIE KAHAZ EXPLAIN HOW TRADITIONAL HAWAIIAN NAVIGATION CENTERS ON USING EVERYTHING AROUND YOU TO FIND YOUR WAY. THE STARS, THE WINDS, THE BIRDS, THE SEA LIFE—YOU HAVE TO OBSERVE EACH ELEMENT OF YOUR SURROUNDINGS BECAUSE WHEN YOU'RE OUT AT SEA, THAT'S ALL YOU HAVE. AS I LISTENED, I REALIZED I'D ESSENTIALLY BEEN DOING THAT THROUGHOUT THIS ROAD TRIP. I'D BEEN OBSERVING THOSE AROUND ME, THEIR STORIES, AND THEIR ADVICE. BUT I'D BEEN OBSERVING MYSELF AS WELL, MAKING NOTE OF THE QUESTIONS I'D SURPRISED MYSELF BY ASKING, AND MY OWN RESPONSES TO OTHERS' QUESTIONS. TAKING IN THE CONDITIONS THAT SURROUND YOU AND USING THEM TO GET YOUR BEARINGS—THAT IS NAVIGATION.

[2] *Hoe uli - n. Steering paddle or oar, rudder, helm.*

I WAS SHOCKED OUT OF MY CONTEMPLATION WHEN AUNTIE KAHAZ ASKED ME IF I'D LIKE TO STEER. THE NEXT THING I KNEW, SHE WAS PLACING THE HOE ULI—AND THE TRUST AND CONTROL THAT COMES WITH IT—INTO MY HANDS. SHE INSTRUCTED ME TO PICK A POINT ON THE HORIZON AND GUIDE US TOWARD IT. THE SUN WAS GETTING LOWER, MAKING EVERYTHING GLISTEN. THE STURDINESS OF THE LONG OAR WAS COMFORTING, AND I COULD FEEL THE VIBRATION FROM THE WATER PASSING THE PADDLE'S BLADE. I WAS SUDDENLY OVERCOME WITH THE PRESSURE OF BEING AT THE HELM. YES, YOU CAN TAKE IN YOUR SURROUNDINGS TO HELP YOU UNDERSTAND WHERE YOU ARE, BUT AT THE END OF THE DAY IT'S UP TO YOU TO STEER, TO MAKE THE CHOICES. HOW DID SHE FIND THE CONFIDENCE TO DO THAT? HOW DO YOU KNOW YOU'RE GOING THE RIGHT WAY? WITH THAT IN MIND, I BLURTED OUT A QUESTION: "IF YOU WERE RANDOMLY DROPPED IN THE MIDDLE OF THE OCEAN WITH NO IDEA WHERE YOU WERE, WOULD YOU BE ABLE TO FIND YOUR WAY?"

"ONLY IF WE KNEW WHERE WE CAME FROM," SHE REPLIED MATTER-OF-FACTLY. I LET THIS SINK IN FOR A MOMENT. I'D NEVER CONSIDERED THE IMPORTANCE OF KNOWING WHERE YOU COME FROM AS A WAY TO UNDERSTAND WHERE YOU'RE GOING. "YOU HAVE TO KNOW WHERE HOME IS IN ORDER TO KNOW NOT ONLY WHERE YOU'RE GOING, BUT HOW TO GET BACK. YOU'RE ALWAYS FINDING YOUR WAY BACK. NO MATTER WHERE YOU GO, YOU'RE ALWAYS GOING HOME."

THOSE WORDS HIT ME DEEPLY. I REALIZED THAT ALL MY LIFE, A PART OF ME WANTED TO JUST GET AWAY BECAUSE I FELT LIKE I WAS STUCK ON THIS ROCK. BUT I SIMULTANEOUSLY WORRIED THAT I'D BE LOST IF I STEPPED OUT INTO THE UNKNOWN. NOW, WITH MY HANDS HELD TIGHTLY TO THE HOE ULI AND THE ISLAND AT MY BACK, I UNDERSTOOD THAT NO MATTER WHERE I GO, I WILL ALWAYS BE ROOTED TO WHERE MY PATH BEGAN. AS I LISTENED TO AUNTIE KAHAZ'S WISE WORDS, IT BECAME CLEAR THAT WHERE YOU COME FROM IS NOT AN ANCHOR THAT HOLDS YOU BACK—IT'S SIMPLY MORE INFORMATION TO HELP YOU NAVIGATE FORWARD. "THE FIRST LESSON WHEN YOU'RE LOOKING AT THE TRADITIONAL HAWAIIAN STAR COMPASS IS, YOU ARE THE CENTER. NO MATTER WHERE YOU GO, YOU ARE ALWAYS THE CENTER."

I AM THE CENTER. I AM STEERING THE SHIP. NO MATTER WHERE I GO, OR HOW FAR I MAY VENTURE OUT, I WILL BE THE CONSTANT THAT IS ALWAYS THERE. STEERING THE CANOE IS NOT PRESSURE; IT'S POWER. THAT DAY OUT ON THE OCEAN GAVE ME THE CONFIDENCE THAT I WILL BE ABLE TO FIND MY WAY NO MATTER WHAT.

CHAPTER 19

GET TO FAILING

Never has a letter had more maligned associations than "F." F is for failure, F is for fake, F is for fear, F is for fraud. F is for f . . . (okay, we walked into that one). It starts in school with the dreaded grade F. Getting an F means you underperformed to the fullest extent. There is no lesson to be learned, no helpful takeaway for bettering your performance the next time. It's no wonder we develop such a deep-seated fear of failure.

Oddly though, despite our fear of it, failure is just part of business as usual—the daily process of missteps and improvement that's part of getting the work done. Even though this is a bona fide fact, we still hold on to outmoded ideas about the shame and fallout of failure.

Organic life itself is the product of millions upon millions of years of trial and error—why shouldn't our lives follow suit? Without failure, you can't improve, modify, or move on. Failure is what gives you the impetus to recraft the beta version of yourself; it redirects your Roadmap. Ultimately, failure is a good thing. Before the first road trip, we couldn't even fathom the idea that successful people failed. But everywhere we've been, accomplished people have shared stories of the failures that changed and improved them.

- **David Neeleman**, the founder of JetBlue, was fired from his high-level VP job at Southwest Airlines. His failures and successes at Southwest helped him create JetBlue.

- **Wanda Sykes**, acclaimed comedian, actress, and Emmy Award–winning writer, bombed on stage before she became a household name.

- **Gina Prince-Bythewood**, the screenwriter of *Love & Basketball*, applied to UCLA's film school and was rejected, so she wrote a letter to the head of the program detailing why they should change their minds and got accepted. "It really set the tone for my career," she says. "It just gave me the confidence to *do* even though people were saying I couldn't."

- **Beverly Donofrio** got a failing grade on her MFA thesis and got fired from a writing job before she wrote her *New York Times* bestselling book, *Riding in Cars with Boys* (which that MFA thesis was an early version of, by the way).

Video game designers often cite studies showing that during a game, the most enjoyable moment for the player is actually when they fail and are spurred to try again. You know the feeling: that moment in *Tetris* when the blocks stack over that top line, or Mario loses his last life, and you feverishly hit "retry" because now you know more about that level, and you know you're one step closer to beating it. Your undeterred video game brain doesn't view starting over as reason to give up, rather you see it as an exciting challenge. You keep going until you save the world (or, until your fingers cramp into a claw).

We thrive on trial and error, on solving problems and overcoming obstacles, and no reward is more satisfying than overcoming failure and seemingly insurmountable challenges. Failure incites movement, and a chance to do better.

272

Using failure as a tool for both self-reflection and further action is something that Paralympian and six-time world champion wheelchair racer Jeff Adams* excels at.

> **"When I go out and speak to students, I talk about races I lost. Because I've learned more in losing. Those are the times when I've grown."**
>
> —**JEFF ADAMS**, *Paralympian*

One of his crucial failures was in the summer games in Barcelona. "I went into the last lap on a breakaway with two other guys, and in my head it was like, 'My life is gonna change today. The last lap is the best thing I do. I'm on a breakaway with only two other guys, and they give three medals. Mathematically, this is working!' But I made a mistake by not checking my equipment enough."

Jeff's chair broke in that last lap, spilling him face-first onto the track.

"I lost. It went from being the best day to the worst day. **We have it so ingrained in us that it's always about winning. Maybe it's about losing, and suffering, and overcoming, and having that courage.** But we don't value that as much as the 'win.' So, I won a race in Sydney, and it was a great day. But what did I learn? That it's fun to have a great day? That's the weird conundrum in life: You learn so much more when things aren't easy, when things aren't fed to you, when things aren't perfect."

✳ ▶ **roadtripnation.com/leader/jeff-adams**

Robert Kiyosaki,* the bestselling author of *Rich Dad Poor Dad*, agrees, and has strong feelings about how we feed into this anti-failure mindset in schools. "We practice making mistakes. In football, it's called practice. In the arts, it's called rehearsal. In a laboratory, it's called an experiment. But if you make mistakes in school, you're punished and labeled stupid.

"The reason that most people aren't successful is simply because they don't fail enough. How do you learn if you don't make mistakes?" In the Marines, Robert practiced failing every day in his plane—he'd shut off the engine mid-flight to master bringing the plane down safely without power—and that ability to handle a failed engine saved his life when the real thing happened in Vietnam. That training and that comfort with failure did more than save his life though, it also *made* his life—that toughness is the key to his success as an entrepreneur.

Consider this: Failure is nothing more than a result. It may not be what you hoped for, but it is an unchangeable fact. You can't fight or hide from facts. Experiencing failure is collecting new information. It's a new fact to process. You now know something that you didn't before. Results—favorable and unfavorable—lead to new actions, more informed actions, more calculated risks, all of which move you closer to the center of your Roadmap.

✳ ▶ **roadtripnation.com/leader/robert-kiyosaki**

Think about instances in your life that you, either now or at some other time, labeled as failures. Using the new definition, list those failures here. But take it a step further. See if you can identify one—or many—lessons you learned from each failure:

FAILURE	WHAT I LEARNED

Take a look at these lists. Your failures may still make you cringe, but that's okay. Focus on what you learned and what you took away from the experience. How have you grown since then? How has your life changed in a good way? How are you doing things differently from how you were before? How are you developing and rebuilding your self-confidence to try again?

Failure itself is not bad. What's bad is the inability to learn or grow from a situation that might not have gone your way the first time. That is true failure.

Craig Brewer,* the renowned director of *Hustle & Flow*, doubled down on this philosophy and urged us to seek out failure. Early in his career, he and a few friends and family members joined forces on a quest to create a masterpiece. Shirking their jobs and responsibilities in favor of pursuing their dreams, they pooled their savings and set out to make the great American film. How did it work out? As Craig revealed with a wistful smile, "It failed, miserably. I mean, there's close to $30,000 of film that sits undeveloped, and I don't think I'll ever develop it." That flop wasn't Craig's last. It was the first in a string of many failures along Craig's road.

Like Craig, we all fail. A lot.

The specter of fear that failure engenders is deep inside all of us. Craig's solution is the old stare-the-demon-in-the-eye approach. Failure is a part of life, a painful part, a rough and messy part, but an unavoidable one. So embrace it.

When Craig met with our crew, one roadtripper, Michael, spoke about how his fear of failure was holding him back from pursuing a film career.

"Are you perfectly clear on the fact that you will fail?" Craig asked. "Are you cool with that? I mean, you know you're going to fail, repeatedly. The only way you're going to get good is if you fail. So get to failing. Get that process going. Don't put that process off, because it's going to hurt more when you're older. Because what ends up happening is people don't want that hurt, so they get married and have kids, and then they blame their families and their circumstances for the fact that they didn't want to fail. . . . **So if you want that enrichment of success, get busy failing.**"

✱ ▶ **roadtripnation.com/leader/craig-brewer**

Randii Wessen,* a systems engineer at NASA's Jet Propulsion Laboratory, applied for the shuttle astronaut program twelve or fifteen times in a row. He has never been accepted. In his files he has rejection letters from grad schools, internships, aerospace companies, and even the very laboratory where he now works. "You can measure the caliber of everything by how it handles adversity," says Randii. "What do you do when you get a lousy grade? What do you do when you get rejected from a university? What do you do when someone dumps you in a relationship? It's how you pick yourself up that makes you stronger, and that really tells you something about the caliber of who you are as a person." With that in mind, Randii left us with this mantra: **"Those who dare, risk defeat. Those who don't, ensure it."**

Failure is never the end of a story; it's not even really a failure. Mistakes, and even epic blunders, are helpful instruments as you make your own road. Take risks. Get to failing! If things don't turn out how you imagined, or you fall flat on your face, modify your method and try again. Failure is an outcome, nothing more. It's a series of lessons to be learned along the way to better versions of yourself.

✳ ▶ **roadtripnation.com/leader/randii-wessen**

277

CHAPTER 20

FIGHTING DOUBT

Doubt is nothing new—it's not a generational thing. From Hamlet to Holden Caulfield, fighting doubt is an old war. It begins early on, in the halls of school, on the playground, in your family home. Are your parents happy with your choices? Do you look good? Do you fit in? Are you doing things that the cool kids like? Our self-confidence gets jammed in the gears of the adolescent Assembly Line.

"My biggest poisonous habit was insecurity, second-guessing myself," says Christina Heyniger, the adventure tourism consultant we profiled in "The Blank Canvas." "I needed someone to approve of what I was doing. In high school I was such a horrible geeky dork, and I wanted so much to be popular. And when I got to college I was the same way. I just wanted to be in the right sorority, and I wanted the right people to like me. . . . I just could not be happy unless some-one was going, 'You're cool!' I didn't even care what *I* thought. I just wanted to make sure all others were happy."

We've probably all learned that the herd lives and dies in high school, and we may shake off some of these insecurities when we say goodbye to our teenage selves, but the template is still set. We fall into the trap of defining our self-worth by the perceived value granted to us by outside forces. Media barrage us with images and concepts of what should make us feel good about ourselves. But none of that, not one ounce of it, has anything to do with our actual authentic selves.

The key to fighting doubt is believing in your own personal worth outside of whatever social strata or Noise-controlled constructs you happen to be cooped up in. That's hard, sometimes impossible. You cannot win the fight against self-doubt by stewing in your own thoughts. Your Roadmap helps. Taking intentional action guided by your Roadmap leads to movement, which leads to change, accomplishment, skill development, creation of meaningful communities, and a sense of satisfaction. **Self-doubt crumbles in the face of a clear understanding of yourself.**

SMALL STEPS BUILD CONFIDENCE

When roadtripper Jason hit the road, he was almost done with his PhD in children's and young adult literature.* He'd already come so far, but his own self-doubt held him back. "The biggest obstacle at the end of the PhD process is probably my lack of self-confidence," he told us. "It's basically something called imposter syndrome, a sense of not feeling worthy enough. I know for me that's my biggest block. The lack of self-confidence made it so easy to think about quitting. There are moments where you want to give up. And it's easier to give up."

Like we've seen with other aspects of self-construction, it's okay to start small. When Jason first sat behind the wheel of the green RV, his anxieties were running high, but the reminders about confidence came back to him. "One of the things that the Leaders stressed," Jason said, before heading out on a long drive, "was that this is something you're always working with. [Nancy Irwin] said confident acts create confidence. So this is my first confident act," he said as he got ready to steer the RV onto the road, "even though I feel completely like I should not be behind the wheel, and so I'm just going to do it and pray that no lives are lost." (Everyone survived; he drove the RV like a champ.)

"When you're loyal to your values, the confident feelings will come," psychologist Nancy Irwin had told him. "People want the reverse. Doesn't work that way. You've gotta have the courage, then at some point you will get the confidence."

> ✱ ▶ **Watch the documentary *Degree of Impact*:**
> **rtn.is/degree-of-impact**

/// Roadmap ///

Sometimes we have to learn what it's like to feel confident. Small accomplishments will help you get into the habit. "When I look at confidence, it starts in small steps," Ivan Joseph, the director of athletics at Ryerson University, told Jason and the rest of the team. "You gain confidence by the first baby steps, and then you look for something else." Accomplishing something, large or small, helps you build the muscle memory of what accomplishment feels like.

"When I first [drove the RV] I was scared, as I think anyone would be," Jason recounted. "And as I did it more, I became less scared. And that fear turned into confidence. First it was, I can drive this out of the campground . . . then, I can drive this on the freeway . . . then, I can drive this in a city. Now I'm driving on the Las Vegas Strip. I would be scared to drive a car on the Las Vegas Strip and then here I am driving a thirty-seven-foot RV—but that confidence wasn't created by myself, on my own; it came from having a good navigator. And also being able to ask for help."

For Colorado State Senator Irene Aguilar, noting accomplishments is key. She told the team, "I think one thing is I have to remind myself of my little successes, and celebrate them and let them be motivators for me to continue."

This is an essential element of overcoming doubt: We have to become the authors of our own internal mantras and replace the toxic messages of the Noise with positive messages of empowerment. Believing in yourself takes practice, and a mantra helps.

Let's start by getting the garbage out. Examine how you talk to yourself. What are the internal statements that reflect your personal self-doubt? What Noise do you whisper to yourself? Things like: "I'm not experienced enough to have a valid opinion," or "Other people are much smarter," or "I don't belong here."

Get that internal Noise out of your headspace . . . and into this space. Use the space in the illustration to write down as many self-doubts as come to mind. Now read your self-doubts aloud. Chances are you'll hear the absurdities of those statements, and once they're out of your head, you can work on any truths you may hear in them.

To suppress the doubt in your own head, pick a positive mantra and repeat it silently each time you find yourself in a moment of fruitless doubt. At first feelings of doubt will tumble out of you, but counteract them by responding with your chosen mantra. The goal is to cut off the Noise earlier and earlier.

SELF: "~~I'm not smart enough.~~" RESPONSE: "I have everything in me to do this."

SELF: "~~I'm not smart . . .~~" RESPONSE: "I have everything in me to do this."

SELF: "~~I'm not . . .~~" RESPONSE: "I have everything in me to do this."

SELF: "I . . ." RESPONSE: " . . . have everything in me to do this."

If learning to deal with self-doubt is like building muscle, then you have to do the reps—again and again, slowly building up the ability to believe in yourself. When Kimberly Bryant, the Black Girls Code founder and CEO, started to explore a venture that would be all her own, she wasn't sure what it would be. It took trying something and putting her idea out there. She didn't yet have the big picture in mind, or a clear vision of where she would end up. In fact, that first step took a long time to actually commit to. "I'm a super planner type— I want to know as much as possible before I make my first move," she says. "So it took me almost a whole year of gnawing on this idea, talking to folks, before I actually jumped into it."

"I think any entrepreneur has a bit of uncertainty when [they're] first starting," she says. "And I think that holds many folks back from making that leap. You have everything that you need to be successful, but the [key] piece is being able

283

to take a leap of faith, and using that belief in yourself to go forward." The more we force ourselves into intimidating situations and test what we're made of, the more confident we become that we can handle the next test. Then, after we've done it enough times, we know that no matter what situation we get thrown into, we can land on our feet because we trust ourselves.

EVERYONE FEELS IT

Even if the small cliffs are too much, if the doubt in your head is borderline crippling, remember, you're not alone. Everyone struggles with self-doubt, in varying forms, every day. Even the people you wouldn't expect.

Pixar's Danielle Feinberg says, "I've found that at every level that I've gone to, those challenges just keep coming back. It isn't like you magically get somewhere where you're like, 'Oh, I know everything and I never have any doubts anymore.' And I think that's another thing to get used to as time goes by; it isn't like you just know it all and you have it all figured out."

Dave Banks* is an acclaimed photojournalist and filmmaker with fourteen Emmy nominations (and one win under his belt), but growing up he struggled with dyslexia that turned into a lasting and deep self-doubt about his abilities. "I was constantly called stupid," says Dave.

In an effort to find a way to understand what he was going through, and get over the doubts he had about his own creative process, he joined an artists' support group. "I had to stop thinking, 'Are they going to like it?'" Dave points out. "I needed a different perception because we can always be self-critical and

* ▶ **roadtripnation.com/leader/david-banks**

we can just beat ourselves up. I needed to get beyond that. What the support group showed me was that other artists had the same feelings as I did, and the same insecurities.

"Screw confidence, just do it. The more risks that you take, the stronger your confidence grows."

Ira Glass, the host and executive producer of *This American Life* introduced in "Skills Pay Bills," shared with us some poignant insights about the power of confidence, noting that it isn't always realistic to conquer doubt, but we can manage. He explains, "Some people feel happy and confident when they wake up in the morning every day, and some people are going to feel doubt and worry. . . . And it's good to acknowledge early which kind you are and make your peace with it. I know no matter what I'm doing, I'm going to wake up worried every single day." Ira's lesson is to not let lingering self-doubt be a deal-breaker for the things you want to attempt in life.

JUST ACT LIKE YOURSELF

Doubt will never abandon us completely, but finding that place where you can be yourself can steady you and give you the courage you need to be who you are.

For poet Fatimah Asghar,* the biggest part of quieting doubt is about getting past the voice that asks: Why would anyone care about me or my pain? "Ignore that voice," she says. "That voice is not necessarily your voice. It's the voice of everyone else around you who's made you feel that way."

* ▶ **roadtripnation.com/leader/fatimah-asghar**

The first time Fatimah performed, she had to sit down on the stage because her knees were shaking so much. "I performed a poem and there was something that woke up," she says, "that made me be like, this is the thing I need to do. The first time I watched someone do spoken word, I was like, 'Oh my god, that is crazy'—to see someone who was confident and able to be like, 'This is who I am.' Never in my life had I dreamed about being able to say, 'This is who I am.' But then I started performing and it felt like a home—like people who would listen to you, people who wouldn't judge you, people who would just sit in a dark room with you and hear you say a poem and then be quiet with you and just respect you in a different way."

"For a long time I apologized for the way I had grown up," she says. "For being an orphan, for not being raised a certain way. You don't owe anybody that; there's enough people trying to erase you, to not erase yourself or your own voice."

"There's enough people trying to erase you, to not erase yourself or your own voice."

—FATIMAH ASGHAR, *poet*

CHAPTER 21

PRACTICE, SCHMACTICE. IT'S DOING THAT MATTERS.

Here's a confession that may be coming very late in the game: There were other road trips before Roadtrip Nation. Years before we set out on our first self-prescribed adventure, we were taking road trips all over the place. Up the coast to visit friends in Santa Cruz. To Utah, Idaho, and Wyoming to get to the snow. There was a road trip from Los Angeles to Seattle, then to Grand Teton National Park in Wyoming, and then back to Southern California. And we even interviewed a few people on that one.

Practice makes perfect! We've all heard it a million times. But in our experience, it's not practice that makes perfect. It's *doing* that does. *Experience* makes perfect. Practice is important, but it barely even qualifies as the start of perfect.

If we had actually set out to practice for starting Roadtrip Nation, we would have taken RV driving classes, studied up on the basics of engine mechanics, learned how to film, taken a course in the art of interviewing, researched what "business casual" means, and forced ourselves to live for a month in one small room on a strict diet of Clif Bars and Grape-Nuts. Much like going to school, this kind of careful practice would have given us useful logistical knowledge

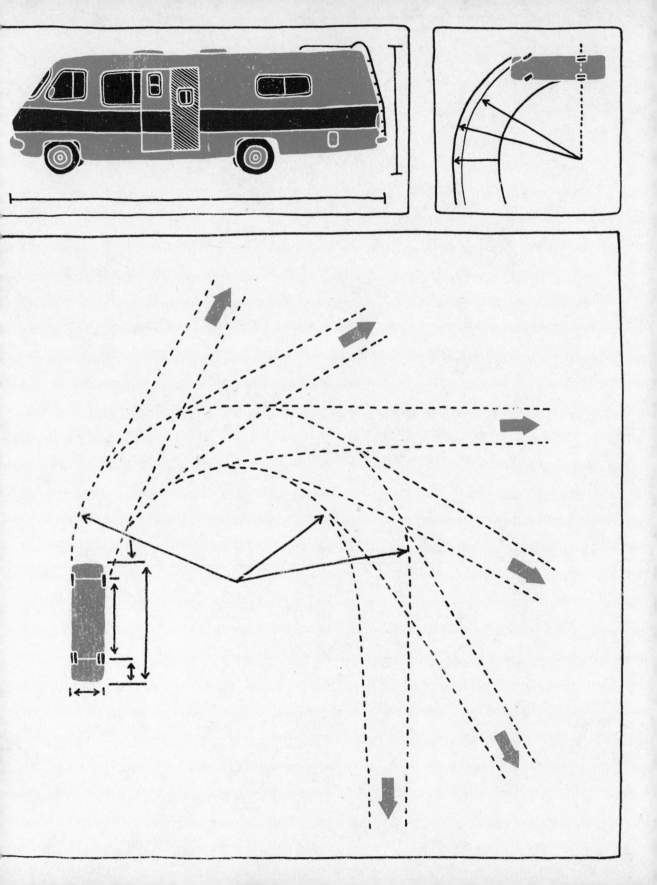

to build on, but it would have lacked the richness we gained from hitting the ground and experiencing. Studying theory can only take you so far. As original roadtripper and cofounder Brian McAllister says, "Being naive and doing is better than studying and not doing."

So, how did forgoing practice pan out? Well, driving an RV with no prior experience was a bit dangerous, for a start. Our regular clothes often made us feel out of place (we once had to split a suit between two of us at the Boston Philharmonic). We never did figure out how to repair a 454 Chevy engine. And, of course, our initial interviews could have been more expertly conducted. But practicing for all that would have paled in comparison to what we learned by doing.

Veronica Belmont* sums it up best. Veronica is a product manager by day and a technology- and gaming-centric video host whose projects have ranged from *Tekzilla*, a weekly tech help and how-to show, to the BBC America show *Gizmodo: The Gadget Testers*, to *IRL*, a show about online life and the future of the web.

When talking about her journey, Veronica exudes a charm that belies her years of struggle. She told us, "When I was in high school and college, I had crippling social anxiety . . . I couldn't go to social events, couldn't talk to people I didn't know very well—the whole panic attack thing. I would just have total breakdowns and not be able to leave my dorm room or my apartment."

❋ ▶ **roadtripnation.com/leader/veronica-belmont**

In front of the camera, cracking jokes and commenting on the gaming world, Veronica's easy confidence prompts us to wonder, what gives? How'd she do it?

Veronica's change came slowly and intentionally. She found a community of like-minded people with whom she could simply be her nerdy self. Veronica admits that she still struggles with feeling uncomfortable; she just doesn't let it stop her from being out there doing. "If I'm emceeing an event or something," she says, "I'll be fine when I'm onstage, and the second I have to actually talk to the people at the event, I'm like [silent awkward face]. But I think that's normal for most people, you know? So it's forcing yourself to take that extra step."

Veronica's philosophy is one we all can follow: Say yes as much as possible, and act on aspirations now.

"If you're really passionate about a topic," Veronica told us, "and you want to work in that field, you should already be making YouTube videos and posting them online. You should be blogging about it. And that way, when you're ready to start applying to jobs, you already have that back catalog [of work] to show to people. Just be doing it."

She didn't say, "You should be practicing." She didn't say, "Imagine your dreams in your mind, and they will become reality." She didn't say, "Start doing" or "You should try to do." She said, "*Already* be doing." And that is the truth about the world we find ourselves in. You can get a book deal on Twitter. You can land a record deal on YouTube. Ten years before we started Roadtrip Nation, the only way to film was to have millions of dollars of equipment, yet by the time we hit the road, equipment was cheap enough that we could cover it with one of our nearly maxed-out credit cards. This ease of access changes the level of competition. Being "successful" is not restricted to the lucky few who have the means and have made it past the gatekeepers. But if we're going to make it amid the fray, we need to jump in and get to doing.

"You should already be doing it."

—**VERONICA BELMONT**, *technology web show creator and host*

ALL EDUCATION IS SELF-EDUCATION

There used to be a time when getting a college degree would set you up for life. And while it is statistically true that, on average, if you have a college degree you're more likely to be healthier and earn more and less likely to end up in jail, the guarantee that you are set for life is no more. Access to knowledge of all kinds is free and plentiful. This is such a basic fact of our lives that it feels ordinary, but it's a revolution that is difficult to overstate. A kid living in an isolated outpost in Antarctica can tap into a million free online courses, take all the basics on Coursera, access millions of instructional videos on YouTube, gain inspiration and insights from hours of TED Talks, or become a better coder than we'll ever dream of—all by just doing.

So build your own education. Augment it. Customize all your learning around the things you're interested in. Focus on what drives you and expand outward from there. Your classes and textbooks are not enough. If you're interested in business, you should also be reading and watching everything you can.

And if you're out of school and working, the same is true. Doing the work you're paid to do is not enough. You've got to do more to keep moving and keep up with new ideas and skills. Go to conferences, learn new ways to apply your knowledge and your interests. Keep building your Roadmap. No matter what you're doing, studying, or working in, it is up to you to continuously learn and expand your knowledge.

James Reeves* is a New Orleans–based creative whose design collective gathers multiskilled artists, designers, and businesspeople. Reflecting on his earlier years as a freelancing designer and musician, he tells us, "You have to have a goal in mind. It's not like you're just going to sit down and say, 'I'm going to learn

* ▶ **roadtripnation.com/leader/james-reeves**

/// *Practice, Schmactice. It's Doing that Matters.* ///

web design.' The only reason I learned that is because we were putting out records and we wanted to tell people about them." James didn't wait to take an expensive course on web design; he approached it as a trial-and-error exercise. He learned Photoshop the same way.

When you self-initiate and curate your own set of skills, experiences, and knowledge, not just for four years of your life, but daily, you not only learn new strengths, you also stay relevant.

If you want to brew beer or start an online business or keep bees or learn video editing or study the finer points of Dostoyevsky, you don't need to quit your job, take out loans, and go to school.

Rosemarie Certo* is a spirited first-generation Italian American and owner of the wildly popular Dock Street Brewing Co., a brewery and pizzeria in Philadelphia. She started brewing beer for the lively dinner parties she threw for friends. At the time, Rosemarie was a teacher turned industrial photographer, but she loved making things with her hands and started selling the beer she was brewing. Rosemarie didn't feel the need to be an expert; she simply began.

You can start learning and doing tonight. Join a Meetup and talk to people who are already doing it. You don't have to be an expert to play.

"In the past it was very common for people to know how to play music, sing songs, cook, garden," says Harrell Fletcher,** a Portland State University art and social practice professor. "[Now] there's always this sense that you have to have all of these skills and all of these formalized ways of doing things or equipment or whatever it happens to be; it's something that I think ultimately alienates

*   ▶ **roadtripnation.com/leader/rosemarie-certo**

** ▶ **roadtripnation.com/leader/harrell-fletcher**

people from the sense that they can just do things." Knowing that we don't need permission to dive into new experiences and places opens up our possibilities and proves that we can and should follow our curiosity. These pursuits not only add color and spark new interests—they can lead to full-fledged lucrative livelihoods.

What we're advocating is not a new idea. It's being self-taught. There's even a word for it: *autodidact.* You don't have to be a mad genius to be self-taught; you just need to follow your own innate curiosity.

auto (self) + didact (teach)

Filmmaker Dave Banks, whom we introduced a bit earlier, hacked his film school education at USC. "When I came out here to California," he recalls, "I had a suitcase and $200 in my pocket. I remember taking the bus from Burbank to USC, because USC had a famous film school. Francis Ford Coppola, George Lucas, all these guys graduated from there. Well, there was no way in hell I was able to afford to go to school or get into that school because I just didn't have the grades. So I'd go to their bookstore and buy all the books that the students were selling back. That's what I studied."

Joe Quesada's starting point to becoming the editor-in-chief of Marvel Comics was very simply loving comic books, despite having little exposure to the mechanics of the industry. "Once I knew I wanted to be in the industry," he tells us, "I started to develop a game plan. I'd missed out on this whole history of comics; it was time to get educated. Which were the better creators, which were the bad creators? I wanted to be like the better creators. That was my roadmap."

/ / / *Practice, Schmactice. It's Doing that Matters.* / / /

Self-study, practice, and discipline kept Joe on target. When an opportunity arose for a portfolio review at DC Comics, Joe spent six weeks hunkered down, working on his comic book portfolio. He didn't wait, he just got to doing, and while doing, he educated himself. He got his foot in the door with the job at DC as an artist, and eventually went on to become Marvel's chief creative officer.

ADD EXPERIENCE—LOTS OF IT

We now know that there's no linear path to a life of satisfaction. So it shouldn't surprise us that we won't always find a path to satisfaction clearly laid out in the pages of a course catalog. Preset educational pathways can give us a general sense of which direction to go. It's fair to think of your education as practice. You're learning and acquiring knowledge. You're learning how to learn, but very rarely are you doing. What goes on inside the four walls of a classroom often doesn't represent real-world realities, so it's important to build a track record of experiences to add to your baseline knowledge.

As NASA engineer Diana Trujillo Pomerantz* told us, "Produce what you put in. Don't just go from class to class." For her, the key was to take a class, but then try that thing in the actual world. Put knowledge into practice and test it out—try all the things, but really do them. Besides, if we're truly following our Roadmap and mixing our Core Interests, we need to be adept in a variety of media to support the robust lives we're after. "The roads that most of my peers took, they were expected," recalls Delfina Eberly,** the director of data center operations at Facebook. "I come from a large Mexican family, I'm first generation, my father was a farm laborer. I wanted something different. I was searching for something to connect to." Although she had no background in the digital world, Delfina found that connection among techies and data crunchers.

* ▶ **roadtripnation.com/leader/diana-trujillo-pomerantz**

** ▶ **roadtripnation.com/leader/delfina-eberly**

/ / / Roadmap / / /

Her path to Facebook was not paved by coursework alone. She took a job in a computer room at a local bank on a whim, then found she actually liked the work and started signing up for all the relevant computer courses she could find. She told us, "I never had worked with computers, and didn't have that kind of training. . . . Rather than shying away from the technology, I leaned into it. I would just sit down and figure it out. And that philosophy has really served me well, even today."

One of the surest ways to stay on your path is to develop your skills and add experience—lots of it—in a variety of disciplines, keeping a deeply grounded center. This is known as having "T-Shaped" skills, where your knowledge is both broad and deep. You have specialized knowledge in your particular field or interest (the stem of the T), but also possess a broad set of skills so you can interact with people outside of your discipline, solve problems, and build relationships (the top bar of the T). When you can connect this idea to your Roadmap, your next steps for self-education become clear (see page 339).

DON'T GO IT ALONE

Don't think that self-education should be done in the dark of your bedroom in front of YouTube. The importance of relationships in self-education is huge. Joe Quesada took advantage of a chance encounter with a comic book artist at his day job to get his foot in the door, and Dave Banks joined a support group of artists.

Tina Roth Eisenberg,* also known as swissmiss, is a prolific designer and the founder of many businesses, such as CreativeMornings and Tattly, that started out as side projects. Growing up in a village of three thousand people in Switzerland, she always craved more action, more energy, more excitement. "I arrived in New York and I remember taking the subway and I noticed how everyone walked as fast as me and talked as fast as me," she says. "I realized in Switzerland I always had to slow myself down. I always felt, I'm a bit too much, I talk a bit too much; I always felt like I had to hit the brakes. I realized once I moved here, *Oh wait a second, they're all in the fast lane.* They all have ideas they're bubbling over with, ideas of things they want to make, and everybody tells you, 'Go, go, do it!' When you surround yourself with like-minded people who are really pushing themselves and want to put out the best work and be the best and dream really big—that's contagious, because that influences what you dream about."

299

Defining your own road in life is at its heart an exercise in self-education. You are learning about yourself—your strengths and your capabilities. Armed with that knowledge, the journey becomes about the energy and commitment you put into it. It doesn't matter as much what school you went to or what your GPA was. What matters is what you do.

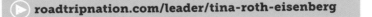 **roadtripnation.com/leader/tina-roth-eisenberg**

CHAPTER 22

WHEN TO VEER AND WHEN TO U-TURN

In life, you have to build momentum. One thing leads to another and doorways open as you forge ahead, developing skills, relationships, and experience. Momentum is easy if all the dominoes start to connect. You just tap the edge of one and watch them fall into each other down the line.

But how often does that really happen?

The challenges to your own personal momentum are almost uncountable, and they are almost certainly unknowable in advance. What is certain is that no matter who you are and how much you plan, sacrifice, and strive, you will still encounter roadblocks, and those roadblocks can really slow your momentum. But how you react to them will define who you are just as much as the circles on your Roadmap.

The moment you hit a roadblock is a critical decision point. Will you give up, or will you overcome the challenge and become a better version of yourself?

We know we've urged you to "get to" failure and to embrace the lessons you can learn from it, but a roadblock is a little different from an isolated instance of failure. It could be a series of failures, or one big one. It could be a major life change, from flunking a class, to a health issue, to getting laid off. Or it could be the nagging sense that, no matter what choices you make, you're still misguided and lost. Whatever the roadblock is, it's something that forces you to question your direction. In order to overcome it, you'll have to face it head on. It's there in front of you, so now what?

First, relax. You're not the only one to experience this. Adversity can be useful. It's a tool that tests your convictions and validates whether you're going the right way. The double-platinum recording artist Jon Foreman, of the band Switchfoot, describes the power of the roadblock as similar to the tension required to make a sound with an instrument: "I used to think that friction—the tension that you feel—is a bad thing. Pain is the enemy. But I don't think that's true. Tension is a good thing. To be pulled tight is almost the only way to make a proper noise on a guitar or a violin." We can't have music without tension, and we can't have growth without the tension that roadblocks create.

Moments of change or growth are almost always preceded by challenging roadblocks. It's only natural—obstacles force us to make choices. The goal is to make sure you deal with the roadblocks you're facing with honesty and intention.

Be in control of your reaction. Don't panic. Don't freeze. Breathe and think. A roadblock does not mean you'll never move forward. It means that there is a situation in front of you that requires thought and attention before you proceed.

Instead of following your first impulse to turn and run, take time to analyze the situation. There are solutions to your problem if you apply reason and turn to your roadmap as your compass. This is not the moment to flee or stop trying. It's the time to take that deep breath and figure out what can be learned from meeting the challenge. Then you get to choose how to react.

All of this requires a willingness to look deeply at the root cause of the setback and to take some time to analyze what it really means for your road ahead. Look at what the roadblock is telling you and balance it against what you know about yourself.

/ / / Roadmap / / /

As a place to start, explore our online Interview Archive by theme, where you'll find interviews with Leaders who have faced the very same obstacles you may be facing (doubt, failure, financial issues, negativity, and so on).

✳ ▶ **rtn.is/themes**

After years on the road observing how people approach and conquer all kinds of roadblocks, we've found that in the face of this challenge you have three basic options: You can veer, you can bust a U-turn, or you can jump the hurdle. Check out the flowchart on pages 308–9 to assess the roadblocks you're facing.

WHEN TO VEER

Veering means being fluid and flexible in your thinking. It means letting yourself think differently about how you might apply yourself to a chosen interest or choosing which subjective truths, in practice, matter the most to you. It is a side step, not a complete abandonment of your direction.

When the roadtrippers met with *Radiolab* host Jad Abumrad, one of them, Megan, was on the fence about her future path as a teacher, after applying to more than one hundred jobs without success. "I'm at that point right now where I really know that I want to teach," said Megan. "But I'm not getting any jobs. So it's kind of that uncertainty principle. And I want to figure out how to better cope with that and how to be more open to Plan B and C and D."

"Well," Jad replied, "what do you define as a teaching position? Maybe that's an elastic term and you can sort of stretch it a little bit. It may not end up looking at all like what you expect. It may shape-shift on you. And the career you thought you were heading toward becomes something very different."

That's the Roadtrip definition of veering: taking something you always considered as rigid as steel and making it bend. And that bend, that flex, can lead you to your next iteration of yourself. Once Megan stopped imagining a teaching job as one thing and one thing only, she saw a host of other possibilities. She realized she could write curricula for an educational nonprofit, work with students at an after-school organization, or give historical tours at an archaeological dig site in Greece. Veering—and being bendable—expands narrow expectations and deftly dances past the Noise of "To do this, I can only be this."

Veering is what you do when you know you have the ability to succeed in an interest area and your drive is unabated, but things aren't quite coming together, demanding that you adjust your original vision a bit. This was the case with astronomer Laura Danly.*

"As a kid, I loved seeing all the Apollo missions and Gemini missions, I wanted to go to space, I wanted to study space, there was never a question in my mind," Laura says. Laura began her career at NASA—the dream job of any astronomer. "As a child, NASA was the be-all and end-all, and here I was at the Hubble Space Telescope—what could be more wonderful than that?

"But other things came into play at that time," Laura remembers. "Most importantly, my life satisfaction; I was not happy." Laura took time to create space (you'll remember this concept from "The Blank Canvas," page 119) with several weeks of trekking through Nepal. Who she was had evolved. She returned with a better understanding of what authentically made her happy—and she knew in her heart it wasn't NASA.

* ▶ **roadtripnation.com/leader/laura-danly**

Now, as a curator at L.A.'s Griffith Observatory, Laura plans the exhibits and planetarium shows, combining her love of science with the arts, which is more in line with her Roadmap. But Laura acknowledges that nothing is static. "I've restarted half a dozen times. Six years ago I was in New York, and that was at age fifty. I was changing at fifty. I hope I'll never stop changing."

Laura's steady stream of jumps has eroded doubt and built up a stockpile of self-confidence. "I remember talking to my sister just before I decided to leave NASA, and saying, 'But I'm scared. I'm scared.' And my sister said, 'Well, what's the other side of being scared?' And I thought, 'What's she getting at? Excitement!' And the minute she said that, I knew that was true. Half of the adrenaline, half of the 'I'm scared, I'm scared!' was 'It could be really great. I'm really excited about this!' . . . So when you're scared, understand why you're scared. If it's legitimate, respect it. But if in fact a good component of your fear is 'I don't know what's on the other side. I don't know what it could be,' then [take a] deep breath. Jump out of the plane. It'll be fine. And I've done enough leaping to know that that's true."

WHEN TO U-TURN

As the term implies, the U-turn is a complete change in course. There's no way to universally gauge the motivation for this deeply personal decision—it will be different for everyone—but there are some obvious signposts that might get you to bust a sharp U-turn. Are you loving what you do? Is it what you thought it would be? Does it feel right in your gut? Do you possess the innate skill your work requires? If you think you lack the skills, do you feel enthusiastic enough to hustle to develop that skill?

If the answers to any of these questions freak you out, remember it's never too late or too early to make the U-turn.

Nat Paynter* is the director of water programs for the humanitarian company charity: water. Previously he worked as a water and sanitation specialist at the World Bank. Before all of that, however, he left a thriving career in publishing, completely changing course to study engineering. For Nat, the signs were obvious. As he puts it, "It got to the point where I hated to fall asleep because I knew I'd have to wake up. I was on the wrong track." The sudden death of Nat's father played a role in his introspection as well. Nat was twenty-five at the time, and he acknowledges that he's not sure he would have woken up and changed course without the perspective that such a loss can bring.

"It was while I was going through this questioning of my career, my father just died, and I was like, *I could just die.* I don't have time to be doing something I'm not excited about. I just said, 'Alright, I've gotta go be happier.'"

Nat began a complete 180 from liberal arts to engineering: This meant redoing his undergraduate degree, sitting in classes with fresh-out-of-high-school college freshmen, and grinning and bearing it while his former coworkers got married and bought houses. But his pursuit of happiness outweighed the embarrassment of admitting a misstep.

JUMP THE HURDLE

On the other hand, maybe what's right for you is to stick to your guns. To maintain your vision, stay the course, and do the work to overcome the hurdle. Maybe the resistance you're encountering is just Noise, and your skills and fervor are sufficient to get you over the hurdle. If your internal monologue is saying, "This is what I want to do, and I will make it work," then the signal from your gut should drown out the Noise. But this doesn't mean you're guaranteed success. Pushing through the barriers requires an honest assessment of your skills and your enthusiasm for the work—and you need to recognize the sacrifice it will take to get you there.

Of the three options, when you jump the hurdle you're definitely choosing the most difficult option. To carry on in the face of a roadblock, you'll likely have to defy a lot of Noise, work hard, and face down odds that might seem impossible.

Mabel Arellanes* has jumped hurdles every single step of the way on her journey to become a lawyer. She dropped out of high school and was pregnant at fifteen, but an attorney gave her an admin job, and Mabel discovered that she loved law. That new focus on law and the drive to get an education got her back to high school, where she told her counselor about her plans.

The counselor looked up at her and said, "*Mijita*, you'll never be able to go to college, because you don't have a social security number." This roadblock seemed immovable, but she went home in tears and told her husband, "I'm going to go to college; I'm going." She got involved with an organization that was advocating for students like her, and helped push through a bill that enabled her to go to college.

Her next roadblock: getting into law school. The first time she applied, she was rejected. Her grandfather pushed her to try again. She waited a year, and this time, she got in. But once she'd graduated, another roadblock: She couldn't take the bar exam because of her lack of legal citizenship. Three attorneys who heard about this setback volunteered to represent her, and she was able to take the test and passed.

Any one of these roadblocks would have been enough to stop someone, no matter how determined. But through it all, Mabel kept this advice in mind: "No matter what you do, make sure you never give up. You're going to go over, you're going to go under, you're going to go around, but never, never give up."

✳ ▶ **roadtripnation.com/leader/mabel-arellanes**

/// When to Veer and When to U-Turn ///

Whatever your roadblock is (or has been in the past), use this flowchart to work out your thoughts. This chart won't include all the nuances of your unique situation, but it's a place to start.

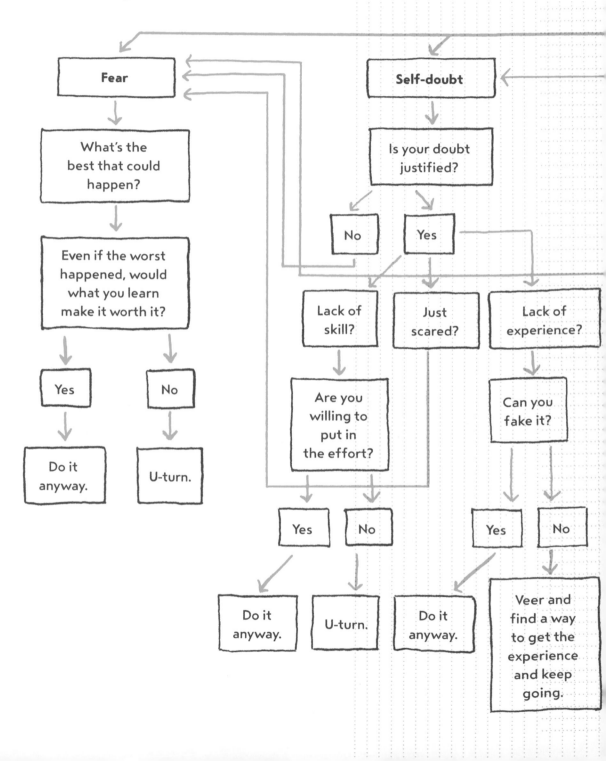

START

WHAT IS YOUR ROADBLOCK?

I can't make a living doing this.

This path doesn't feel right.

Is this feeling from the Noise?

Is this direction consistent with your Roadmap?

How much do you really need?

Yes

No

Yes

No

What can you give up?

You're on the Assembly Line. Go back to your Roadmap.

Still struggling to get by?

Are you sure?

Are you scared?

Is this just self-doubt speaking?

It's just not turning out the way you thought.

Yes, and it's a problem.

Yes, but I can figure it out.

Are you worried about money?

Veer and look at other possibilities within your Roadmap.

Do it anyway.

Veer and reevaluate your Roadmap.

U-turn.

CHAPTER 23

DISTINCTION IS EVERYTHING

On the road one day in Vermont, after a twenty-four-hour drive and our seventh and final interview of the day, we met with Michael Jager,* the creative director who cofounded design groups JDK Design and Solidarity of Unbridled Labour. Whenever we heard fellow designers mention Michael, it was with quiet awe; he's been producing groundbreaking work that elevates design and branding to a paradigm-shifting art for his whole career. He evoked a quiet confidence that seemed, unlike so many others, to come not from a manufactured act, but from his core—he was simply being himself.

Michael summed up all that we were hoping to find on the road. He began with an observation that has become, after the thousand-plus interviews we've done, a universal trait we've recognized in people living meaningful lives. In Michael's words, "If you look at examples of people who have been successful— not monetarily successful, but wholly successful in their lives, they are generally distinctive individuals. And it can be a farmer in the boonies of Vermont or Montana, or it can be the most progressive artist in New York City. They will both have self-confidence in what they're doing, and they'll have a point of view. They'll have a philosophy that they'll back up."

As Michael said, **"Distinction is everything."**

✳ ▶ **roadtripnation.com/leader/michael-jager**

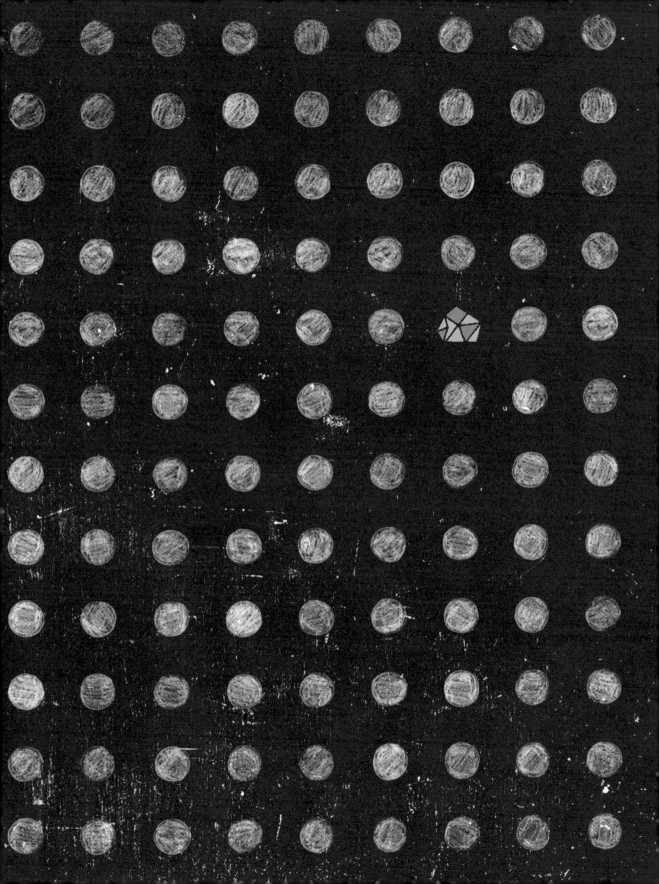

"If you decide you're gonna be a sculptor, or you decide you're gonna be an architect, or you decide you're gonna be a kick-ass accountant, if you really believe it, and you wear it on your shoulder, and you really do it with distinction, the world will conspire to support you."

—MICHAEL JAGER, *cofounder and creative director, JDK Design*

Knowing who you are and unabashedly chasing the things that reflect your true sense of self—these are the fundamental elements that break us free from the Assembly Line and support us as we forge our own roads in life. It's only when we take a stand on behalf of our identity that we're able to rid ourselves of the dissonance and discontent that plagues so many of us. How can life be meaningful and satisfying if it doesn't reflect who we really are?

The quiet self-confidence that we witnessed in Michael stemmed from his unwavering conviction. He knows who he is, and at every crossroad, he allows his sense of self to point him in the direction that is best for him.

Zen Master Bon Soeng* told us, "The greatest gift you give to the world is when you discover who you are and you manifest that." There's joyous freedom in that statement. You don't have to find a cure for cancer. You don't have to make the *Forbes* list of wealthiest people. You don't have to be the next tech genius. Being the most authentic person you can is a gift to you, your family, and the world, because the life you lead will be authentically yours.

Out on the road, listening to people like Michael—these distinctive individuals who act with intention and spirit—people with a point of view, it's impossible not to begin to imagine the best versions of ourselves. Once we accept that real fulfillment is possible, the only thing that makes sense is to throw ourselves entirely into the pursuit of it. Staring out the window between interviews, we daydream of all the things we'd be doing in an ideal world. We dream of our most authentic and inspired selves. It's our hope that at some point between these pages, your own daydreams tumbled out of hiding and began to look like real possibilities. That's one of the most valuable lessons from the road: **A person can only be as great as the dreams they allow themselves to imagine.**

✳ ▶ **roadtripnation.com/leader/bon-soeng**

"No matter what you do, you've got to use as much energy and brain power as you've got, to do it as well as you can do it, all the time. Because you don't get the days back. You don't get the hours back. You don't get the minutes back. Do the things that make you feel like you've spent your time well, and at the end you'll be happy, if not proud of your life."

—**ANDREW LINS**, *conservator, Philadelphia Museum of Art*

The most well-spent and fulfilled lives begin with dreams, because without them, we're not truly ourselves—we're what others tell us we can be. Your vision for yourself is a start, but of course it's nothing without action. Whenever a new generation of roadtrippers returns from the road and passes on the keys to the green RV, they, too, must put their dreams into action. Realizing what's possible is both an affirmation and a provocation to grab the reins, to dive in, to try something that pushes your sense of self to the next version.

As entrepreneur Paola Santana told us, "There is not a path. You have to create your path. By definition you are creating adventure, and adventure is an *adventure*. If there was a path there wouldn't be anything new to discover."

Just like each of our road trips comes to a bittersweet end, this book has run out of pages. So, what have you begun to imagine yourself doing? Have you let yourself believe that what you dream isn't just possible, but inevitable? Because now it's time to own it—it's time to put your dream on the street.

"Attempt the impossible. Do the crazy. Stand on a limb, and teeter. I say teeter away! Reach! Leap! Attempt things that everyone says can't be done. Run! Jump! Move. Walk. Get your crazy done! You are your bravest self. And when I say brave, I don't mean the quiet courage that it takes to raise a child, I mean the courage to do what no one else is doing. These are the years to climb a mountain! These are the years to break an arm. These are the years to fall in love, and recover, and fall in love again, and recover. Make love in a hundred different cities, shave your head, or take a year off from your life to do something that makes no sense to anyone else! Do it. Do it. Do it now! Live it! If you want to write, if you want to make film, anything you want to do—you have to live to be able to do it first. So live! Live! Live! Live! LIVE! Get it out of your system so that when you have an ankle that is sore, and you have bills to pay, and you have a kid to watch at night, there are no regrets behind you. The heaviest thing you'll have to carry as you move forward is regret. Make sure you're not carrying too much."

—STACEYANN CHIN, *poet and memoirist*

PROJECTS

As we've done our best to lay out in this book, finding the open road happens in the act of doing; that's where momentum builds. Self-construction is a continual process rooted in action, and while you likely took small steps as you read each chapter, we also wanted to provide some bigger, bolder opportunities for action.

The projects that follow aren't recipes in a cookbook; they're more like open-ended lab experiments meant to help you take action with your Roadmap. They will help you discover whether an interest truly connects with who you are; they'll reinforce positive aspects of the path you're on and will help you sidestep the distractions and roadblocks. We've left room for you to keep notes as you start thinking about each project.

The level of effort you put into these is for you to decide. You can dip a toe in, you can dive in headfirst, or you can use these to help solidify your own ideas about your Roadmap. Do one, do them all, or use them as inspiration to make up your own.

Just be doing.

PROJECT #1: TALK WITH SOMEONE WHO'S LIVING YOUR ROADMAP

TIME COMMITMENT: About one hour of prep and one hour of conversation

COSTS: $0 to $

TOOLS/SUPPLIES: Pen and paper, a phone, a willingness to open up and listen

GOAL: To speak with someone who inspires you and learn how they got to where they are in order to gain insights and guidance for your own path in life

BIG IDEA: Roadtrip Nation started with a pretty simple thought: If you don't know what you want to do in life, find someone who's doing what you're interested in and ask them how they got there.

No matter what you want to do or what kinds of roadblocks stand in your way, there's a strong likelihood somebody out there is already doing it and/or has found ways to navigate through similar obstacles—so go learn from them! Talking with people is how we've been able to collect all of the insights in this book, and now it's your turn to find your own insights. You don't need a big green RV or a video production crew to make it happen. By simply doing some research and picking up the phone, or emailing, or reaching out on social media, you can make a connection that could profoundly impact your life.

Levels of Engagement

LOW: Interview a friend or colleague about their path in life, perhaps over lunch or coffee.

MEDIUM: Find and reach out to an inspiring Leader within a reasonable proximity to you, then take a trip over to interview them.

HIGH: Why stop at one? You can interview as many people, in as many industries, from as many different walks of life as your heart desires! Take it from us—after decades on the road and thousands of interviews, once you get the bug, it can be hard to stop . . .

Before you start, here are some FAQs:

I. WHY SHOULD I DO IT?

No profile in a book, no story your friend told you, no idea will ever stand in as a surrogate for real, firsthand experience. The conversations you have will be acts of discovery, revealing the challenges and the excitement that await you on your Roadmap.

2. WHAT WILL I GET OUT OF IT?

This is your chance to confirm or reject the ideas you've been chewing on. There's priceless value in getting advice and insights from someone who is living a life in line with your own vision for yourself.

3. ISN'T THIS THE SAME AS NETWORKING?

No! Networking conversations are the career equivalent of speed dating—each party is on their best behavior, hiding the flawed truths behind a perfectly packaged mask of corporate politeness. The goal of networking isn't to have a deep and meaningful conversation about the tribulations of life; it's to further your own personal occupational agenda. And while that's useful once you've narrowed down your interests, when you're trying to figure out how to build a fulfilling work life, you have to go deeper and get personal—you have to talk about LIFE in all of its glories, doubts, and pitfalls. **THAT'S** what a Roadtrip Nation conversation is all about.

STEP ONE: WHO TO INTERVIEW?

A Leader can be anybody with experiences and stories you can learn from. For the most impactful interviews, look for someone who's living out the things you're interested in. Most importantly, find someone who loves what they do. There are plenty of doctors, but you want a doctor who is inspired every day, not someone who's counting the days till retirement. You're looking for insights and stories from someone who is living their own open road. Take some time online and do research, and remember to use your Roadmap as your guide.

1. The Foundation and Core Interests from my Roadmap are:

    _____

    _____

    _____

2. Brainstorm a few job titles and/or companies that embody your Roadmap:

    _____

    _____

    _____

    _____

    _____

    _____

/ / / Roadmap / / /

Now it's time to put on your detective hat. Do a bit of research to find out if any of those jobs or companies are in your area. If so, check if their websites have an "about" page or staff member bios. Is there any contact info listed? Are you in school, or have you graduated from somewhere? If so, research alumni from your school who have gone on to do the things you hope to do. And don't forget to utilize the powers of social media sites like LinkedIn, Facebook, and Instagram as great tools to discover people with similar interests, as well as find direct lines to contact them. Get ready to slide into those DMs!

STEP TWO: THE COLD CALL

Roadtrip Nation essentially began as a excuse for us to talk with really interesting people. We pass on that excuse to you. When you make your first cold call or write that cold email, feel free to say something like this:

"Hi! My name is _____ and I'm interviewing inspiring individuals to learn how they got to where they are today in the hope that it will help me on my own road in life. I would love to talk with you about how you got to where you are today."

There are so many ways to contact people these days, but we believe in the power of the old-school phone call! It remains the most direct, personal, and effective way to break the ice and secure an in-person meet-up. If you're nervous, that's perfectly natural, but we've found that facing and overcoming the fear of cold calling often leads to the development of a life skill that will benefit you for years to come.

Here are a few tips from our years of experience picking up the phone:

▶ Be ready to tell the people you call exactly who you are and why you are trying to talk with your Leader.

▶ Make sure you've done your research on the Leader; knowing his or her name, job title, and other information may help you get a "yes."

▶ Practice leaving a voicemail so you can get your request down to a short one-minute message.

▶ If you blank out, just remember: Be your genuine self. The person you talk to might end up being your mentor, friend, or guide as you define your own road.

▶ We caution against reading from a script because it can sound too robotic, but jotting a few essential notes on a sticky note is a good way to ensure you remember any critical information!

STEP THREE: THE INTERVIEW!

The magic of a Roadtrip Nation–style interview is that it's a casual, organic conversation. Instead of over-preparing and sticking to a rigid structure, we recommend preparing a few key points, then remaining open-minded and ready to follow wherever the conversation may lead.

1. **Begin the interview by introducing yourself,** and we're not just talking about saying your name. Take two to three minutes to give your Leader some context for the conversation. A good introduction will set the tone for the conversation. Don't be afraid to **make it personal.** Don't be afraid to be vulnerable. If you'd like someone to open up to you and give you the honest and personal details of their life, you have to open the door first. By sharing information about yourself and being honest about what you're struggling with, you're inviting them to do the same. Also, if you don't give them the personal context for why you'd like to talk to them and what you're looking for, their advice will probably be too general to matter.

   Practice summarizing these key ideas into a concise introduction:

   ▶ Who are you, and where are you currently at in your life?

   ▶ What are some of your hopes and dreams for your future, and what do you currently see as the biggest roadblocks that stand in your way?

   ▶ What compelled you to reach out to this person in particular?

▶ What are you hoping to get out of this conversation?

_____

_____

_____

_____

_____

2. **Ask them an opening question.** The best way to get things rolling is to ask an open-ended question that allows them to share as much or as little as they feel is relevant. For example, the tried-and-true Roadtrip Nation opening question is: *Where were you when you were just starting off on your path, and how did you get to where you are today?*

Asking a question like this is like opening a floodgate. Once they're off and rolling, sharing their story with you, there's really only one thing left to do . . .

3. **Listen, and ask follow-up questions!** The best way to avoid this becoming a stiff, standard, informational interview is to stay present, listen intently, and ask follow-up questions based off of what you're hearing. If they mention something you'd like to hear more about, ask them to elaborate on it! If they skip over a period in their story, ask them to fill in those blanks for you! Asking follow-ups will guide the conversation toward what's interesting and important to you and ensure that the conversation stays relevant to your life. Some of the best follow-up questions are the most simple. Don't overthink it; just let it flow.

4. **Have go-to questions ready, just in case.** Sometimes we just hit a blank. That's okay! Brainstorm a list of go-to questions you can always fall back on if the conversation hits a lull.

    Here are a few Roadtrip Nation classics to get you started:

    ▶ What kind of expectations or external pressures were on you when choosing your path, and how did you deal with them?

    ▶ Did you ever question whether this was the right path for you?

    ▶ What were the biggest roadblocks you faced, and how did you get past them?

    ▶ What was the biggest risk you took on the path to getting where you are?

    ▶ What is your personal definition of success?

    Brainstorm your own here:

    _____

    _____

    _____

    _____

    _____

    _____

5. **Ask a final wrap-up question.** At this point, you will have received tons of great information and advice, but it's helpful to give the Leader a chance to sum it all up and express the most important takeaways from the conversation. Here is how we typically end our interviews: *I'd like to be respectful of your time, so with that in mind I just have one last question: What would be your parting piece of advice for me as I continue on my path?*

6. **Reflect.** Take time to capture what you've learned from the conversation while it's still fresh. Whether you journal it, record a rambling voice memo on your phone, or use another way to synthesize your thoughts, immediately capturing your takeaways is the best way to ensure the key lessons of the conversation really sink in.

Go to rtn.is/interview to learn more!

PROJECT #2: SELL YOUR GOODS/ SERVICES ONLINE

TIME COMMITMENT: Medium to high

COSTS: $0 to $$$

SET-UP TIME: +/– five hours to get rolling

TOOLS/SUPPLIES: Variable; a camera and computer, a collection of goods or services you want to put out into the world

GOAL: Capitalism! Nah, just kidding. Well, sort of. But truly, there's nothing like getting paid—even on a small scale—for doing something you love. If people are willing to pay for what you're selling, and what you're selling is at the center of your Roadmap, then it is validation that you're going in the right direction.

BIG IDEA: This is a perfect project for makers and doers; whether it's train whistles, custom furniture, your editing and writing services, or screen-printed T-shirts of your golden retriever, you can put it out there. Or perhaps you're more of an entrepreneurial spirit who's really into buying and selling vintage sunglasses—the idea is to get out there and let people respond to your vision. And it doesn't have to be things. You can put your services up for sale on a freelance site or contribute to collaborative projects on sites like Quirky.com. This is how you put your dream on the street or on the Internet.

Levels of Engagement

LOW: Make one thing, or describe your talent, and open your store.

MEDIUM: Make a few things and see what happens.

HIGH: Build a whole brand identity around your products or services and then market 'em, and unleash 'em for all to enjoy.

Before you put your goods and services in the world, here are a few questions to think about:

1. WHAT CAN I MAKE/DO?

What things are made or done at the center of your Roadmap? Chances are, if you're doing this project, you've already got something in mind. And if you don't, no worries. Start thinking about how your Roadmap can fill a specific public need.

2. HOW MANY THINGS SHOULD I MAKE BEFORE I OPEN MY STORE?

Best to start with at least one. But the truth is, you can start with zero. If you lack the upfront cash to get you started, look at Kickstarter! It's filled with thousands of projects that are sold before a single thing is made.

3. WHAT INTERESTS AM I MAGNIFYING?

The goal isn't as much to make money (just yet) as it is to experiment with what it feels like to put your work out there. The idea of being a painter is one thing, but what is it like to be a painter? This is your low-touch way to answer that question.

4. WHAT IS UNIQUE ABOUT THE THING(S) I'M MAKING/DOING?

The market is glutted with the same products and services, so what's unique about your work? The way you package it, how it looks and feels? Or the story behind it?

Choose a Venue

There are tons of different storefronts out there you can use. The obvious one is Etsy, but there are others geared toward specific interest verticals.

▶ **Etsy:** Offers users their own digital storefronts to sell goods; mostly geared toward those who make handmade things.

▶ **Shopify:** An easy way to build your online store from scratch. You can even use related apps to edit photos, resize objects, and customize your site.

▶ **Quirky:** Collaborate on product development. Easy way to jump in without having to do everything.

▶ **Kickstarter:** Crowdsource funding for creative projects that run the gamut of ideas.

▶ **Amazon:** One of the best ways to sell online. You can start fast without having to set up your own website, immediately tapping into their hundreds of millions of existing customers.

▶ **Squarespace:** This easy-to-use web-hosting platform provides slick design templates for portfolios, storefronts, and blogs.

▶ **Brick-and-mortar:** Tap your local craft fair, farmers' market, or other small outlet.

Put It Out There

Once you're ready, it's time to make people aware of what you have to offer. Start with the easy: friends. Go word of mouth and share it through your social media networks. Write to bloggers who have similar interests and see if they'll spread the word.

Some Tips

▶ **Start Small.** Keep it easy. Start with a few products. See what interests people. Watch how they react to what you have and iterate from there.

▶ **Tell a Story.** As you work on your store, think of the entire experience as a story: your story, and the story of how these things have come to be made. People like to know the history of their goods, and they want to feel like the things they're buying aren't just things, but a bigger vision that says something to the world. Think about how you can highlight an aspect of your product that makes you stand out from everyone else. Maybe your old-timey-styled letterpress greeting cards are created on a vintage letterpress owned by your great-grandfather; maybe the materials for everything you make are locally sourced; or maybe you donate 10 percent of your proceeds to a worthy cause. Those unique elements will invest the consumer and differentiate you from the herd.

▶ **Be Aware.** It takes a special type of person to like the entire process of creating, from building something, to marketing it, selling it, and dealing with feedback. As you go through this experience, observe the things you like and dislike. If you dislike enough of the process, start to look at how you can focus your life around the parts you do like.

▶ **Going Bigger?** If you're getting some good results, take it more seriously. There are hundreds of books on how to run a successful Etsy store, and Etsy encourages you to join Etsy teams (**etsy.com/help/article/332**) to get feedback and learn more from other sellers.

Inspiration

To show you how it's done and to get you motivated, take a look at a few stores we patronize. Remember that you don't have to go it alone; sites like Threadless or Cotton Bureau rely on the creative output of a wide community of people—and it's easy to use their services (and those like them) to test the waters.

Joey Roth: joeyroth.com

Gemma Correll: society6.com/artist/gemmacorrell

Threadless: threadless.com

Jon Contino: Society6.com/artist/joncontino

Cotton Bureau: CottonBureau.com

Bandcamp: bandcamp.com

Retrofit Comics: retrofitcomics.com

Yellow Owl Workshop: yellowowlworkshop.com

Reflection

Now that you've given it a shot, what are your thoughts about getting your work out there?

1. *What have you learned about your work process through building the store?*

2. *Which part of the process did you like the most (conceptualizing, designing, making, teaching, the logistics)?*

3. *Did your connection to your Core Interests grow or weaken?*

4. *Which part of the store would you like to improve? Which part is working well?*

PROJECT #3: TRAVEL TO A NEW PLACE

TIME COMMITMENT: Partial day or longer

COSTS: $0 to $$$

SET-UP TIME: A few evenings of planning plus the length of the stay

TOOLS/SUPPLIES: Map, computer, camera, maybe a notebook and a pair of snazzy sunglasses

GOAL: To get in proximity to what you want, sometimes you need to create distance between you and your routine. The idea is to put yourself in a new headspace by visiting a new locale that lives and breathes your Roadmap or at least corresponds to a Core Interest or two. It doesn't have to be a glamorous destination; it's just about seeing things in a new light.

BIG IDEA: Take something you're interested in and seek out a location or an event that supports that interest within your time and budget. Get out of your comfort zone. Maybe it's a visit to the Maker Faire in the Bay Area to see the latest in gadget wizardry, or it could be a day-long field trip to see *The Starry Night* by van Gogh in New York City. What matters is finding a way to go somewhere new where the things you're interested in are thriving.

Levels of Engagement

LOW: Take an afternoon adventure.

MEDIUM: Make the most of a weekend trip.

HIGH: Turn your next vacation into a full-fledged Core Interest exploration.

Before you start, here are some questions to consider:

I. THE CORE INTEREST FROM MY ROADMAP THAT I'M EXPLORING IS:

_____ .

2. I'M WILLING TO INVEST $ _____ IN THIS EXPERIENCE.

3. HERE ARE FIVE PLACES WITHIN MY BUDGET THAT SUPPORT MY CORE INTEREST:

1.

2.

3.

4.

5.

4. HOW WILL I GET THERE?

a. *Walk*

b. *Bicycle*

c. *Public transportation*

d. *Car*

e. *Boat*

f. *Plane*

g. *All of the above*

PLANNING RESOURCES

Meetup: Find people gathering in almost any city in the world, based on common interests.

Lonely Planet: Travel resources for places to stay and visit.

Couchsurfing: Find a cheap place to sleep and interact with locals.

Airbnb: A step up from sleeping on a couch, while still meeting locals.

Once you've narrowed down your list from five spots and settled on one, here's a mini photo scavenger hunt to make this trip more focused. Want to share your experiences with your fellow readers? Share your photo scavenger hunt online and use the hashtag **#RoadmapBook**:

▶ Trip planning: Take a screenshot of your Google Maps route, snap a pic of you drawing on a physical map, document your hotel reservation, your three Lonely Planet guidebooks, and anything else that completes the picture (pun intended).

▶ Share a photo that represents your Core Interests in this new place.

▶ Share pictures of people who are getting paid to work at something directly connected to the Core Interests and/or Foundation on your Roadmap.

▶ Get out of your comfort zone and try a food you've never had before. Could be a specific dish you've never tried or a staple that reminds you of your mom's home cooking. Capture the rusty street cart serving bacon-wrapped hot dogs or a foreign candy bar you've never heard of.

▶ Take a photo of a moment where you felt you were out of your comfort zone.

▶ Make a self-portrait in which the expression on your face sums up the experience you had in this new place.

Inspiration

Here are a few examples of locations that live and breathe a particular interest. Ideally you'd head out to the epicenter of your interest, but if you can't take the time or spend the cash, find your local equivalent.

▶ **Austin, TX:** Live-music capital of the world.

▶ **Los Angeles, CA:** Dive into space at the Jet Propulsion Laboratory in Pasadena and Griffith Observatory in LA. Then head over to SpaceX headquarters a bit farther south.

▶ **Rome, Italy:** This city is an ultimate mix of architecture and history. From the Colosseum, built in 72 A.D., to the Pantheon, the Vatican, and Baths of Caracalla, Rome is awash in the past.

▶ **Washington, D.C.:** Museums. History. Politics.

▶ **Orange County, CA:** Center of the action-sports industry with companies like Quiksilver and Volcom tucked into the warehouses just off the coast. P.S. We're here, too!

▶ **Silicon Valley, CA:** Technology and start-up capital of the world.

▶ **Marfa, TX:** An unlikely modern art mecca in the West Texas desert.

▶ **Paris, France:** Plunge into the art scene at the Louvre, one of the world's largest museums that also was once a palace. Then saunter down idyllic cobblestone streets to such landmarks as the Musée d'Orsay, the Centre Pompidou, and Rodin Museum.

▶ **St. Louis, MO:** Visit the City Museum if you're into creating immersive interactive experiences.

▶ **Hong Kong, China:** The Hong Kong Science & Technology Parks are home to all things engineering, science, and just about anything techy.

▶ **Nagoya, Japan:** The center of the auto industry in Japan. Like Detroit in its heyday.

▶ **Milan, Italy:** Widely considered the global capital for fashion.

▶ **Queenstown, New Zealand:** The center point for extreme sports.

▶ **Florence, Italy:** The mecca of art history and the birthplace of the Renaissance.

▶ **Zurich, Switzerland:** One of the world's main hubs of international banking and finance.

▶ **Nairobi, Kenya:** This prominent social center is full of international aid and development organizations, including United Nations Environment Programme and the African headquarters for the UN.

Grab a few magazines or sift through a few blogs related to your Core Interests. Where are the hot spots for your interests? What are the names and places that keep popping up? Maybe it's New Orleans for jazz or Portland, Oregon, for coffee. If there's a way to get close, take a tour of a facility or just be immersed in the environment of people engaged in worlds that align with your Roadmap.

Reflection

After your outing, take some time to look back on the experience. Here are a few questions to think through:

1. *How did it feel to get out of your comfort zone and dive into someplace new?*

2. *Reflect on what it was like to see people living lives built around your Core Interests.*

3. *What did you like and what didn't you like about the Core Interest(s) you explored?*

PROJECT #4: CREATE YOUR OWN SEMESTER

TIME COMMITMENT: As long as it takes, but we'll call it a semester

COSTS: $0 to $$$

SET-UP TIME: A few hours' planning, and then the number of hours you want or need to invest in classes, practical applications, and sharing

TOOLS/SUPPLIES: Depends on the type of class you create and your own budget

GOAL: To create your own immersive experience to learn and develop skills that tie into or support your Roadmap

BIG IDEA: Create your own "semester" in which you learn what you want to learn, experience what you want to experience, and are challenged in a way that you want to be challenged. Design an experience that is right for you and that connects to your Roadmap. Do it on your own time and within your own budget.

Look at your Roadmap. Create your semester based on a mashup of your Core Interests and Foundation. Focus on the overlaps of all three. How can you fill in the gaps of your expertise and accumulate skills on your own time in your own way?

Levels of Engagement

LOW: Complete an online course on a subject, skill, or topic aligned to your Core Interests.

MEDIUM: Complete an online class aligned with your Core Interests with a final project/demonstration of your learning.

HIGH: Take multiple classes aligned with your Core Interests, combined with any of the other projects or experiences, with a final project or demonstration of your learning.

The Core Interest category I want to pursue:

_____

Before you start, here are some questions to consider:

I. WHAT DO I WANT TO LEARN?
It can be as small as learning a new program or as large as learning a new language. Work the answer to this question into a statement such as "I want to learn how to letterpress postcards" or "I want to learn how a social media strategy is developed."

340

2. HOW MUCH TIME DO I HAVE TO DEDICATE MYSELF TO THIS? ARE WE TALKING NIGHTS AND WEEKENDS FOR A FEW MONTHS OR JUST A WEEKEND PROJECT?

3. HOW MUCH MONEY DO I WANT TO INVEST IN THIS?

Semester Design

▶ **The Coursework:** Figuring out the content area of your semester is the first place to start.

▶ **Online Classes:** There are hundreds of online sites dedicated to providing free and open coursework. From renowned universities to no-budget YouTube tutorials, there's an endless range of possibilities to help you learn information or develop new skills. Most free, open online courses require completion of assignments, or assigned reading (usually online articles), and possibly online discussions with others enrolled in your class. Browse around and find classes that are most relevant to your Roadmap.

▶ **My Classes**

_____

_____

_____

_____

_____

Here are a few places that offer free, open, or subscription-based online coursework:

Coursera
Offers courses from more than eighty different schools

edX
Courses with a focus on art, technology, and science

Udacity
Courses with a focus on new technology, modern programming, science, and critical thinking

Khan Academy
Courses with a focus on chemistry and other sciences

Peer 2 Peer University (P2PU)
Online courses meant to work hand-in-hand with traditional education

Udemy
An online platform that allows professors to host open courses

Skillshare
A community-based marketplace for professionals and teachers to share their skill sets

General Assembly
A platform that connects professionals with learners in creative fields

Academic Earth
Offers 750 courses from a variety of schools

Open Education Consortium
Offers a broad range of courses

MasterClass
Online classes for any skill level, taught by the best in the world

Required Reading

Every class you take in a traditional school setting has required reading, so why not add some to your nontraditional semester? Whether it's buying yourself a subscription to a magazine; creating a space online to track articles, op/eds, or stories you'd like to read; or even following a relevant blog, you can supplement your online coursework with as much outside content as you have time for—or can afford.

Instead of spending a ridiculous amount of money at a college store on text-books, just think what $100 at a local bookstore will buy—or make a list of materials to check out from the local library or tap into Google Books.

▶ **My Reading Materials**

_____

_____

_____

▶ **Mentorship/Apprenticeship**
Rather than just being a receptacle for information, put your learning into action. Find a mentor in a related field, or see if you can volunteer your time at a business or organization that interests you. Look for an internship or, if you like film, find a student project that you can volunteer for.

▶ **Possible Mentors**

_____

_____

_____

_____

_____

▶ What's My Final?

You want to have something to show for all the learning you are committing yourself to. Maybe it's a new art piece for your portfolio, a new skill on your LinkedIn profile, a physical display of what you have been crafting, building, or drawing, or a presentation you'd like to give to someone in the field. Regardless of what you decide, make a commitment to complete it.

My final is ————————————— Due ——————————

Electives

Since this semester can be pretty much whatever you want it to be, we want you to think big. Here is a suggested menu of experiential activities you can choose from if you want to add depth to your coursework. You can also look for ways to use other projects in this book to work within your semester:

▶ Join a group, organization, or Meetup of like-minded people interested in learning the same thing.

▶ Follow someone on any social media outlet.

▶ Travel to a new place, your own "study abroad" equivalent.

▶ Talk to someone in your Core Interests field.

▶ Take an online class or do a tutorial in something outside your "field of study."

▶ Start a YouTube channel.

▶ Create an online forum.

▶ Create a yearbook of photographs recording your progress.

▶ Try to teach what you learned to someone else.

▶ Take a field trip!

▶ Watch some TED Talks or films that connect to your vision.

▶ Get crafty! Use your hands to create a visual representation of what you're learning.

▶ Design an infographic.

▶ Volunteer at an organization related to your Core Interests.

Reflection

Consider this your course evaluation. Take some time to think about how your semester helped you align with your Roadmap or revealed course corrections you need to make.

345

PROJECT #5: FIND YOUR NICHE

TIME COMMITMENT: One to ten hours a month

COSTS: $0 to $$

SET-UP TIME: Two hours

TOOLS/SUPPLIES: A computer, some form of transportation (to meet people, unless you're going virtual), and a readiness to talk to and learn from others

GOAL: To find, create, or join a community of like-minded people involved in at least one of your Core Interests whom you can learn from and exchange ideas with

BIG IDEA: Look at your Roadmap and try to find (or create) the community at the intersection of your Foundation and Core Interests. We all have at least one skill, either one we're just starting to explore, or one we're fairly confident we can grow into. A big part of learning is surrounding yourself with dedicated people of similar interests who can join you in a collective effort to grow. By sharing and swapping tips in a setting like this, you will not only expand your capabilities but also get the lay of the land (industry, company, and so on). Reach out to fellow enthusiasts and become better together, whether you're exploring your interest in yoga, knitting, blogging, web design, guitar, or *World of Warcraft*.

Levels of Engagement

LOW: Find an online forum you can contribute to that is centered around your interest or skill. We could list some here, but there is actually a message board for every interest (we just found one for jellyfish farming!).

MEDIUM: Create a members-only Facebook group, compile a mailing list, send out a monthly newsletter. Join an existing gathering.

HIGH: Start a group of your own on Meetup.com or elsewhere, create flyers and put them on car windshields, or just find a group that you can commit to with real-life people.

Before you start, here are some questions to consider:

1. ARE YOU MISSING SOMETHING? WHAT INTERESTS DO YOU HAVE WITH-OUT ANYONE TO SHARE THEM WITH?

You probably have a few interests that you've never explored fully because they're not the type of things your friends are into. Try to think deeply about the untapped and unexplored interests that aren't part of your current social circle.

2. IN PERSON OR ONLINE, LOCAL OR COMMUTING?

How far are you willing to travel? Do you want to start out virtual and then roll into something in person, or are you ready to jump in?

3. TO JOIN OR CREATE?

Is there a gathering of people that already exists around your Core Interests or is this something you're going to have to start up on your own?

Some Tips

▶ **Community looks different to each of us.** Some people find it easier to connect online; others need faces to look at and group activities to tag along on. Find what feels right for you.

▶ **Don't feel like you have to have something to contribute.** It is okay (at the start) to join a book club or go to the local gathering of hobby wielders and just observe. As you get comfortable, you can jump in with a question or contribution, but for now the main idea is to get yourself out there among others who share the same interests.

Thoughts

▶ Everyone needs a community. Simply put, it reminds us we're not alone, and sometimes that's all the motivation we need to pursue our goal.

▶ It can be hard to really gauge your strengths and weaknesses without interaction with and feedback from others. The people you meet in a community can act as a mirror, reflecting both the good and the "may need some work."

▶ Everyone is a teacher, and that includes you! Communities build reciprocal relationships, so soak up all you can while also imparting your ideas to others.

▶ You don't need to be an expert to join a community or start a group. Exploring for the sake of exploration is enough of a motivator.

Once You're In, Find a Niche Mentor

If you really want to go the extra mile, turn your involvement in your new community into a quest to find a mentor—your Mr. Miyagi (if you've drawn a blank, just do a search for "Karate Kid"). Once you've identified someone, ask them to be your mentor. Have a heartfelt message in mind and describe what you seek to learn from them. Look for a way to create repetition in your mentorship: low touch might be just asking them to respond to an emailed question once a month; high touch could be having a conversation over a meal each month. Find something that works for you and your mentor, then put it into practice.

Reflection

1. *Once you got among people who shared the same Core Interest, did you find yourself more excited about that Core Interest?*

2. *What have you learned about the communities that exist around your Core Interest?*

3. *What do you want to investigate deeper?*

PROJECT #6:
[Invent Your Own Project]

TIME COMMITMENT:

COSTS:

SET-UP TIME:

TOOLS/SUPPLIES:

GOAL:

BIG IDEA:

350

Levels of Engagement		
LOW:		
MEDIUM:		
HIGH:		

Some questions to get started:

I. WHAT AM I DOING?

2. WHY AM I DOING THIS?

3. HOW DOES THIS GET ME CLOSER TO MY OPEN ROAD?

4. HOW AM I PUSHING MY COMFORT ZONE?

5. WHERE DO I START?

▶ **First . . .**

I'll accomplish this by _____ .

▶ **Second . . .**

I'll accomplish this by _____ .

▶ **Third . . .**

I'll accomplish this by _____ .

▶ **Fourth . . .**

I'll accomplish this by _____ .

Measure Success

How will I measure my success in this project?

Inspiration

Things related to this project that inspire me:

Reflection

My notes, discoveries, and takeaways from this project.

ACKNOWLEDGMENTS

Like just about anything in this world, making a book takes a village. Everyone here at Roadtrip Nation, past and present, had a hand (or two) in creating this book you're reading. From our sales and program management teams who find and build the relationships that fuel our projects; to the producers, directors, and editors who tackle logistics, film for weeks while living in an RV, and turn hours of footage into story arcs that move us; to our creative and marketing teams who bring ideas and stories to life, share them, and measure their impact; to the project management team who makes sense of the crazy things we do and keeps us on track; to our education and events teams—and all of our roadies!—who bring this content to students all over the country; to our product and software engineering teams who transform ideas and sketches on a whiteboard into clickable magic; to the IT, admin, and facilities teams that keep this place (and our RVs) together and running; to the accounting team that literally and figuratively keeps fuel in our tanks; and the HR folks who support this big, crazy team. They all deserve recognition, but the names would fill more pages than we have, so we'll simply say: To our team, we couldn't do this without you. Thank you. And to the dozens of roadtrippers and hundreds of Leaders who have opened their lives up to us and shared what they've learned. This work doesn't happen without you. We're forever grateful.

To the folks who were essential to our first edition, especially John Woldenberg, Lorena Jones, and Monique Adcock. And to the team that made this second edition, extra extra thanks to Allyson Campion, our editor Deanne Katz, Jennifer Tolo Pierce (who's been with us for editions one and two), Freesia Blizard,

Mikayla Butchart, Barbara Genetin, Claire Gilhuly, Joyce Lin, Magnolia Molcan, Margo Winton Parodi, Cecilia Santini, and Cynthia Shannon.

Seriously, what started as a hare-brained idea to paint an RV green and travel the country interviewing people about how they found work they love has grown into a movement, something larger and far more meaningful than anything we could have ever imagined when we were trying to fix our fuel tank a few weeks into the first road trip.

Finally, to you, the one reading this book! The work we do starts in our office and out on the road, but this movement continues because of you. You keep it going by reading this book and by applying the stories and advice to your own life in any way, however big or small. Now we're passing the keys to you. Go out there and become who you want to be.

INDEX

A

Abumrad, Jad, 104–7, 215, 303

Academic Earth, 342

Adams, Jeff, 273

addiction, 61–62

Adjacent Possible, 215–17, 260

Aguilar, Irene, 281

Ahmad, Raza, 238

Amazon, 331

Andrade, David, 67

apprenticeships, 343

Arce, Julissa, 122–23

Arellanes, Mabel, 307

Arlington, Mara, 174

Asghar, Fatima, 285–87

Assembly Line
  dangers of, 33, 34

  myopic view from, 166

  Noise as furnace of, 41

  personal, 29

  questions for, 35–38

  safety of, 30, 34

  stepping off, 30, 33 38–39

  stuck on, 32–33

B

Baker, Gerard, 42

Banks, Dave, 284–85, 295, 299

Barlow, John Perry, 20

Bassett, Scout, 17, 66

Beachley, Layne, 111, 112–13

Belmont, Veronica, 290–92

Benstein, Elise, 172

Bethea, Clarence, 61–62

Blank Canvas
  change and, 125

  getting to, 119, 120, 122–27

  letting go and, 119, 125–27

Bolles, Gary, 229

Boyle, Greg, 66

Brewer, Craig, 276

Brickell, Barry, 185–87

Brilliant, Larry, 161

Brown, Ron, 246, 248

Brown, Warren, 93–94

Bryant, Kimberly, 124, 283–84

Burks, Jewel, 191

Bushnell, Brent, 158–59

Byron, Kari, 17, 246

C

career
  choosing, 130, 132

    interests and, 132, 134, 142

Carroll, Gregory, 70–71

Carroll, Kevin, 238, 240–41

certainty, avoiding, 103–4

Certo, Rosemarie, 294

Cham, Jorge, 43, 150–51

change
  challenge vs., 102–3

    fear and, 125

    inevitability of, 13, 223

Child, Julia, 248

Chin, Jimmy, 79–80

Chin, Staceyann, 315

Chow, Malia, 135

Clark, Deon, 82–84, 86, 87, 190

Clark, Karen, 260–61

classism, 52

Clinton, Bill, 246

community, finding your, 346–49

confidence, building, 280–81, 284–85

Conrad, Robin, 137

Core Interests. *See* interests

Coursera, 342

courses, online, 341–42

Cowan, Zachariah, 82–84, 86–87

criticism, 46

Cruz, Dominick, 42

D

Danly, Laura, 304–5

Dash, Damon, 108

death, dress-rehearsing for, 125

decisions
importance of making, 212

deferred life plan, 76–77, 256

delaCruz, Art, 225–26

Del Valle, Elaine, 57–58, 65

Denman, Pete, 63–65

Dennison, Brandon, 236–37

Desai, Mihir, 261–62

discrimination, 52

distinction importance of, 310, 312–14

doing vs. practicing, 288, 290–97, 299

Donofrio, Beverly, 272

doubt
fighting, 279–86

sources of, 279

as universal struggle, 284–85

dream jobs, existence of, 170–75

dreams, importance of, 313–14

Dunye, Cheryl, 159

dyslexia, 63–64

E

Eberly, Delfina, 296–97

Echelman, Janet, 197

Echols, Michael, 108, 110

Eckert, Cindy, 78

education, 204–5, 235, 293–97, 299, 339–45

edX, 342

Eisenberg, Tina Roth, 299

Enriquez, Juan, 99–100

Etsy, 330, 332

F

failure
examples of, 272

fear of, 270, 276

as good thing, 270, 272–77

roadblock vs., 301–2

fallback plan, 84

Farley, Chris, 97

Feinberg, Danielle, 160, 284

Fletcher, Harrell, 294–95

flexibility, importance of, 96–97

Foreman, Jon, 302

Forman, Zaria, 157, 174–75

Foster, Cheryl, 151–52, 256

Foundation
combining Interests and, 154, 156, 158–63

concept of, 147

constancy of, 150

discovering your, 148–49

ignoring, 152

Franklin, Ben, 215–16

French, Antonio, 66

359

G

Gand, Gale, 248

gap year, 79

Gardner, Chris, 17, 52, 54–56, 65

General Assembly, 342

Glass, Ira, 42, 197–99, 204, 285

Gonsalves, Dennis, 159

Gradman, Eric, 158–59

H

Halpern, Charna, 96–97, 224

happiness, defining, 257

Harris, Shamayim "Mama Shu," 167

Harrison, My, 188

Hatfield, Tinker, 232

Hawking, Stephen, 64

Heller, Brittan, 92

Helmstadter, Theo, 101–2

Heyniger, Christina, 123–24, 279

hurdle, jumping the, 306–7

hustle
examples of, 238, 241, 246, 248–52

importance of, 238, 241, 244, 246, 247

questions about, 252–53

Roadmap and, 251

I

Inglis, Mark, 102–3

interests
combining Foundation and, 154, 156, 158–63

core, 140–41

discovering, 134–35, 144

earning a living and, 201

pursuing, 132, 134

skills and, 196–200

interviewing, 320–27

Irwin, Nancy, 230, 280

J

Jackson, Raven, 174

Jager, Michael, 310, 312, 313

Johnson, Jeff, 30, 31, 45

Joseph, Ivan, 281

Jude, Wilburn, 236–37

K

Kahape'a-Tanner, Bonnie, 265–68

Kamen, Dean, 161

Kamkar, Samy, 225

Kasliwal, Mansi, 42

Khan Academy, 342

Kickstarter, 331

Kim, Jim Yong, 161

King, Billy, 142, 144

Kiyosaki, Robert, 274

Kopcso, Katie Carr, 204

Kuchenbecker, Katherine, 133

Kurzweil, Ray, 161

Kwon, Elaine, 50–51

L

Laggner, Jakob, 216

Lateiner, Bogi, 43, 45

Laverde, Catalina, 66, 204, 205

Lee, Gabrielle, 74–76, 80

Legend, John, 17, 245

Legohn, Lisa, 67, 202–3, 232

Leser, Kimberly, 204

letting go, 18, 52, 65, 119, 125–27, 130

life
deferred, 76–77, 256

nonlinear nature of, 90–97

to-do list vs., 119

Lifehacker Night School, 342

Linklater, Richard, 44–45, 48

Lins, Andrew, 314

living in beta, 99–107

lost, being, 11, 20–21, 26, 88, 176–81

Love, Tristan, 67

Lynn, Peter, 172, 173

M

MasterClass, 342

Matthews, Airea Des, 33–34

Matthews, Jessica, 161

Maynard, Kyle, 67

McAllister, Brian, 290

McCain, Artina, 153

mentors, 343, 349

momentum, building, 301

money, necessity of, 195

Monroe, Van Taylor, 177–81, 191

Morris, William, 175

Mullen, Rodney, 111–12, 113

Myers, Mike, 97

N

Neeleman, David, 272

networking, 321

Ng, Lillie, 161

niche, finding your, 346–49

Noise
dangers of, 44

definition of, 41

distinguishing between useful feedback and, 48–50

examples of, 42–43

as furnace of Assembly Line, 41

internalized, 50, 51

overcoming, 44–47, 48, 50–51

sources of, 41

subjective truths vs., 187

O

Obregon, Rosa, 145

O'Brien, Soledad, 250–51

O'Connor, Sandra Day, 249–50

Okura, Eiko, 110

online courses, 341–42

online sales, 328–33

OpenCourseWare Consortium, 342

opportunity cost, 259–60

overthinking, 261

P

Pacheco, Keakealani, 264–69

Page, Peter, 108

Parcheta, Carolyn, 135

Passacantando, John, 187–88

passion,
as destination, 88, 93

following, 88, 93, 195

identifying, 90, 94

Paynter, Nat, 306

Peer 2 Peer University, 342

Phukan, Indira, 156

Piailug, "Papa" Mau, 266

Pierce, Charles Sanders, 261, 262

plausibility, embracing, 166–67

Pomerantz, Diana Trujillo, 296

Poneman, Jonathan, 257–58

Pouisima, Leila, Hokulani Kaaekuahiwi, 135–36

practicing vs. doing, 288, 290–97, 299

Prince-Blythewood, Gina, 272

projects
Create Your Own Semester, 339–45

Find Your Niche, 346–49

Invent Your Own Project, 350–55

Sell Your Goods/ Services Online, 328–33

Talk with Someone Who's Living Your Roadmap, 320–27

Travel to a New Place, 334–38

Q

Quesada, Joe, 295–96, 299

Quirky, 328, 331

R

racism, 52

Reeves, James, 293–94

regrets, 255–57, 262, 315

Reid, Morris, 246, 248

Remer, Roy, 119–21, 125, 127

résumés
best, 74

building, 69, 71, 74

Reynolds, Penny Brown, 39

risks
dangers and rewards of, 255, 257

perceived vs. actual, 259–60

regrets and, 255–57, 262

taking, 255–56, 260–62

roadblocks
approaches to, 303–9

as critical decision points, 301

failure vs., 301–2

flow chart, 308–9

inevitability of, 301

overcoming, 52, 54–65

power of, 302

Roadmap
concept of, 154

creating, 156, 160–63

as guide, 208–9, 212

hustle and, 251

possibilities in, 161

taking action with, 212, 215–21, 319

talking with someone who's living your, 320–27

Roadtrip Nation,
  history of, 6, 11–13,
    16–17, 288, 290

  productions of, 7

  website, 9

Robertson, Beverly, 90

Robinson, Evin, 60

Rodrigues, John, 159

Rosenberg, Steven, 161

Rosenthal, Mila, 91, 93

Ruiz, Raul, 43

S

sales, online, 328–33

Salopek, Paul, 86–87

Santana, Jessica, 59–61,
  65

Santana, Paola, 147–48,
  314

self-construction
  core of, 71

  phases of, 18–19

  process of, 19

  unending nature of, 21,
    154, 224, 319

self-education,
  293–97, 299, 339–45

semester, creating your
  own, 339–45

Shallal, Andy, 174

Shopify, 330

Siemionow, Maria, 161

Simmons, Christine, 17,
  228

skills
  bridging gaps in,
    231–32, 234–35

  common, 227

  concept of, 196

  developing, 196–99,
    204–5

  identifying, 234

  importance of, 196

  interests and, 196–200

  T-shaped, 297

Skillshare, 342

Smith, Brooklyn, 165–66

Smith, Vicki, 95–96, 212,
  244

Snyder, Window, 150

Soeng, Bon, 313

Song, Hannah, 159, 161

Squarespace, 331

Steltzner, Adam, 217–19

Sterling, Debbie, 174

subjective truths
  balancing, 189

  concept of, 182

  discovering, 184–85,
    192–93

  examples of, 182,
    190–91

  listening to, 185–88

  Noise vs., 187

  truths vs., 182

  as value system,
    188–91

success
  definitions of, 108,
    110–17

  distinction and, 310

  effort and, 244

  money and, 108

  out-of-the-box thinking
    and, 31

  society's formula for,
    29

Sykes, Wanda, 272

363

T

Thompson, Ahmir "Questlove," 250

thresholds, marking, 120

travel, 334–38

Trujillo, Diana, 43

truth. *See* subjective truths

U

Udacity, 342

Udemy, 342

U-turns, 305–6

V

Vaynerchuk, Gary, 46–47

veering, 303-5

W

Walker, Magnus, 94–95

Ward, Jes, 191

Weatherhead, Andrea, 142–44

Wessen, Randii, 277

Williams, Wendy, 247

Witte, Willie, 176–81

Woolcott, Richard, 199–200

worklife integration, 77–81

Z

Zahn, Laura, 231–32

NOTES

NOTES

NOTES

NOTES

ROADTRIP NATION MANIFESTO

SO, WHAT DO YOU WANT TO DO WITH YOUR LIFE?

Everywhere you turn, people try to tell you who to be and what to do. We call that the Noise. Block it. Shed it. Leave it for the conformists.

This is a movement about being true to who you are. Self-construction rather than mass production.

Define your own road in life instead of traveling down somebody else's. Listen to yourself. Your road is the open road. Find it.

Find the open road.